STATE LEVEL PUBLIC ENTERPRISES IN INDIA

STATE LEVEL PUBLIC ENTERPRISES IN INDIA

R.K. MISHRA

J KIRANMAI

GYAN PUBLISHING HOUSE

NEW DELHI-110002

State Level Public Enterprises in India
Rs. 690

ISBN: 81-212-0954-4

Published in 2007 in India by
Gyan Publishing House
5, Ansari Road, Darya Ganj,
New Delhi-110002
Phones : 23282060, 23261060
Fax : 011-23285914
E-mail : books@ gyanbooks.com
Website: www.gyanbooks.com

Lassertype Setting by: Rudra Computer Graphics
Printed at : Salasar Imaging System, Delhi

Contents

Preface

The State Level Public Enterprises (SLPEs) are an important component of the public enterprise system in India. They are instruments of public policy implementation at the hands of the state governments and affect the lives of a vast number of people in India. Engaged in multifarious activities, the SLPEs carry huge investments and a large number of personnel. However, there financial performance has become a cause of great concern. The Department of Public Enterprises, Government of India vide their communication no. 16(3) / 2006 – GM dated 13th December 2006 invited the Institute to prepare a Status Report on SLPEs.

This study contains information about the status of the state level public enterprises under different state governments and UT administrations. The study incorporates the problems and issues faced by the SLPEs and recommendations for improving their performance. We hope that this study will be a precursor to a full-fledged report on the SLPEs in India to fill the void in this important area of information sharing and research at the initiative of the Department of Public Enterprises, Government of India which so thoughtfully promoted this study.

We express our gratitude to Dr R C Panda, IAS, Secretary, Department of Public Enterprises, Government of India, for entrusting the study on the SLPEs to the Institute. Shri K D Tripathi, IAS, Joint Secretary, Department of Public Enterprises, Government of India encouraged us from time to time to complete the study and enrich its contents. We are indebted to Dr A K Rath, IAS, Additional Secretary and Financial Advisor, Ministry of Steel, Government of India for enlightening us on the various facets of functioning of Public Enterprises. We are grateful to Shri P C Cyriac, Director and Shri M R Nair, Consultant, Department of Public Enterprises for their guidance and suggestions. Dr P Rama Rao, President, IPE, motivated us from time to time in completing this study. We are immensely grateful to him for the motivation.

We express our gratitude to Ms S Laitha, Senior Administrative Officer (Research), Ms Ch Lakshmi Kumari, Assistant Professor and Shri P A Naidu for the inputs provided in the completion of this work.

R K Mishra
J Kiranmai

Introduction

1. State Level Public Enterprises in India: A Macro Analysis

- The State Level Public Enterprises (SLPEs) are an important component of the public enterprise system in India. 1,129 SLPEs had an investment of Rs. 2,59,187 crore as on March 31 2005.
- The contribution of SLPEs to the GDP is about five per cent
- Although SLPEs constitute 80 per cent of the total investment of the Central Public Enterprises (CPEs), they are more than the number of the CPEs. The average investment in an SLPE is 15 per cent of a CPE.
- The total investment in the SLPEs increased from Rs. 77,730 crore in 1990-91 to Rs. 2,59,187 crore in 2004-05.
- The lion's share of total investment belong to the utility enterprises.
- The compound average growth rate (CAGR) of total investment for the period 1990-91 to 2004-05 was 8.85 per cent.
- The various categories in which the SLPEs could be classified include manufacturing, financial, promotional, trade & service, utility and welfare enterprises.
- The manufacturing enterprises dominated the scenario in terms of typology of the SLPEs followed promotional, utility, welfare, financial, and trading and services.
- The preference for creating economic and social infrastructure was responsible for preferring enterprises with economic and social orientation.

- The capital employed was 85 per cent of the total investment in the SLPEs pointing to the fact that the SLPEs system was not organic.
- The net worth as a percentage of total equity was shade lower than seven per cent pointing to a negligible growth and erosion of shareholders' basic capital.
- The total revenues as a percentage of total investment presented a very weak picture. It points to the lack of marketing drive, quality consciousness and soft targeting in the SLPEs.
- All the states faced the challenge of unlocking the vast untapped value in the SLPEs in terms of their market potential.
- On an average, net profits for all the states taken together as a percentage of the revenues earned were -2.7 per cent in 1990-91 shooting up to -5.49 per cent in 2004-05.
- The CAGR for net profit during the period 1990-91 to 2004-05 was -13.79 per cent.
- The net losses incurred by the SLPEs not only wiped out their total profits but also were responsible for the phenomenon of loss making.
- The story of the SLPEs is one of accumulating losses and creating a huge pile in this regard.
- The accumulated losses of the SLPEs increased from Rs. 10,999 crore in 1991-92 to Rs. 60,517 crore in 2004-05.
- The impact of the non-viable working of the SLPES was very adverse on the state finances hinting at the possibility of a significant turnaround through the restructuring of the SLPEs.
- The proliferation in the number of SLPES and investments therein has compelled the state governments to re-look their SLPEs portfolio.
- Whereas some states were open to both privatisation and / or restructuring, there were others such as Kerala, West Bengal, Tripura and Bihar which rejected the privatisation option and decided to go in for only restructuring/ closure including the reference to BIFR (Board for Industrial and Financial Reconstruction).

- The state governments have preferred to set up expert committees to advice about the retention of the SLPEs portfolio.
- The state governments adopted different techniques ranging from cold privatisation (i.e., non-privatisation reforms to transfer of ownership and closure of the SLPEs).
- Kerala, West Bengal, and Tripura preferred cold privatisation whereas Punjab, Haryana, Karnataka, Orissa and Andhra Pradesh opted for transfer of ownership through trade sale, divestment of majority stake and sale of equity by private placements. Tamil Nadu has preferred mergers and amalgamations.
- The various states have not been able to establish an adequate mechanism to deal with the problem of social safety net.
- Privatisation and Restructuring of the SLPEs was fraught with a number of serious problems.
- The political ideology and support of the chief of the state such as Andhra Pradesh, Karnataka, Punjab, Maharashtra, West Bengal and Kerala was responsible for the creation of conducive climate for privatisation in these states.
- Another very important factor responsible for privatisation was the preference of the private sector to buy/take over the manufacturing enterprises.
- The size of the SLPEs in terms of investment also weighed as an important consideration
- Andhra Pradesh Government appointed a Committee to report on Restructuring of SLPEs. A three-tier machinery consisting of Department of Public Enterprise, Implementation Secretariat and Cabinet Sub-Committee on Privatisation, was evolved to effect disinvestments.
- S C Jha Commission (2002) on Bihar state finances, suggested privatisation and restructuring of most of its SLPEs.
- Gujarat constituted a High Level Committee (1994) to formulate broad guidelines in this regard.
- Haryana has set up a High Power Cabinet Sub Committee (2002) for Public Sector Restructuring.

- Kerala set up an Enterprise Reforms Commission (ERC) to have a re-look at the portfolio of SLPES
- Karnataka Government set up Linn Committee (1996) to suggest privatisation, deregulation and merger of SLPEs and later set up a Public Sector Restructuring Commission (2000)
- Maharashtra Government constituted the Maharashtra Board for Restructuring State Enterprises (MBRSE) in August 2001
- Madhya Pradesh has embarked on an Integrated Public Resource Management Programme [2001] under which an integrated Public Enterprises Reform was envisaged, with loan and technical assistance grant from the Asian Development Bank (ADB)
- Orissa set up a Cabinet Sub-Committee (1996) under former Deputy Chief Minister which suggested closure and privatisation of certain units
- Punjab set up a Disinvestment Commission in January 2001 which submitted its draft report in June 2002. The government had set up a Directorate of Disinvestment to process the Disinvestment Commission's recommendations or come up with *suo moto* reports in consultation with the Commission
- Rajasthan set up a committee on "Re-organisation, strengthening and Disinvestment of SLPEs and Industrial Development"
- Tamil Nadu set up the S.V.S. Raghavan Committee (1997) for streamlining and restructuring SLPEs and to initiate privatisation process
- West Bengal is contemplating to close down loss making SLPEs and welcomes private participation in state run enterprises
- The privatisation programmes of Andhra Pradesh , Orissa and Uttar Pradesh received the support of DFID and were carried out with the support of foreign consultant. The Madhya Pradesh and Gujarat programmes received the support of Asian Development Bank and were also carried out with the support of foreign consultants.

- The disinvestment/ privatisation of CPEs began since the launching of New Economic Policy in July 1991 where as privatisation of SLPEs was resorted to much before in the case of the states.
- The states preferred Trade Sale as the modality of privatisation as compared to the partial disinvestment and strategic sale by the Central Government.
- The states preferred an independent legislation to executive privatization as compared to the executive action in the case of the central government.
- The privatisation exercise in the state governments was not target based whereas the Central Government laid down the targets of money to be mobilized through disinvestment/ privatisation.
- The privatisation experiences of the various State Governments revealed that effective due diligence expedites privatisation; it is easier to privatise smaller enterprises; and manufacturing enterprises possess a greater appeal for privatisation.
- There should be a nodal agency to deal with the issues of common interest to all SLPEs.
- The state governments should have institutional arrangements and well thought out procedures for selecting CEOs of SLPEs.
- The state governments should set up a procedure by which the administrative ministries have periodic discussions on the programme of each SLPE and arrive at an action plan / MoU.
- All enterprises in the state sector should prepare a corporate plan for an appropriate time period based on an analysis of their strengths and weaknesses, and a realistic assessment of resources which could be mobilized.
- The Comptemporary & Auditor General (CAG) should revamp the system of appointment of auditors in the SLPEs for clearing the arrears of annual reports and accounts .
- The public financial institutions should appraise the investment proposals of the SLPEs more carefully.
- It would be advisable for the state governments to set apart some funds for sponsoring through nodal agencies studies

/ training programmes relevant to SLPEs in academic institutions within or outside the state.

2. *State Level Public Enterprises in India: State-wise Analysis*

- There are 28 states and 7 union territories. It is proposed to discuss the state-wise dimensions of the SLPEs in India pertaining to the various states and the union territories.
- Andhra Pradesh (AP) had 54 SLPEs with an investment of Rs. 33,914 crore as on March 31 2005. The enterprises incurred a net loss of Rs. 393 crore. The accumulated loss of these enterprises was of the order of Rs. 2,215 crore as on the same date. These enterprises received budgetary support of Rs. 4,957 crore during 2004-05.
- The SLPEs in AP had less sensitization about corporate governance. These enterprises faced both the internal and external problems. The 4 P's of marketing has a great potential to further improve the performance of the SLPEs. The state government has not been able to evolve a satisfactory performance evaluation system for these enterprises.
- Assam had 42 SLPEs with an investment of Rs. 4415 crore as on March 31 2005. The enterprises incurred a net loss of Rs. 671 crore. The accumulated loss of these enterprises was of the order of Rs. 5268 crore as on the same date. These enterprises received budgetary support of Rs. 754 crore during 2004-05.
- Sickness has marred the functioning of the SLPEs. The improper selection of top level executives, their frequent transfers and lack of management expertise in the functional areas of management have emerged as the major handicaps confronting these enterprises. The operational snags have undermined productivity of the SLPEs.
- Arunachal Pradesh had 5 SLPEs with an investment of Rs. 20 crore as on March 31 2005. The enterprises incurred a net loss of Rs. 6.40 crore. The accumulated loss of these enterprises was of the order of Rs 0.59 crore as on the same date.
- The SLPEs need to effect improvement in technology and developing human resources.

- Bihar had 54 SLPEs with an investment of Rs. 5,407 crore as on March 31 2005. The enterprises incurred a net loss of Rs. 747 crore. The accumulated loss of these enterprises was of the order of Rs. 5,163 crore as on the same date. These enterprises received budgetary support of Rs. 778 crore during 2004-05.
- The SLPEs lack clarity of vision and mission. Financially, there are bankrupt. There is a need to improve the work culture. Operationally, the enterprise face the problems of inventory management, scheduling and balancing, plant layout, etc.
- Chattisgarh had 10 SLPEs with an investment of Rs. 1,059 crore as on March 31 2005. The enterprises incurred a net profit of Rs. 5.75 crore. The accumulated profit of these enterprises was of Rs. 10.76 crore as on the same date. These enterprises received budgetary support of Rs. 165 crore during 2004-05.
- The division of assets and liabilities with Madhya Pradesh continuous to be an issue. The management development and training as also specialized skills in project management are required for the improved functioning of the SLPEs. Concepts and skills need to be provided in infrastructure management related issues.
- Delhi had 15 SLPEs with an investment of Rs. 9,694 crore as on March 31 2005. The enterprises incurred a net loss of Rs. 1,693 crore. The accumulated loss of these enterprises was of the order of Rs. 7,143 crore as on the same date. These enterprises received budgetary support of Rs. 1,500 crore during 2004-05.
- The National Capital Territory of Delhi enterprises suffer from the problem of subsidization, net worth erosion, sub-optimal asset utilisation and non-performing asset.
- Gujarat had 50 SLPEs with an investment of Rs. 21,195 crore as on March 31 2005. The enterprises incurred a net loss of Rs. 755 crore. The accumulated loss of these enterprises was of the order of Rs. 7,207 crore as on the same date. These enterprises received budgetary support of Rs. 5,372 crore during 2004-05.

- The nodal agency controlling the performance of the SLPEs needs to be accorded a superior status and greater autonomy. There is scope for further amalgamations and merger of the SLPEs.
- Goa had 15 SLPEs with an investment of Rs. 586 crore as on March 31 2005. The enterprises incurred a net loss of Rs. 47 crore. The accumulated loss of these enterprises was of the order of Rs. 189 crore as on the same date. These enterprises received budgetary support of Rs. 30.60 crore during 2004-05.
- Professionalsation of the management cadres is the prime need. The marketing functions require to be strengthened. The enterprise in the manufacturing need to improve the supply chain management.
- Haryana had 29 SLPEs with an investment of Rs. 9,847 crore as on March 31 2005. The enterprises incurred a net profit of Rs 68 crore. The accumulated loss of these enterprises was of the order of Rs. 1,028 crore as on the same date. These enterprises received budgetary support of Rs. 1,376 crore during 2004-05.
- The managerial deficiencies have been the prime factors responsible for the dismal show. The boundary management practices were not forceful. Subsidization of the services through the SLPEs hindered there performance.
- Himachal Pradesh had 21 SLPEs with an investment of Rs. 3,683 crore as on March 31 2005. The enterprises incurred a net loss of Rs. 77 crore. The accumulated loss of these enterprises was of the order of Rs. 763 crore as on the same date. These enterprises received budgetary support of Rs. 107.51 crore during 2004-05.
- Many SLPEs are duplicating functions. The operating systems have become outdated. The debt-equity ratios need reformulating.
- Jharkhad had 7 SLPEs with an investment of Rs. 816 crore as on March 31 2005. These enterprises received budgetary support of Rs. 645.15 crore during 2004-05.
- The enterprises face the problem of cash management, inexperience in project appraisal, and division of assets and liabilities by the of Government of Bihar.

- Jammu and Kashmir had 23 SLPEs with an investment of Rs. 2,994 crore as on March 31 2005. The enterprises incurred a net loss of Rs. 5 crore. The accumulated loss of these enterprises was of the order of Rs. 1,056 crore as on the same date. These enterprises received budgetary support of Rs. 94.45 crore during 2004-05.
- The SLPEs in J&K has operational problems in all the areas of management. They suffered from very low capacity utilisation.
- Karnataka had 82 SLPEs with an investment of Rs. 35,197 crore as on March 31 2005. The enterprises incurred a net profit of Rs. 378 crore. The accumulated profit of these enterprises was of the order of Rs. 808 crore as on the same date. These enterprises received budgetary support of Rs. 5,387 crore during 2004-05.
- The nominee directors need to perform with greater vigilance. Corporate planning related issues deserve greater attention. Privatisation programmes should gain a higher tempo. Working capital problems are very acute.
- Kerala had 109 SLPEs with an investment of Rs. 11,045 crore as on March 31 2005. The enterprises incurred a net loss of Rs. 55 crore. The accumulated loss of these enterprises was of the order of Rs. 2,343 crore as on the same date. These enterprises received budgetary support of Rs. 237 crore during 2004-05.
- The state should go for mergers to remove duplication of activities among the SLPEs. The sick enterprises need to be turnaround. Agencies like Restructuring Internal Audit Board (RIAB) have to improve their visibility and effectiveness. Supply chain management should improve.
- Madhya Pradesh had 40 SLPEs with an investment of Rs. 5,862 crore as on March 31 2005. The enterprises incurred a net profit of Rs. 59 crore. The accumulated loss of these enterprises was of the order of Rs. 4,062 crore as on the same date. These enterprises received budgetary support of Rs. 1,450 crore during 2004-05.
- The nodal agencies is not proactive. The top and middle management are weak. The management development and training need greater attention.

- Maharashtra had 82 SLPEs with an investment of Rs. 20,549 crore as on March 31 2005. The enterprises incurred a net loss of Rs. 1,179 crore. The accumulated loss of these enterprises was of the order of Rs. 4,604 crore as on the same date. These enterprises received budgetary support of Rs. 6,430 crore during 2004-05.
- The asset utilisation ratio is poor. The incremental capital output ratio requires improvement. The Maharasthra Board for Restructuring State Enterprises (MBRSE) should be empowered through appropriate amendments in its legislation.
- Manipur had 16 SLPEs with an investment of Rs. 135 crore as on March 31 2005. The enterprises incurred a net loss of Rs. 3 crore. The accumulated loss of these enterprises was of the order of Rs. 22 crore as on the same date. These enterprises received budgetary support of Rs. 0.50 crore during 2004-05.
- Most of the enterprises are sick. Sweeping internal and external reforms are required to improve the performance of the SLEPs.
- Mizoram had 5 SLPEs with an investment of Rs. 68 crore as on March 31 2005. The enterprises incurred a net loss of Rs. 4 crore. The accumulated loss of these enterprises was of the order of Rs. 25 crore as on the same date. These enterprises received budgetary support of Rs. 2.79 crore during 2004-05.
- The entrepreneurship in the state is hampered by infrastructural bottle necks. The executives in the SLPEs lack project management concepts and skills.
- Meghalaya had 13 SLPEs with an investment of Rs. 848 crore as on March 31 2005. The enterprises incurred a net profit of Rs. 5 crore. The accumulated loss of these enterprises was of the order of Rs 346 crore as on the same date. These enterprises received budgetary support of Rs. 46 crore during 2004-05.
- Lack of professionalisation is obstructing the growth of the SLPEs. A heavy dependence on deputationists marred the effective functioning of the SLPEs.

- Nagaland had 15 SLPEs with an investment of Rs. 52 crore as on March 31 2005. The enterprises incurred a net loss of Rs. 2 crore. The accumulated loss of these enterprises was of the order of Rs. 25 crore as on the same date. These enterprises received budgetary support of Rs. 6 crore during 2004-05.
- The SLPEs in Nagaland face the resource crunch, infrastructural problems and net worth erosion.
- Orissa had 70 SLPEs with an investment of Rs.12,417 crore as on March 31 2005. The enterprises incurred a net loss of Rs. 571 crore. The accumulated loss of these enterprises was of the order of Rs.2,669 crore as on the same date. These enterprises received budgetary support of Rs. 126 crore during 2004-05.
- The nodal agency has to improve its effectiveness through a better understanding of corporate governance, restructuring, privatisation and technology upgradation.
- Punjab had 57 SLPEs with an investment of Rs. 14,023 crore as on March 31 2005. The enterprises incurred a net profit of Rs. 72 crore. The accumulated loss of these enterprises was of the order of Rs.1,953 crore as on the same date. These enterprises received budgetary support of Rs. 8,781 crore during 2004-05.
- The function of corporate strategy is in a very poor shape in Punjab. The nodal agency has to improve its effectiveness through a better understanding of corporate governance, restructuring, privatisation and technology upgradation.
- Pondicherry had 11 SLPEs with an investment of Rs. 453 crore as on March 31 2005. The enterprises incurred a net loss of Rs. 7 crore. The accumulated loss of these enterprises was of the order of Rs. 146 crore as on the same date. These enterprises received budgetary support of Rs. 29 crore during 2004-05.
- The internal systems need to be strengthened. The coordination with the government departments need to be improved. There is a high untapped potential in terms of capacity buildup.

- Rajasthan had 24 SLPEs with an investment of Rs. 13,818 crore as on March 31 2005. The enterprises incurred a net profit of Rs. 146 crore. The accumulated loss of these enterprises was of the order of Rs. 274 crore as on the same date. These enterprises received budgetary support of Rs. 1,545 crore during 2004-05.
- The enterprises are run in a country club style. The strategic functioning needs to be given its due importance.
- Sikkim had 15 SLPEs with an investment of Rs. 141 crore as on March 31 2005. The enterprises incurred a net loss of Rs. 3 crore. The accumulated loss of these enterprises was of the order of Rs. 57 crore as on the same date. These enterprises received budgetary support of Rs. 1 crore during 2004-05.
- The organisations are very small in size being run by unprofessional management teams and characterized by duplication of activities and gross lack of marketing orientation.
- Tamil Nadu had 68 SLPEs with an investment of Rs. 14,178 crore as on March 31 2005. The enterprises incurred a net loss of Rs. 1,032 crore. The accumulated loss of these enterprises was of the order of Rs. 5,251 crore as on the same date. These enterprises received budgetary support of Rs. 2,564 crore during 2004-05.
- Costing, budgeting, pricing and internal audit systems have to be revamped. The SLPEs portfolio needs to be revisited.
- Tripura had 10 SLPEs with an investment of Rs. 287 crore as on March 31 2005. The enterprises incurred a net loss of Rs. 19 crore. The accumulated loss of these enterprises was of the order of Rs. 176 crore as on the same date. These enterprises received budgetary support of Rs. 23 crore during 2004-05.
- Logistics and supply chain management are the key problems. The marketing orientation is very weak and lack of coordination is the key limiting factor.
- Uttaranchal had 10 SLPEs. Most of the SLPEs are promotional and utility enterprises. The government intends to promote public-private partnership for undertaking ventures in different areas.

- The problems of the SLPEs are a baggage inherited from the erstwhile UP SLPEs. The executives lack a good grounding in concepts and skills in project management. The computerization and balance scorecard introduction could pep- up the performance of the SLPEs.
- Uttar Pradesh (UP) had 94 SLPEs with an investment of Rs. 18,952 crore as on March 31 2005. The enterprises incurred a net loss of Rs. 1,813 crore. The accumulated loss of these enterprises was of the order of Rs. 10,589 crore as on the same date. These enterprises received budgetary support of Rs. 7,411 crore during 2004-05.
- Overstaffing has crippled the functioning of the SLPEs in UP. Internal management systems are unsound. The interference from the government impedes their working. Productivity in organisations is extremely low. The enterprises suffer from duplication of activities.
- West Bengal had 84 SLPEs with an investment of Rs. 17,802 crore as on March 31 2005. The enterprises incurred a net loss of Rs. 749 crore. The accumulated loss of these enterprises was of the order of Rs. 9,257 crore as on the same date. These enterprises received budgetary support of Rs. 3,365 crore during 2004-05.
- The early retirement scheme has attracted a trenchant criticism. Asset utilisation is abysmally low. Duplication of activities mars the working of the enterprises. Capacity utilisation is very low.

1

State Level Public Enterprises in India: A Macro Analysis

1. Introduction

The State Level Public Enterprises (SLPEs) are an important component of the public enterprise system in India. As per the Institute of Public Enterprise (IPE) database, there were 1,129 SLPEs as on March 31, 2005 with an investment of Rs..2,59,184 crore. The contribution of the SLPEs to the Gross State Domestic Product (GDP) is about 5 per cent as compared to 10 per cent by the Central Public Enterprises (CPEs). The role of SLPEs can be assessed from the total turnover as a percentage of the GDP. There was no consistent pattern among states and this percentage generally varied from 1 to17 per cent of the Gross State Domestic Product, with most states falling in the range of 6 to15 per cent. Although, the SLPEs constitute 80 per cent of the total investment of the CPEs, they are more than four times the number of the CPEs. The average investment in an SLPE is 15 per cent of a CPE. However, the SLPEs in terms of the resource use and control depict a different picture as compared to their counterparts in the central sector in that they directly impact the functioning of the state economies and have a greater exposure to the state political systems. The SLPEs are characterized by weak middle management systems as they do not have on their rolls the requisite number of professionally qualified mangers. The top management in these enterprises comprises mostly an IAS CEO and nominees of the state governments drawn from civil services, defeated politicians and political party in power. The financial performance of the SLPEs bears the brunt of these shortcomings. Between 1990-91 and 2004-05, the SLPEs continued to incur net losses and showed the chronic tendency of accumulating losses. The macro analysis provides in the beginning an overview of the SLPEs in India in terms of various financial parameters followed by the general scenario in regard to their privatisation. The differentiating features of privatisation of the SLPEs vis-à-vis the CPEs have been outlined to bring out the challenges that the various state governments have to meet in reconsidering the retention of their portfolios of the SLPEs. The summing up provides the conclusions to formulate an appropriate policy in this regard.

2. Financial Performance and Fiscal Impact

2.1 Total Investment

The total investment comprises sum total of the investments in the form of equity and debt capital by State Government and others which includes the Central Government, holding company and financial institutions.

Table 1 shows the total investment in the SLPEs. The total investment in these enterprises for all the states taken together increased from Rs. 77,730 crore in 1991 to Rs. 2,59,184 crore in 2005. The lion's share of about 85 per cent total investment belonged to utility enterprises. The major portion of total investment was shared by Andhra Pradesh, Delhi, Gujarat, Karnataka, Maharashtra, Punjab, Rajasthan, Tamil Nadu, Uttar Pradesh and West Bengal. The Compound Average Growth Rate (CAGR) of total investment for the period 1990-91 to 2004-05 was 8.85 per cent. The investment grew at a slower pace during the period 1990-91 to 1996-97. The growth was much faster upto during the 1997-98 to 2003-04. However, investment levels declined during 2003-04 and recorded a marginal increase in 2004-05. Bihar, Delhi, Gujarat, Kerala, Punjab, Tamil Nadu, Rajasthan and Uttar Pradesh registered the decline due to closure of some enterprises or change in ownership.

Chart 1
All States : Total Investment

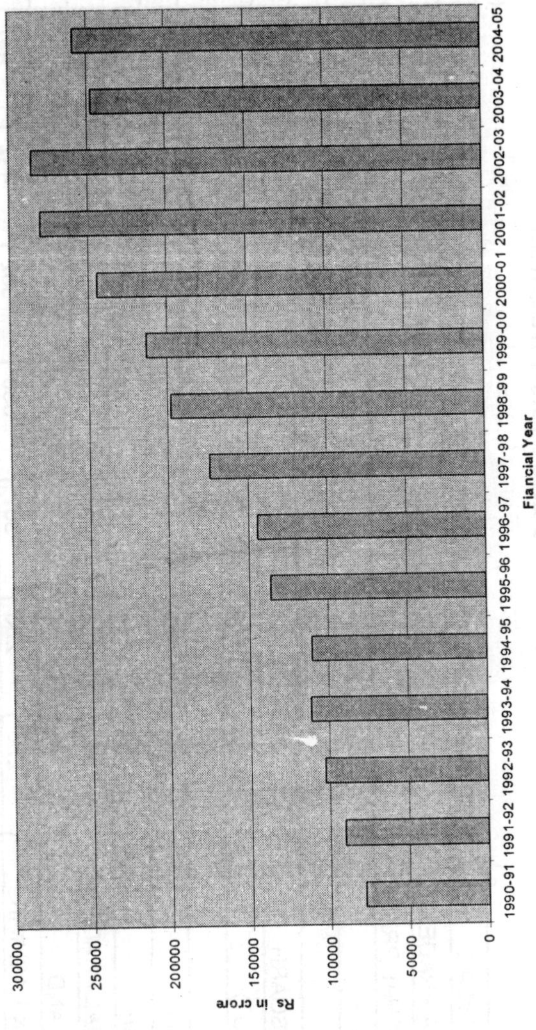

Table 1 All States : Total Investment

(Rs in crore)

STATE / YEAR	*1990-91*	*1991-92*	*1992-93*	*1993-94*	*1994-95*	*1995-96*	*1996-97*	*1997-98*
ANDHRA PRADESH	6086	7030	8364	10487	12751	13255	11761	23016
ARUNACHAL PRADESH	30	32	39	38	48	45	52	42
ASSAM	2284	2599	2853	3078	3302	3512	3632	3826
BIHAR	~	~	~	~	~	~	~	5336
CHATTISGARH								
DELHI (UT)	5734	6863	7475	8742	10232	11185	11171	13361
GOA	140	178	203	247	328	401	468	581
GUJARAT	6536	7207	7729	8161	9101	10156	11081	11743
HARYANA	434	444	471	464	511	663	1510	1633
HIMACHAL PRADESH	1088	1185	1233	1288	1598	1739	1948	2593
JHARKHAND	-	-	-	-	-	-	-	0
JAMMU & KASHMIR	258	280	307	338	382	442	497	1032
KARNATAKA	4566	5398	6167	7505	8504	10867	13353	13245
KERALA	3466	3931	4811	4829	5471	6375	7692	9162

(Contd.)

(Contd. Table 1)

STATE / YEAR	1998-99	1999-00	2000-01	2001-02	2002-03	2003-04	2004-05
ANDHRA PRADESH	26672	29793	29476	31162	33209	30842	33914
ARUNACHAL PRADESH	35	33	26	27	27	23	20
ASSAM	3859	3602	3627	3870	4180	2454	4415
BIHAR	5408	7963	7955	9895	9287	7132	5407
CHATTISGARH					0	113	1059
DELHI (UT)	16131	18419	19070	21484	10964	10964	9695
GOA	668	420	467	494	598	598	598
GUJARAT	16472	18288	21046	27613	31098	18435	21195
HARYANA	1465	1458	1658	1888	8957	9441	9847
HIMACHAL PRADESH	2662	2452	3842	4941	5103	3683	3683
JHARKHAND	-	-	-	-	0	198	645
JAMMU & KASHMIR	1196	1503	2018	2554	2889	2362	2994
KARNATAKA	18163	19879	23667	27231	29231	30011	35197
KERALA	11503	11444	14991	15998	10891	11900	11045

(Contd.)

(Contd. Table 1)

STATE / YEAR	1990-91	1991-92	1992-93	1993-94	1994-95	1995-96	1996-97	1997-98
MADHYA PRADESH	519	565	674	697	722	859	854	945
MAHARASHTRA	6450	6990	8743	9157	9892	10524	14310	15542
MANIPUR	52	59	64	114	122	127	129	134
MEGHALAYA	341	380	399	407	412	431	438	476
MIZORAM	23	21	23	22	22	23	24	31
NAGALAND	209	220	237	250	355	98	180	196
ORISSA	2272	2583	2754	3049	3323	3465	5782	6698
PONDICHERRY (U.T.)	48	88	100	116	142	176	214	272
PUNJAB	5493	6083	6711	7338	8138	9061	9826	11533
RAJASTHAN	3145	3591	4235	5017	6105	6683	7486	8988
SIKKIM	88	68	76	71	75	91	85	50
TAMIL NADU	4720	5426	5568	6397	7933	8830	9705	10739
TRIPURA	78	87	96	101	105	119	130	153
UTTAR PRADESH	10867	12383	14170	15118	16310	16988	18573	24441
WEST BENGAL	3541	3957	4286	4634	4896	5771	6374	7621
Total	77730	90983	102670	111757	110780	136301	144471	141169

(Contd.)

(Contd. Table 1)

STATE / YEAR	*1998-99*	*1999-00*	*2000-01*	*2001-02*	*2002-03*	*2003-04*	*2004-05*
MADHYA PRADESH	928	845	1061	1230	5585	5133	5862
MAHARASHTRA	16661	17833	19531	20597	17898	20817	20549
MANIPUR	141	155	161	175	135	135	135
MEGHALAYA	468	488	587	628	701	567	848
MIZORAM	30	37	41	62	66	69	68
NAGALAND	208	82	75	81	81	52	52
ORISSA	7652	8229	9779	12981	12395	12417	12417
PONDICHERRY (U.T.)	324	369	402	419	425	437	453
PUNJAB	12712	12505	13942	16944	19753	13824	14023
RAJASTHAN	10179	11566	14983	16535	12891	14077	13818
SIKKIM	57	44	65	81	130	139	141
TAMIL NADU	10332	8591	12489	14489	10590	13665	14178
TRIPURA	143	123	146	164	172	172	172
UTTAR PRADESH	25561	27541	31897	32754	32754	20214	18952
WEST BENGAL	8193	9230	10954	15819	25554	17802	17802
Total	197823	212892	243956	280116	285564	247676	259184

(Source : Database on SLPEs, Institute of Public Enterprise, Hyderabad)

2.2 Typology

Table 2 presents the sectoral distribution of the various SLPEs. The various categories in which the SLPEs have been divided include manufacturing, financial, promotional, trade and service, utility and welfare sectors. The manufacturing enterprises are followed respectively by promotional, utility, welfare, financial and trading and services enterprises. The manufacturing enterprises dominated the scenario because the various state governments emulated the central government in giving a fillip to industrialization. The trading and services enterprises received an encouragement to provide export thrust and create a suitable infrastructure of services at the state level. The promotional enterprises were set up to orient social activities with an economic tinge at the state level. The welfare enterprises were a new breed of the SLPEs set up to provide economic support to the backward classes of society, comprising scheduled castes, scheduled tribes, minorities, women and handicapped. Andhra Pradesh, Assam, Gujarat, Karnataka, Kerala, Maharashtra, Tamil Nadu, Uttar Pradesh and West Bengal showed a preference for manufacturing, promotional and financial enterprises. Maharashtra, Kerala and Uttar Pradesh setup a large number of welfare enterprises. The

Chart 2

All India : No. of SLPEs Category-wise as on March 31, 2005

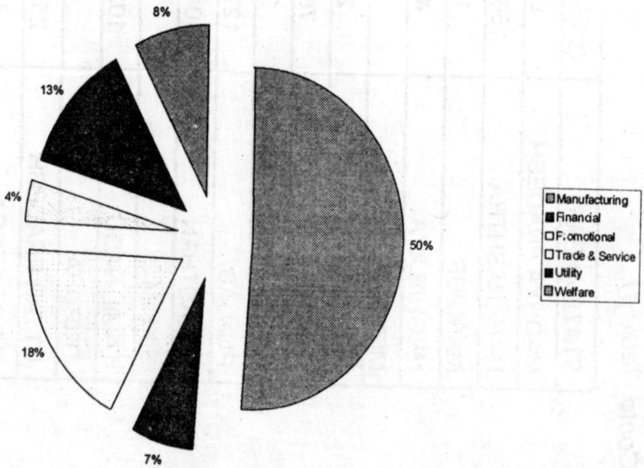

Table 2 All India: No. of SLPEs Category-wise as on March 31, 2005

		Manufacturing	Financial	Promotional	Trade & Service	Utility	Welfare	Total
1	Andhra Pradesh	28	5	13	5	8	1	54
2	Arunachal Pradesh	2	1	2	0	0	0	5
3	Andaman and Nicobar	1	0	1	0	0	0	2
4	Assam	28	2	5	1	10	3	42
6	Bihar	40	2	4	2	4	2	54
5	Chattissgarh	2	1	1	2	4	0	10
7	Delhi	1	2	2	0	6	4	15
8	Goa	6	2	4	0	2	1	15
9	Gujarat	25	6	7	4	4	4	50
10	Haryana	10	2	5	2	7	3	29
11	Himachal Pradesh	6	1	10	0	2	2	21
12	Jammu & Kashmir	12	5	2	0	2	2	23
13	Jharkhand	1	0	4	0	2	0	7
14	Karnataka	35	2	20	3	15	7	82
15	Kerala	77	3	12	4	3	10	109
16	Lakshwadeep	1	0	0	0	0	0	1

(Contd. Table 2)

(Contd. Table 2)

		Manufacturing	*Financial*	*Promotional*	*Trade & Service*	*Utility*	*Welfare*	*Total*
1	Andhra Pradesh	28	5	13	5	8	1	54
17	Madhya Pradesh	15	2	7	3	4	9	40
18	Maharashtra	34	4	16	1	4	12	71
19	Manipur	11	1	2	0	1	1	16
20	Meghalya	5	1	6	1	0	0	13
21	Mizoram	3	1	1	0	1	0	6
22	Nagaland	3	1	2	0	0	0	6
23	Orissa	47	5	7	2	7	2	70
24	Pondicherry	5	0	3	0	1	2	11
25	Punjab	24	2	17	6	6	1	56
26	Rajashtan	12	3	4	1	9	0	29
27	Sikkim	4	2	2	1	1	1	11
28	Tamil Nadu	33	6	13	3	24	5	85
29	Tripura	3	3	3	0	1	0	10
30	Uttar Pradesh	53	5	21	2	7	16	104
31	West Bengal	52	7	10	1	9	3	82
	Total	**579**	**77**	**206**	**44**	**144**	**91**	**1,129**

Source : Database on SLPEs, Institute of Public Enterprise, Hyderabad

preference for economic and social infrastructure might have been responsible for the respective choice. Andhra Pradesh, Delhi, Karnataka, Orissa, Tamil Nadu and West Bengal have a major share in the utility sector enterprises. The utility enterprises comprised the state road transport corporations and the unbundled power sector enterprises.

2.3 Capital Employed

The capital employed comprises the sum total of the investment in the next fixed block and working capital. The net fixed assets indicate the investments in gross fixed assets minus accumulated depreciation. The investment in working capital represents the excess of current assets over current liabilities. The capital employed is also represented by the sum total of investments arising out of equity, long-term debts and internal resources.

Table 3 represents the investments by way of net fixed assets and working capital. Such investments are financed by debt, equity and internal funds. The capital employed was Rs. 73,300 crore in 1991. It increased to Rs. 2,44,773 crore in 2004-05. The CAGR for capital employed was 8.78 per cent during the period under reference. The capital employed was 85 per cent of the total investment pointing to the fact that the SLPEs system was not organic and required artificial respiration from time to time. The states where this phenomenon had a forceful presence included Delhi, Goa, Haryana, Himachal Pradesh, Jammu & Kashmir, Karnataka, Kerala, Maharashtra, Orissa, Punjab, Tamil Nadu, Uttar Pradesh and West Bengal. Rajasthan turned-out to be an exception indicating the appreciation for viable and self liquidating project management as the strength of the top management of the SLPEs and the policy makers in the State Government.

2.4 Net Worth

The net worth is derived by subtracting intangible assets, accumulated losses and fictitious assets from paid-up capital, and reserves and surpluses.

Though the net worth showed the trend to increase manifold indicated in Table 4, turned out to be a shade lower than 7 per cent

Chart 3
All India : Capital Employed

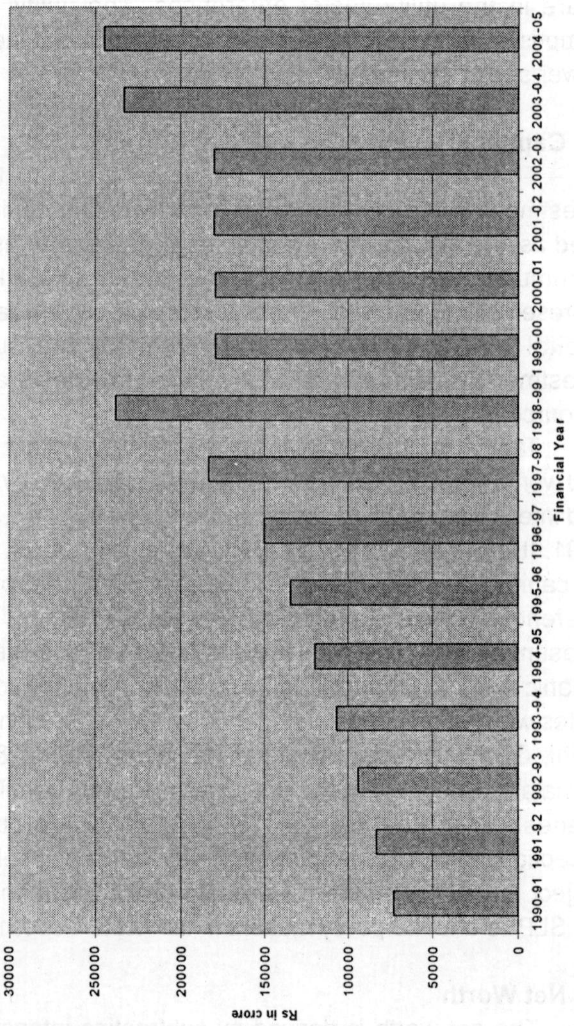

Table 3 All India : Capital Employed

(Rs.in crore)

STATE / YEAR	*1990-91*	*1991-92*	*1992-93*	*1993-94*	*1994-95*	*1995-96*	*1996-97*	*1997-98*
ANDHRA PRADESH	6438	7456	8848	11053	13384	14312	12769	29443
ARUNACHAL PRADESH	24	27	34	51	52	74	89	39
ASSAM	1984	2283	2509	2676	2881	3057	3203	3356
CHATTISGARH								
DELHI	6957	9503	10910	11385	9744	11776	14161	5907
GOA	137	178	207	230	336	391	460	576
GUJARAT	6501	7325	7979	8599	9824	11233	12803	16987
HARYANA	439	447	511	497	585	669	731	1720
HIMACHAL PRADESH	1031	1117	1185	1233	1425	1573	1716	2312
JAMMU & KASHMIR	401	409	366	302	271	260	292	791
KARNATAKA	5120	5718	6447	7325	8384	9629	13063	12634
KERALA	2823	2701	2957	3414	4087	4736	5717	7147
MADHYA PRADESH	546	581	709	772	804	976	980	1124

(Contd.)

(Contd. Tab;e 3)

STATE / YEAR	*1998-99*	*1999-00*	*2000-01*	*2001-02*	*2002-03*	*2003-04*	*2004-05*
ANDHRA PRADESH	28429	22504	22115	20670	21402	22202	25314
ARUNACHAL PRADESH	34	31	37	32	32	0	0
ASSAM	2519	2389	2110	2128	2128	1586	1267
CHATTISGARH			0	0	0	50.81	352
DELHI	6533	7688	8692	9745	10851	10851	10851
GOA	391	432	455	640	483	684	619
GUJARAT	15541	27674	37066	25839	23913	33573	30052
HARYANA	1970	1936	2303	2531	2493	7123	8210
HIMACHAL PRADESH	2373	2155	3584	3814.1	3575	0	4941
JAMMU & KASHMIR	1597	1981	2493	2515	3075	3075	5274
KARNATAKA	18033	19253	21561	25092	25092	29926	39671
KERALA	9600	9953	11270	12285	12680	0	0
MADHYA PRADESH	1073	924	1039	977	903	7315	2917

(Contd.)

(Contd. Tab;e 3)

STATE / YEAR	*1990-91*	*1991-92*	*1992-93*	*1993-94*	*1994-95*	*1995-96*	*1996-97*	*1997-98*
MAHARASHTRA	11820	13137	15891	17399	17739	19428	20362	21370
MANIPUR	38	113	41	41	41	43	19	18
MEGHALAYA	325	353	388	414	424	450	454	434
MIZORAM	117	143	179	207	236	268	314	341
NAGALAND	-37	-61	-79	-100	-209	-36	23	24
ORISSA	2070	2395	2752	2703	3187	3520	5925	6639
PONDICHERRY (U.T.)	54	118	131	165	181	189	197	236
PUNJAB	5228	5452	6296	7200	8533	9513	9712	11463
RAJASTHAN	4180	4771	5486	6489	8037	9221	10479	12155
SIKKIM	30	44	49	48	41	41	36	47
TAMIL NADU	5945	6874	7336	8385	10220	11965	13200	14965
TRIPURA	51	63	66	66	58	66	78	86
UTTAR PRADESH	8144	8599	9407	12109	14925	15643	17218	25073
WEST BENGAL	2935	3529	3717	4416	4831	5909	6292	7921
Total	73301	83277	94323	107080	120018	134903	150291	182807

(Contd.)

(Contd.Tab;e 3)

STATE / YEAR	*1998-99*	*1999-00*	*2000-01*	*2001-02*	*2002-03*	*2003-04*	*2004-05*
MAHARASHTRA	23316	17422	16402	15730	15471	22218	21757
MANIPUR	0	0	0	0	0	27	27
MEGHALAYA	442	427	480	448	448	423	686
MIZORAM	343	54	48	49	48	50	50
NAGALAND	19	40	26	48	48	18	18
ORISSA	6639	6639	6639	6639	6639	5458	0
PONDICHERRY (U.T.)	133	287	306	306	324	324	382
PUNJAB	2676	3081	4066	7354	7354	20373	17114
RAJASTHAN	64733	16612	17220	21991	21700	15933	19736
SIKKIM	61	65	70	61	61	0	0
TAMIL NADU	15292	6035	5633	5631	5631	16945	18055
TRIPURA	50	46	22	18	17	17	17
UTTAR PRADESH	27510	27881	11512	11441	11441	15466	17338
WEST BENGAL	8788	3609	4048	3847	3818	19251	20122
Total	238095	179117	179198	179831.1	179627	232889	244770

(Source : Database on SLPEs, Institute of Public Enterprise, Hyderabad)

Table 4 All India : Net Worth

(Rs.in crore)

STATE / YEAR	*1990-91*	*1991-92*	*1992-93*	*1993-94*	*1994-95*	*1995-96*
ANDHRA PRADESH	1245	1370	1579	3160	3109	4048
ARUNACHAL PRADESH	5	7	9	12	18	22
ASSAM	-535	59	29	27	-135	-261
BIHAR	0	0	0	0	0	0
DELHI	-596	-788	-1022	-955	1432	1858
GOA	63	90	110	126	234	277
GUJARAT	961	1161	1430	1702	2103	2518
HARYANA	93	125	167	227	257	334
HIMACHAL PRADESH	726	794	829	912	1205	1370
JAMMU & KASHMIR	86	22	-39	-117	-186	-279
KARNATAKA	1115	1226	1342	1756	1886	2852
KERALA	425	370	-544	383	600	713
MADHYA PRADESH	175	1784	251	265	277	294
MAHARASHTRA	3186	4909	4853	3937	4156	4294

(Contd.)

(Contd. Table 4)

STATE / YEAR	*1996-97*	*1997-98*	*1998-99*	*1999-00*	*2000-01*	*2001-02*	*2002-03*
ANDHRA PRADESH	4317	6413	6572	4042	4157	4199	4450
ARUNACHAL PRADESH	26	24	17	11	16	9	9
ASSAM	-619	-925	26	-12	-13	-10	27
BIHAR	0	4	5	7	7	7	8
DELHI	-69	288	320	275	415	525	93
GOA	311	357	311	128	94	83	72
GUJARAT	3002	4743	4619	4777	5690	4971	4992
HARYANA	372	463	475	213	232	292	300
HIMACHAL PRADESH	1578	23	27	7	11	6	6
JAMMU & KASHMIR	-341	782	761	931	868	837	576
KARNATAKA	3594	3284	4619	4790	4897	6545	6545
KERALA	968	1123	2640	2488	2492	3881	4101
MADHYA PRADESH	323	343	341	275	279	240	247
MAHARASHTRA	4610	8001	3703	3703	3703	3703	3703

(Contd.)

(Contd. Table 4)

STATE / YEAR	*1990-91*	*1991-92*	*1992-93*	*1993-94*	*1994-95*	*1995-96*
MANIPUR	9	0	15	58	52	43
MEGHALAYA	312	348	378	407	423	450
MIZORAM	14	15	17	21	22	23
NAGALAND	-118	-143	-166	-189	-300	-57
ORISSA	891	1044	1299	1167	1099	1244
PONDICHERRY (U.T.)	30	77	86	87	105	112
PUNJAB	996	1148	2744	2901	3194	3298
RAJASTHAN	-237	513	647	837	970	1522
SIKKIM	13	15	15	14	8	14
TAMIL NADU	1210	1605	1175	1668	2280	2328
TRIPURA	39	46	53	57	57	66
UTTAR PRADESH	-38	57	111	-44	82	-65
WEST BENGAL	-359	-426	72	149	640	1361
Total	11053	13248	17664	21676	27669	32855

(Contd.)

(Contd. Table 4)

STATE / YEAR	*1996-97*	*1997-98*	*1998-99*	*1999-00*	*2000-01*	*2001-02*	*2002-03*
MANIPUR	37	35	34	34	34	34	34
MEGHALAYA	454	442	450	64	67	1	1
MIZORAM	24	26	20	6	8	11	12
NAGALAND	-4	-8	-18	0	0	0	0
ORISSA	1261	72	3	-26	-51	-55	-51
PONDICHERRY (U.T.)	123	182	86	260	274	287	304
PUNJAB	4304	4354	201	201	201	201	201
RAJASTHAN	1911	2868	3034	3131	3151	3055	3041
SIKKIM	17	21	5	0	0	0	0
TAMIL NADU	3199	3570	3311	3311	3311	3311	3311
TRIPURA	74	83	13	-11	-6	-4	-3
UTTAR PRADESH	-280	352	4204	4124	2066	3003	3003
WEST BENGAL	1320	1555	876	800	800	800	800
Total	35352	43620	44124	33736	33615	38429	44631

(Source : Database on SLPEs, Institute of Public Enterprise, Hyderabad)

of the total equity which pointed to a negligible growth in net worth and erosion of shareholders' basic capital in terms of real investment prices appearing to be a great cause of concern. The equity erosion occurred in Assam, Delhi, Goa, Kerala, Maharashtra, Mizoram, Meghalaya, Nagaland, Pondicherry, Sikkim, Tripura, Uttar Pradesh, and West Bengal. These were precisely the states where the subsidies accounted for major portion of the losses incurred.

2.5 Total Revenue

This represents the top line of an enterprise. This provides cushion against contingencies and the cover to meet expenses. This should grow at least at a compound annual growth rate of 10 percent to set off the loss caused by the real rate of inflation and meet the challenges of productivity arising out of technological

Chart 4
All India: Total Revenue

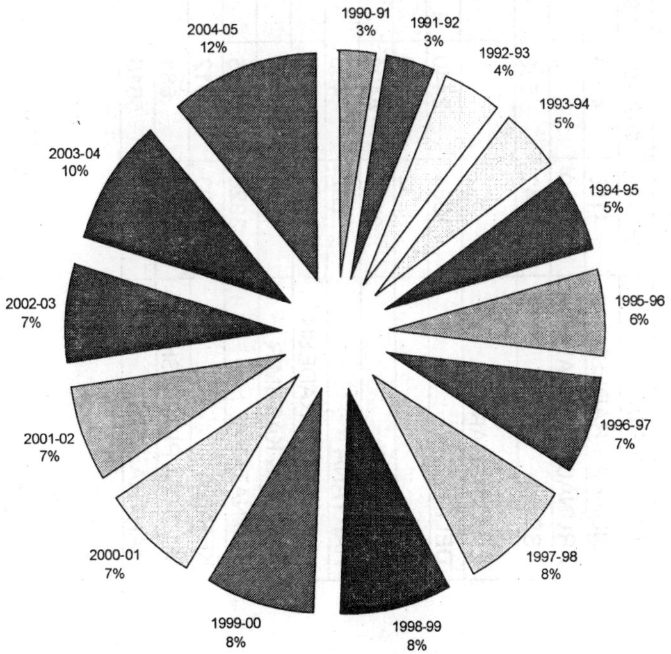

Table 5 All India : Total Revenue Earned

(Rs.in crore)

STATE / YEAR	1990-91	1991-92	1992-93	1993-94	1994-95	1995-96	1996-97
ANDHRA PRADESH	4168	4914	11161	5494	6626	7675	7817
ARUNACHAL PRADESH	19	19	25	29	31	27	36
ASSAM	542	568	584	625	702	1051	896
CHATTISGARH							
DELHI	1984	2440	2895	3341	3554	3900	4563
GOA	32	39	55	63	93	99	100
GUJARAT	3676	4408	4768	5460	6279	7652	8935
HARYANA	302	435	463	526	599	665	631
HIMACHAL PRADESH	362	408	473	530	602	693	816
JAMMU & KASHMIR	119	100	132	134	146	195	232
KARNATAKA	3328	3795	4202	5038	6074	7092	7214
KERALA	1803	2012	2456	2512	2939	3356	3771
MADHYA PRADESH	551	681	899	957	931	1063	1328
MAHARASHTRA	4743	5616	6729	8002	9235	11079	12393

(Contd.)

(Contd. Table 5)

STATE / YEAR	*1997-98*	*1998-99*	*1999-00*	*2000-01*	*2001-02*	*2002-03*	*2003-04*	*2004-05*
ANDHRA PRADESH	12956	13529	11605	9261	9665	9981	31901	34332
ARUNACHAL PRADESH	22	21	16	13	11	10	0	0
ASSAM	830	77	74	59	65	74	109	1115
CHATTISGARH							32	355
DELHI	4002	4543	4933	1848	1852	1821	0	0
GOA	123	131	121	124	73	95	157	202
GUJARAT	9983	11274	10262	11701	13437	13318	11635	13807
HARYANA	608	458	369	337	280	233	9939	1177.9
HIMACHAL PRADESH	264	309	245	223	302	320	453	453
JAMMU & KASHMIR	351	400	363	392	439	424	0	0
KARNATAKA	5478	8812	9588	10196	11708	11708	0	0
KERALA	4603	5432	6246	7341	7332	7443	0	0
MADHYA PRADESH	1383	1506	1209	1270	980	1078	5619	6330
MAHARASHTRA	13072	13568	15154	14083	14851	15423	17665	19427

(Contd.)

(Contd. Table 5)

STATE / YEAR	1990-91	1991-92	1992-93	1993-94	1994-95	1995-96	1996-97
MANIPUR	8	11	11	9	13	10	8
MEGHALAYA	53	64	67	85	86	110	120
MIZORAM	7	7	11	13	14	15	19
NAGALAND	4	6	4	1	1	1	2
ORISSA	1099	1371	1479	1683	1920	2562	3071
PONDICHERRY (U.T.)	17	115	133	153	174	175	178
PUNJAB	1245	1478	1659	2291	2803	3179	3621
RAJASTHAN	1302	1807	2348	2821	3372	4201	4778
SIKKIM	20	29	26	25	23	34	41
TAMIL NADU	5224	6058	7264	8097	9764	11478	13398
TRIPURA	14	16	15	16	12	15	17
UTTAR PRADESH	4276	5073	5989	6896	7697	8844	9343
WEST BENGAL	1215	1515	1768	2101	2531	2895	3353
Total	36112	42986	55616	56902	66222	78066	86681

(Contd.)

(Contd. Table 5)

STATE / YEAR	*1997-98*	*1998-99*	*1999-00*	*2000-01*	*2001-02*	*2002-03*	*2003-04*	*2004-05*
MANIPUR	8	0	0	0	0	0	0	0
MEGHALAYA	127	126	36	39	18	22	211	279
MIZORAM	1306	13	0	0	0	0	1	1
NAGALAND	19	23	20	15	12	10	1	1
ORISSA	7293	6124	5401	4880	3572	2005	0	0
PONDICHERRY (U.T.)	163	136	155	211	199	215	362	362
PUNJAB	4185	3200	2509	2298	1807	1665	1357	14660
RAJASTHAN	5611	6205	7441	3731	3750	3689	11185	11185
SIKKIM	46	36	30	24	13	11	0	0
TAMIL NADU	15184	12094	7271	7560	7560	7560	0	0
TRIPURA	14	12	6	5	4	2	0	0
UTTAR PRADESH	12014	12878	11981	13369	7911	7911	13685	13528
WEST BENGAL	3721	3489	2579	1893	1534	1268	8896	9935
Total	103366	104393	97612	90873	87375	86284	113208	127150

(Source : Database on SLPEs, Institute of Public Enterprise, Hyderabad)

advances and reorganization of business processes. This should be at least three times of the investment. The private sector multiple is five times. The multiple in the case of private sector enterprises abroad is eight times. The CAGR for total revenue for the period 1990-91 to 2004-05 was 9.8 per cent. Table 5 shows that total revenues was about 46 per cent of the total investment in 1990-91 and 53 per cent in 2004-05. The total revenue comprised the income from mainstream operations and other yields. The total revenue scenario tells many untold facts concerning lack of marketing drive, quality consciousness and soft targeting. The states which earned more than average on a rupee of investment were only handful. In 2004-05, such states included Gujarat, Madhya Pradesh, Maharasthra and West Bengal. All the states in the country faced the challenge of unlocking the vast untapped value in the SLPEs.

Net Profit After Tax

The net profit after tax comprises profits net of all expenses, interest and taxes. They determine the scope for and extent of allocations to reserves, dividends and surpluses.

Net profit after tax is the be all and end all of all businesses. It is not only that top line is important for a business but it is also essential to ensure that the bottom line is positive. Net profit making helps in updating the technology, contribute to an organic growth and provide a unified direction. It adds to building up reserves and surpluses and higher earnings per share. Net profit making is the core element of corporatisation which takes place through the concept of equity participation, limited liability, setting up the strategic business units and practicing responsibility accounting. The operationalisation of these concepts creates a harmonious internal environment where the different units/ product groups and services could compete with one another to improve their efficiency. Profitability strikes an optimum tradeoff between the demand side factors (revenues) and the supply side factors (costs) in a competitive regime.

The net profits should at least be equivalent to prime lending rate or 10 per cent of the revenues earned which the bench mark is prescribed in financial management. Table 6 shows that the net

Table 6 All India : Net Profit After Tax

(Rs in crore)

STATE / YEAR	*1990-91*	*1991-92*	*1992-93*	*1993-94*	*1994-95*	*1995-96*	*1996-97*
ANDHRA PRADESH	-105	-275	-208	4	-14	-188	-224
ARUNACHAL PRADESH	0	1	2	2	7	4	4
ASSAM	-142	-273	-222	-316	-293	-155	-418
CHATTISGARH							
DELHI	-318	-342	-173	-357	-235	-434	-508
GOA	1	1	2	-1	9	-4	-5
GUJARAT	135	101	169	154	172	261	294
HARYANA	10	26	33	39	55	17	30
HIMACHAL PRADESH	-16	-24	-6	9	9	27	-36
JAMMU & KASHMIR	-29	-79	-66	-91	-76	-96	-70
KARNATAKA	76	94	-59	-54	68	66	-62
KERALA	-169	-201	-139	-78	-16	-35	-197
MADHYA PRADESH	7	2	23	14	9	1	14
MAHARASHTRA	123	143	187	406	536	567	255

(Contd. Table 6)

STATE / YEAR	*1997-98*	*1998-99*	*1999-00*	*2000-01*	*2001-02*	*2002-03*	*2003-04*	*2004-05*
ANDHRA PRADESH	142	147	-108	-29	22	-188	346	393
ARUNACHAL PRADESH	-1	-4	-5	1	-5	-1	-4	-6
ASSAM	-448	-54	-53	-67	-61	-691	-727	-671
CHATTISGARH						0	4	6
DELHI	-1019	-1410	-1435	535	-584	-768	0	-1693
GOA	2	-4	-9	-11	-20	-18	0	0
GUJARAT	178	178	-240	-279	-641	-517	-1181	-755
HARYANA	84	32	58	14	59	-178	20	68
HIMACHAL PRADESH	-113	-162	-168	-81	-141	-77	-77	-77
JAMMU & KASHMIR	-109	-129	-126	-84	-70	249	305	-5
KARNATAKA	-22	17	44	40	45	45	143	378
KERALA	-165	-111	-156	-271	-711	-100	-146	-55
MADHYA PRADESH	-15	-22	16	16	19	-16	-5	1
MAHARASHTRA	249	249	211	-302	-620	-951	-1161	-1179

(Contd.)

(Contd. Table 6)

STATE / YEAR	1990-91	1991-92	1992-93	1993-94	1994-95	1995-96	1996-97
MANIPUR	-2	-2	-2	-5	-5	-8	-7
MEGHALAYA	-4	-3	-4	-2	-1	-3	-3
MIZORAM	-14	-18	-20	-22	-28	-36	-36
NAGALAND	-20	-24	-24	-22	-114	-247	-21
ORISSA	-3	-11	-1	-70	-81	70	-141
POND'CHERRY (U.T.)	1	5	2	-7	-7	-19	-25
PUNJAB	-74	32	-111	-10	60	280	86
RAJASTHAN	-94	81	72	112	99	241	132
SIKKIM	0	1	0	-1	-8	-4	-1
TAMIL NADU	70	284	251	280	361	226	70
TRIPURA	-9	-10	-10	-12	-13	-14	-15
UTTAR PRADESH	-174	24	-10	-190	83	-215	-694
WEST BENGAL	-187	-193	135	-120	-143	-150	-175
Total	-938	-632	-314	-341	434	151	-1502

(Contd.)

(Contd. Table 6)

STATE / YEAR	*1997-98*	*1998-99*	*1999-00*	*2000-01*	*2001-02*	*2002-03*	*2003-04*	*2004-05*
MANIPUR	-9	-8	0	0	0	0	-3	-3
MEGHALAYA	-2	-2	-3	-3	-3	-35	-27	5
MIZORAM	-46	-42	-2	-2	-2	-2	-4	-4
NAGALAND	-8	-13	-1	-2	-2	-2	0	-2
ORISSA	-221	-529	-386	-82	65	-189	-571	-571
PONDICHERRY (U.T.)	-17	-17	-19	-12	-12	-3	-6	-7
PUNJAB	-42	-84	-105	-166	-318	-318	-901	73
RAJASTHAN	73	29	351	236	269	-18	11	146
SIKKIM	1	0	0	0	0	-3	-22	-3
TAMIL NADU	104	-90	-289	-190	-160	320	97	-1032
TRIPURA	-17	-3	-9	-9	-15	-17	0	0
UTTAR PRADESH	-391	243	-508	-485	-485	-2355	-1308	-1813
WEST BENGAL	-158	-881	-856	-985	-1739	-1392	749	-749
Total	-2602	-4104	-6529	-10136	-6762	-6997	-4468	-7555

(Source : Database on SLPEs, Institute of Public Enterprise, Hyderabad)

profits for all the states taken together for the various years of the study, excepting 1994-95, and 1995-96 were negative. On an average, net profits for all the states take together as a percent of the revenues earned were -2.7 per cent in 1990-91 shooting up to -5.49 per cent in 2004-05. The CAGR for net profit for the period 1990-91 to 2004-05 was -13.79 per cent. Assam, Delhi, Gujarat, Haryana, Maharashtra, Uttar Pradesh and West Bengal have been major net loss earners during 2004-05. The net losses incurred by these states not only wiped out the total profits of the profit making states but also were responsible for the phenomenon of loss making.

2.7 Accumulated Losses

The story of the SLPEs is one of accumulating losses and creating a huge pile in this regard. The accumulated losses of the SLPEs increased from Rs. 10,999 crore in 1991-92 to Rs. 60,517 crore in 2004-05. Table 7 shows that the loss leaders comprised Andhra Pradesh, Arunachal Pradesh, Assam, Bihar, Delhi, Goa, Gujarat, Kerala, Jammu and Kashmir, Karnataka, Orissa, Pondicherry, Sikkim, Tamil Nadu, Uttar Pradesh and West Bengal.

2.8 Total Impact on State Finances (TISF)

The financial performance of the SLPEs has a great bearing on the fiscal health of the state governments. This impact could be explained in terms of two measures. The Total Impact on the State Finance (TISF) could be shown in terms of annual outflows (sum of outflows resulting from change in state equity and debt and state subsidy and grants to SLPEs) plus the opportunity cost of investments in the SLPEs. The Gross Fiscal Impact on State Finances (GFISF) is another measure which is computed by added the sum total impact on state finances and value of guarantees outstanding given by the state SLPEs. Table 8 shows the TISF as a percentage of Tax Revenue of all the states.

Charts 6 & 7 below represent the ratio of TISF to states' own tax revenue and the ratio of GSISF to states' own tax revenue. Both the charts very clearly show the adverse impact of the non-viable working of the SLPEs on the state finances in India and hint at the possibility of a significant turnaround through the restructuring of the SLPEs.

Chart 5

All India : Accumulated Losses

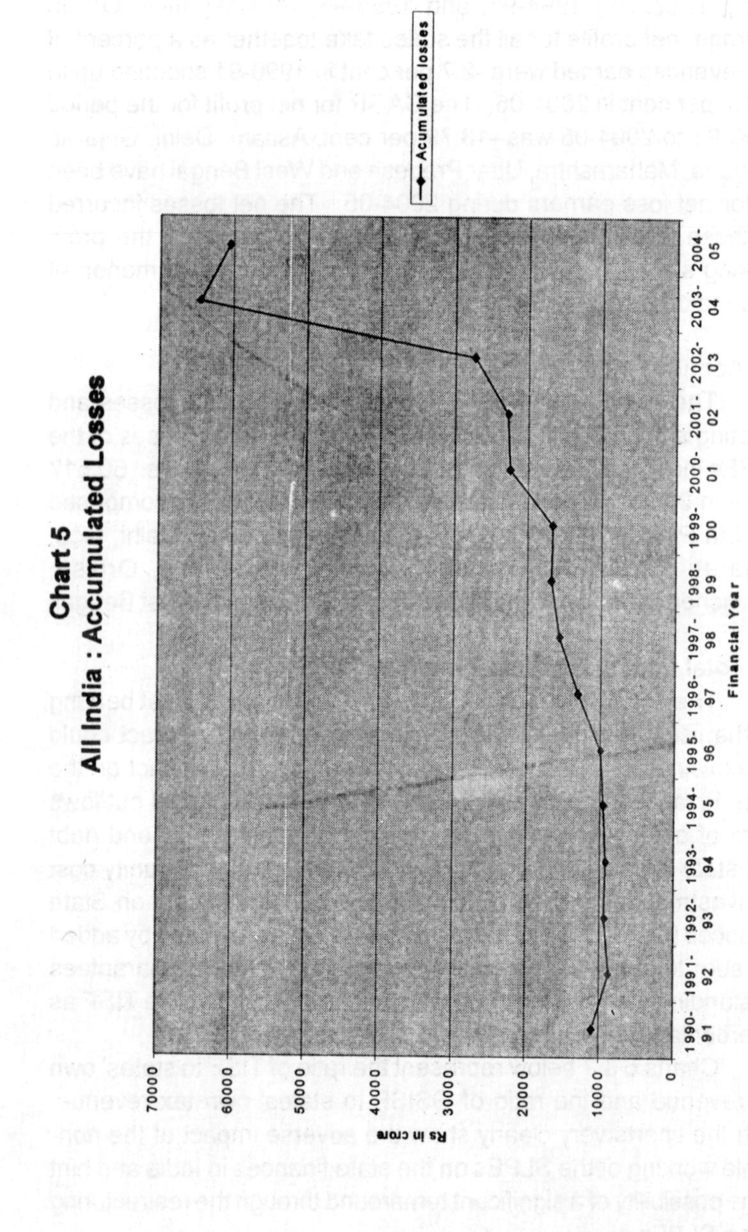

Table 7 All India : Accumulated Losses

(Rs in crore)

STATE / YEAR	*1990-91*	*1991-92*	*1992-93*	*1993-94*	*1994-95*	*1995-96*	*1996-97*
ANDHRA PRADESH	652	991	1276	734	774	1074	1504
ARUNACHAL PRADESH	1	1	2	2	4	6	4
ASSAM	875	1140	1190	1095	1462	1648	2045
BIHAR	0	0	0	0	0	0	0
CHATTISGARH	0	0	0	0	0	0	0
DELHI	1565	2016	2726	3414	4226	5319	4395
GOA	8	12	11	15	11	19	35
GUJARAT	444	480	499	550	640	667	740
HARYANA	86	87	89	100	112	123	140
HIMACHAL PRADESH	108	129	105	158	161	170	193
JAMMU & KASHMIR	132	178	253	346	425	535	619
KARNATAKA	644	681	718	904	919	946	967
KERALA	808	941	1109	1214	1247	1415	1625
MADHYA PRADESH	11	21	33	47	47	89	109

(Contd.)

(Contd. Table 7)

STATE / YEAR	1997-98	1998-99	1999-00	2000-01	2001-02	2002-03	2003-04	2004-05
ANDHRA PRADESH	2002	2124	2155	2021	1916	1758	2872	2215
ARUNACHAL PRADESH	5	8	11	12	15	(+)15	(+)5	(+)0.59
ASSAM	2433	875	2423	3013	3052	691	727	670
BIHAR	2303	2370	5047	5047	5047	9668	9610	5163
CHATTISGARH	0	0	0	0	0	0	4.48	10
DELHI	5348	6769	8235	9915	10148	10940	7965	7206
GOA	48	55	52	61	82	(+)141	0	0
GUJARAT	939	1041	1456	1971	2271	1201	1211	1027
HARYANA	191	203	148	178	218	(+)180	0	0
HIMACHAL PRADESH	392	384	374	434	576	772	762	762
JAMMU & KASHMIR	1016	1159	1311	1402	1535	782	917	1056
KARNATAKA	959	1856	1588	1779	2209	2209	843	808
KERALA	1825	2320	2806	3214	3464	1896	2134	-2343
MADHYA PRADESH	105	117	184	191	289	3016	4062	-4062

(Contd.)

(Contd. Table 7)

STATE / YEAR	*1990-91*	*1991-92*	*1992-93*	*1993-94*	*1994-95*	*1995-96*	*1996-97*
MAHARASHTRA	403	449	200	211	203	233	427
MANIPUR	29	34	37	47	56	68	72
MEGHALAYA	117	129	142	149	168	185	225
MIZORAM	6	7	10	11	13	16	19
NAGALAND	188	213	239	263	379	134	156
ORISSA	157	163	217	234	413	433	751
PONDICHERRY (U.T.)	1	1	1	5	16	41	73
PUNJAB	563	579	719	849	872	7872	715
RAJASTHAN	747	672	616	530	461	442	334
SIKKIM	3	4	5	7	13	17	18
TAMIL NADU	318	355	389	405	477	773	1067
TRIPURA	57	75	87	99	109	122	139
UTTAR PRADESH	1668	1717	1803	2094	2126	2365	2828
WEST BENGAL	1410	1667	1864	2001	2203	2332	2520
Total	10999	8754	9262	9109	9526	9936	13122

(Contd.)

(Contd. Table 7)

STATE / YEAR	1997-98	1998-99	1999-00	2000-01	2001-02	2002-03	2003-04	2004-05
MAHARASHTRA	841	1197	1300	4270	1740	2450	3649	-4603
MANIPUR	79	84	0	0	0	21.	21.	21
MEGHALAYA	256	272	299	341	371	407	340	346
MIZORAM	21	15	19	23	21	16	21.	24
NAGALAND	165	179	5	7	7	7	0	25.
ORISSA	1413	2192	2403	2687	2778	2002	2668	2668
PONDICHERRY (U.T.)	73	95	141	161	186	7.58	132	146
PUNJAB	1140	1168	777	911	942	942	2056	1953
RAJASTHAN	289	275	416	509	578	287	312	274
SIKKIM	22	34	29	27	30	33.95	58.01	57.58
TAMIL NADU	1303	1884	2254	2254	2254	(+)570	4205	5251
TRIPURA	152	128	92	140	158	165	0	0
UTTAR PRADESH	3180	4578	3012	3604	3560	8905	10673	10589
WEST BENGAL	2719	3764	4037	4936	6459	8557	9256	9256
Total	15616	16781	16697	22463	22764	27353	64486	60517

Chart 6

TISF as percentage of state own tax revenues (1997-2002)

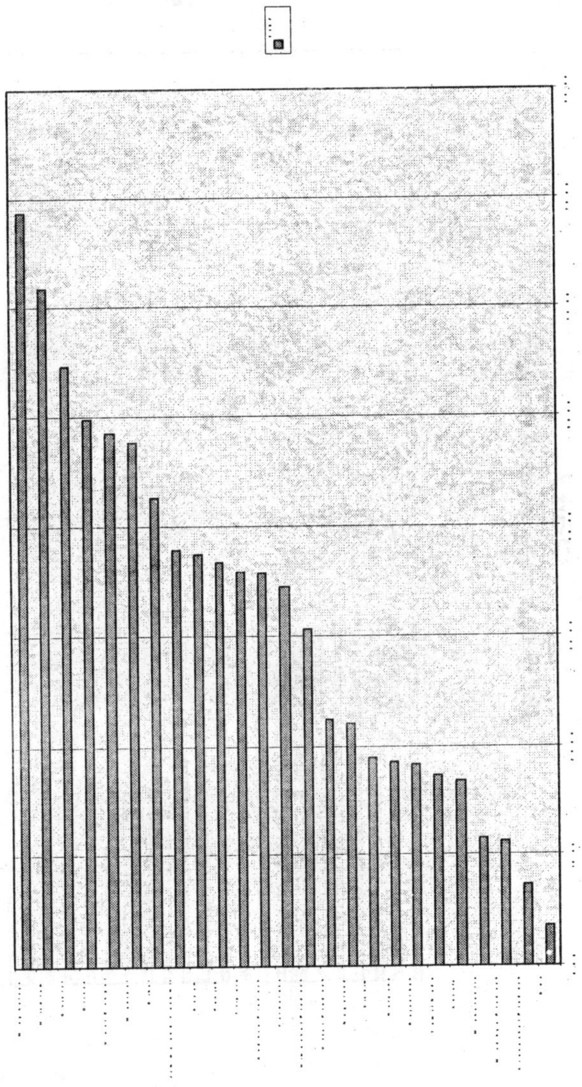

Chart 7

GSISF to states' own tax revenue

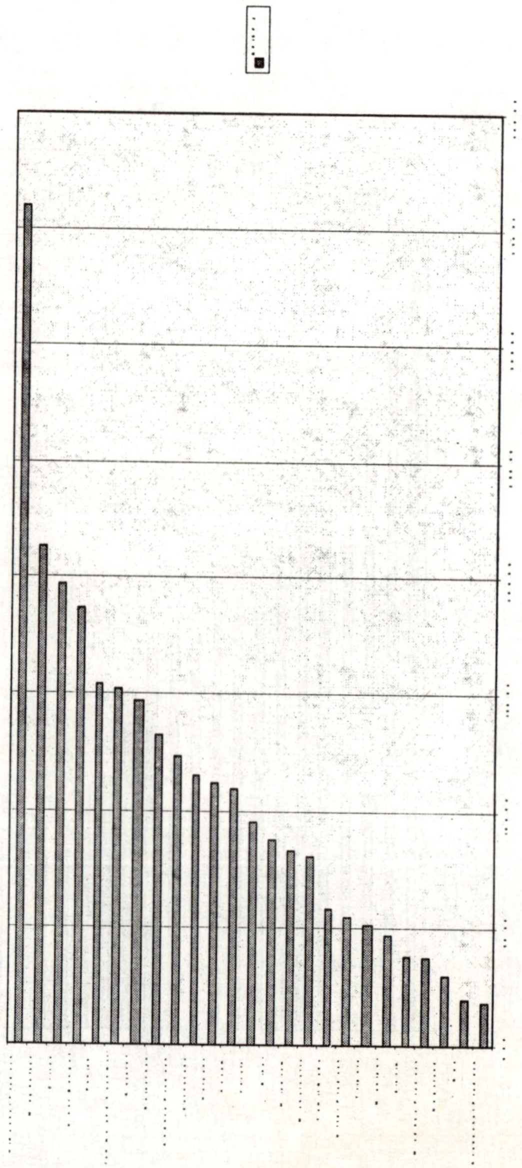

Table 8 Fiscal Impact: All States

Year	*TISF / TRS*	*GFISF/ TRS*
1996-97	35.76	115.54
1997-98	37.45	113.50
1998-99	38.19	114.48
1999-00	14.81	107.41
2000-01	30.20	129.97
2001-02	30.91	137.42
Average	31.22	119.72

3. Privatisation Scenario

3.1 Privatisation Policy

As noted earlier, there is a proliferation in the number of SLPEs and an investment therein has grown phenomenally. This has compelled the state governments to have a re-look of their SLPEs portfolio to decide as to which enterprises they wanted to retain and which ones they considered to privatise, windup or restructure whereas some states are open to both privatisation and /or restructuring, there were others such as Kerala, West Bengal, Tripura and Bihar which rejected the privatisation option and decided to go in for only restructuring/closure including the reference to BIFR (Board for Industrial and Financial Reconstruction).

Some states such as Madhya Pradesh, Karnataka and Kerala have announced detailed policies regarding the SLPEs portfolio. The government of Maharashtra in their industrial policy resolution announced the intention to privatise the SLPEs.

3.2 Privatisation Mechanism

The state governments have preferred to set up expert committees to advice about the retention of the SLPEs portfolio. The Government of Kerala appointed the Vijayachandran Committee and brought out a White Paper on the SLPEs in Kerala. The Institute of Public Enterprise undertook a study on behalf of the Asian Development Bank to recommend the portfolio for retention to the Government of Madhya Pradesh. The S.V. Raghavan Committee made specific recommendations for closure, privatisation and restructuring of the SLPEs in Tamil Nadu. Besides Kerala, which set up an independent machinery to handle restructuring of the SLPEs, Punjab, Andhra Pradesh, Karnataka, Maharashtra, Orissa and U.P also setup independent machinery on restructuring/privatisation/disinvestment.

3.3 Privatisation Techniques

The state governments adopted different techniques ranging from cold privatisation (i.e., non-privatisation reforms to transfer of ownership and closure of the SLPEs). Kerala, West Bengal, and Tripura preferred cold privatisation whereas Punjab, Haryana, Karnataka, Orissa and Andhra Pradesh opted for transfer of ownership through trade sale, divestment of majority stake and sale of equity by private placements. Tamil Nadu has preferred mergers and amalgamations.

3.4 Social Safety Net

Although the various states realized the significance of Social Safety Net in the wake of privatisation, they could not establish an adequate mechanism to deal with this issue chiefly because of shortage of funds. However, Punjab was the first state to set up a State Renewal Fund on the pattern of the National Renewal Fund. Tamil Nadu, Maharashtra, Rajasthan, Karnataka, Madhya Pradesh, took their own initiatives in this regard. The National Renewal Fund did not extend any assistance to the states.

3.5 Privatisation Impediments

Privatisation and Restructuring of the SLPEs was fraught with a number of serious problems. Some of the state governments did not have comprehensive understanding of the technicalities and accountability which formed an important part of the privatisation process. The adjustment of labour force through VRS emerged as a complex issue. There were no arrangements put in place for a pre investigation audit of all the activities concerning privatisation/restructuring in the absence of which a lot of witch hunting made its presence felt. The political ideology also acted as an obstacle in the case of certain states. The location of the states, in particular the north eastern states, obstructed the privatization.

3.6 Privatisation Success

The political ideology and support of the chief of the state such as Andhra Pradesh, Karnataka, Punjab, Maharashtra and Kerala was responsible for the creation of conducive climate for privatisation in these states. The public opinion was significantly moulded by the opinion of the state chiefs and the policy makers. The effectiveness of the machinery created for privatisation lent further support to this phenomenon. The appeal of the enterprise

Table 9 Status of SLPEs in India as on March 31st, 2005

State	*Total Number of Enterprises*	*No. of SLPEs Privatized*	*Profit making*	*Loss making*
Andhra Pradesh	54	30*	24	20
Arunachal Pradesh	5	-	-	4
Assam	42	-	3	36
Bihar	54	-	9	40
Chattisgarh	10		3	4
Delhi	15	-	7	4
Goa	15	-	-	-
Gujarat	50	3	22	25
Haryana	29	1	14	14
Himachal Pradesh	21	-	7	11
Jammu & Kashmir	23	-	6	13
Jahrkhand	7	-	-	-
Karnataka	82	-	39	28
Kerala	109	-	38	70
Lakshadweep	1	-	-	-
Madhya Pradesh	40	-	15	14
Maharashtra	71	-	21	54
Manipur	16	-	4	8
Meghalaya	13	-	3	9

(Contd.)

(Contd.Table 9)

State	Total Number of Enterprises	No. of SLPEs Privatized	Profit making	Loss making
Mizoram	6	-	0	5
Nagaland	6	-	0	3
Orissa	70	1	14	42
Pondicherry	11	-	5	5
Punjab	56	1	12	24
Rajasthan	29	1	11	8
Sikkim	11	-	5	8
Tamilnadu	85	-	48	19
Tripura	10			
U.P.	104	-	56	29
West Bengal	82	-	18	63

* *includes co-operatives.*

and the readiness of the private sector coupled with the negotiating skills displayed in the sale talks also contributed to the success of privatisation. Some states opened a dialogue with the employees of the enterprises put on privatisation list and were able to weaken their resistance or draw their support. Another very important factor responsible for privatisation was the preference of the private sector to buy/take over the manufacturing enterprises. The size of the SLPEs in terms of investment also weighed as an important consideration. These enterprises were mostly in the investment category of Rs.50 - Rs.60 crore. Some states did not insist on full payment of privatisation proceeds and allowed the buyers to pay in installments spread over 2 - 4 years. They also made the buyers agree to not effect immediate retrenchment. The status of SLPEs privatisation is given in Table 9.

4 Privatisation Practices: State-Wise

4.1 Andhra Pradesh

Andhra Pradesh Government appointed a Committee to report on Restructuring of SLPEs. The Committee known as the Subramanyam Committee (1995), had two non-official members. The Commissioner of Public Enterprises was a Member and

Convenor of the Committee. The Committee recommended 9 SLPEs for winding up, 2 enterprises for 100 percent disinvestment, 10 enterprises for partial disinvestment and restructuring, 2 enterprises for restructuring and 5 enterprises for cost reduction and re-orientation. The Committee's recommendations are under implementation.

A three-tier machinery consisting of Department of Public Enterprise, Implementation Secretariat and Cabinet Sub-Committee on Privatisation, was evolved to effect disinvestments. As a part of economic restructuring in the first phase, the government focussed on 12 small and medium SLPEs including some cooperative mills, whose restructuring and privatisation did not involve complex institutional and social issues. The Adam Smith Institute (ASI) was appointed as the consultant.

The government also launched a safety net project for the redressal of social grievances. During the implementation of Phase I, seven more SLPEs were added. In Phase II, covering a period of 5 years between 2001 to 2005, 68 SLPEs have been identified for privatisation. It is however interesting to note that Andhra Pradesh emerged as a leader in privatisation in mid 1980s by the sale of Allwyn Nissan and later Hyderabad Allwyn Limited.

4.2 Bihar

S C Jha Commission (2002) on Bihar state finances, suggested privatisation and restructuring of most of its SLPEs. The Commission observed that one of the noticeable features of Bihar's poor financial management is the non-performance of a large number of state-owned corporations and companies. They have continuously added liabilities and financial burden, the returns on their borrowings and investments turned out to be nil or negative. The total estimated investment in the 54 SLPEs of Bihar, was Rs. 5407 crore. Their accumulated losses stand at Rs. 5163. Most of the SLPEs are entirely defunct. They are surviving on financial life support from the state government. The Jha Commission has suggested to liquidate the companies and use the proceeds to settle liabilities. The Bihar government has initiated liquidation proceedings for several SLPEs but only on paper.

4.3 Gujarat

Gujarat constituted a High Level Committee (1994) to formulate broad guidelines in this regard. On the recommendation of the HLC, the State Government formed a Standing Committee (1995) under the Chairmanship of the Chief Secretary to formulate general principles, broad guidelines and modus operandi to be followed for the disinvestment, privatisation, winding up and restructuring of the SLPEs. The Standing Committee submitted its recommendations in January 1996 which were approved in principle by the Cabinet. The Gujarat Government approved a Comprehensive Public Sector Restructuring Programme (PSRP) and turned out to be one of the most successful state governments in winning the confidence of the workers in working out mutually agreed schemes for closure of non-core enterprises. The Government decided to set up a social safety net and a State Renewal Fund with a substantial budgetary provision. As a part of safety net, Gujarat has made elaborate arrangements for counselling, retraining and redeployment of workers with financial support from the ADB.

4.4 Haryana

Haryana has set up a High Power Cabinet Sub Committee (2002) for Public Sector Restructuring. Six rice mills and one mill owned by Haryana State Cooperative Supply and Marketing Federation have been closed. A Food & Fruit processing plant owned by Haryana Agro Industries Corporation was closed as a measure of reform.

4.5 Kerala

Kerala had 114 SLPEs of which 77 were manufacturing enterprises. The SLPEs employed 1,11,249 personnel. An Enterprise Reforms Commission (ERC) was set up to have a re-look at the portfolio of SLPEs which looks into the recommendation of the Kerala Industrial Revitalisation Fund Board (KIRFB). KIRFB functions through the Restructuring and Internal Audit Board (RIAB). RIAB evolved a seven-fold categorisation of the SLPEs for restructuring and disinvestment. Group-I enterprises having negative net worth and obsolete product range were identified for closure. Group II enterprises having negative net worth and incurring continuous losses due to operational reasons, have to undergo a comprehensive restructuring exercise to attract private investments. Group III enterprises having positive net worth but incurring losses were proposed to be revived and made attractive for private investments. Group IV enterprises having positive net worth and good record of profit earning are proposed to be further strengthened through private participation and accessing capital markets. Group V enterprises consisting of social enterprises were proposed to be retained in the state sector with budgetary support. Group VI enterprises comprising public utilities were proposed to be monitored by the ERC and retained in the state sector with the cost burdens to be passed on to the consumers. Group VII enterprises consisting developmental and infrastructure agencies were to be examined case-by-case for their continuation in the state sector.

4.6 Karnataka

Karnataka Government set up Linn Committee (1996) to suggest privatisation, deregulation and merger of SLPEs and later set up a Public Sector Restructuring Commission (2000), headed by Shri. P. Padmanabha, IAS (Retd.) as full time Chairman and two part time expert members, has submitted a report since then on restructuring of fifteen PSUs and a policy on public sector reforms and privatisation has been brought out by the Karnataka State Bureau of Public Enterprises. The policy document also outlines institutional mechanisms for implementation. The Karnataka Government has also structured a voluntary retirement scheme which is similar to what is being adopted by the Government of Kerala.

4.7 Maharashtra

Maharashtra Government constituted the Maharashtra Board for Restructuring State Enterprises (MBRSE) in August 2001. In January 2002, the state finance department identified 13 of the state government's 65 public sector units to be referred to the MBRSE. Of these, 6 have been referred to the Board so far. These are Maharashtra Land Development Corporation (MLDC),

Ahmednagar-based Chitale Distillery and Mafco, Haffkine Biopharmaceutical Corporation, Maharashtra State Road Transport Corporation (MSRTC), and Maharashtra Fisheries Development Corporation (MFDC). The Board has recommended closure of MLDC, privatisation of Chitale Distillery and restructuring of MAFCO, MSRTC and MFDC. It has returned to the government its proposal to restructure HBC because any restructuring was to entail fresh infusion of capital and the Maharashtra's State Enterprises (Restructuring and Other Special Provision) Act, 2000, does not permit this. The Board asked the state government to refer HBC once again to it for privatisation. Other SLPEs identified but not referred to the Board included Meltron, nine textile mills of Maharashtra State Textile Corporation (MSTC), Konkan, Vidarbha and Marathwada Development Corporations and Maharashtra Scooters, which falls under the Western Maharashtra Development Corporation (WMDC). In case of Maharashtra Scooters, the government is in talks with Bajaj Auto for the sale of 27 percent of its stake in the company. Some other enterprises likely to be referred to the Board included Maharashtra State Farming Corporation (MSFC), Gorgaon Film City, and Kolhapur Film City.

4.8 Madhya Pradesh

Madhya Pradesh has embarked on an Integrated Public Resource Management Programme [2001] under which an integrated Public Enterprises Reform was envisaged, with loan and technical assistance grant from the Asian Development Bank (ADB). As a part of reforms, the Government proposes to strengthen SLPEs in which government ownership is required to meet public purpose, close down those which are chronically sick and loss making and restructure and divest the remaining enterprises to achieve greater efficiency, increase market discipline and have a wider dispersion of ownership. Accordingly, an Empowered Committee, headed by the Chief Secretary to Government and supported by a Technical Secretariat, was set up. It was also decided to transfer the responsibility of restructuring of SLPEs from the Administrative Departments to the Department of Public Enterprises, in order to accelerate the reform process.

4.9 Orissa

Orissa set up a Cabinet Sub-Committee (1996) under former Deputy Chief Minister which suggested closure and privatisation of certain units. Orissa availed financial assistance from the Department for International Development (DFID), UK. Government, for implementing the reform programme.

4.10 Punjab

Punjab set up a Disinvestment Commission in January 2001 which submitted its draft report in June 2002 which is under consideration. The following principles were followed for recommending restructuring, disinvestment and closure of SLPEs: (a) strategic and viable SLPEs be retained; (b) strategic but non-viable SLPEs be retained if their viability can be restored by necessary measures like outsourcing of activities, (c) non-strategic SLPEs be disinvested either by direct sale or through strategic sale. SLPEs to be disinvested should be freed form the administrative departments by allowing the implementation authority to take over their management. The safety net to employees of SLPEs should be rationally chalked out through an adequate compensation package/ retraining for deployment; (d) non-strategic SLPEs, which cannot be revived and in which no expression of interest by private parties is forthcoming, should be liquidated and the management of the SLPEs should be transferred to Punjab State Asset Management Authority for speedy disposal of assets. The Punjab State Asset Management Authority was proposed to be set up through legislation.

The Commission recommended the following process for disinvestments:

(i) Each SLPE should be examined on its merits.

(ii) Management, labour and general public should be given an opportunity of being heard.

(iii) Privatisation should not be confined only to loss making units

(iv) VRS/ retrenchment/compensation, cost of retraining, for redeployment, and retiring of long term debts of SLPEs should be the first, second and third charge respectively on the sale proceeds from SLPEs to be disinvested.

(v) The proceeds from disinvestments should be placed in a disinvestment fund.

The government had set up a Directorate of Disinvestment to process the Disinvestment Commission's recommendations or come up with *suo moto* reports in consultation with the Commission. There is a three-tier structure to deal with disinvestments. There is a Cabinet Committee on Disinvestment chaired by the Chief Minister. There is the core group of officers chaired by the Chief Secretary. The Disinvestment Directorate is the implementation agency. Punjab has put 5 SLPEs on fast track disinvestment. These included Punjab Tractors Limited, Punjab Alkalis, Punjab Communications, Punjab Tourism Development Corporation and Electronics Systems Punjab Limited. Advisors was appointed in case of 3 of these 5 SLPEs. A time frame of 6-8 months was conceived to complete disinvestments in these enterprises. The Punjab Government plans to use both the financial and strategic sale mode to privatise its SLPEs

The Draft Report of the Disinvestment Commission has covered 29 SLPEs with their 11 subsidiaries and 9 apex cooperative institutions. The state has provided total resources of Rs.14,023 crore out of which Rs. 3,466 crore was equity investment in these enterprises as on March 31, 2005. The equity investment in 2004-05 was Rs. 14,023 crore. The government has incurred an accumulated loss of Rs -1,953 crore on the investment in these enterprises till March 31 2005.

4.11 Rajasthan

Rajasthan set up a committee on "Re-organisation, strengthening and Disinvestment of SLPEs and Industrial Development". The Government appointed an Expert Committee i.e., Mathura Das Mathur Committee on the restructuring of SLPEs. The Committee suggested privatisation of public enterprises which were low on both public purpose and profitability. A study of 11 SLPEs in Rajasthan suggests winding up of Rajasthan Land Development Corporation, Rajasthan Cooperative Sheep & Wool Marketing Federation Ltd., Rajasthan State Mineral Development Corporation Ltd., Rajasthan State Agro Industries Corporation Ltd. and Rajasthan Jal Vikas Nigam Ltd. and it has suggested restructuring of Rajasthan State Hotels Corporation Ltd., Rajasthan Tourism Development Corporation Ltd. Rajasthan State Minerals

& Mining Corporation Ltd., Rajasthan State Seeds Corporation Ltd., Rajasthan State Handloom Development Corporation Ltd. and Rajasthan State Road Transport Corporation. As per another study the enterprises recommended for priority closure are Rajasthan Electronics Ltd., Rajasthan State Granite & Marbles Ltd., Rajasthan Tungsten Development Corporation and Rajasthan State Agro Industries Corporation. The enterprises in the list of closure include Hitech Precision Glass Ltd. and Rajasthan State Handloom Corporation Ltd. This study suggested mergers between Rajasthan Tourism Development Corporation and Rajasthan Hotels Corporation; Rajasthan Mineral Development Corporation and Rajasthan Minerals and Mines Ltd. As noted earlier, the departmental enterprises at Deedwana, Rajasthan Electronics Ltd. and Rajasthan Land Development Corporation Ltd. were lying closed/defunct for many years. The Rajasthan State Electricity Board is undergoing a reforms exercise as a part of which a State Regulatory Commission has been set up. Two SLPEs namely, Rajasthan State Tanneries Ltd., and Rajasthan State Salts prominently figured in the realm of privatisation.

4.12 Tamil Nadu

Tamil Nadu set up the S.V.S. Raghavan Committee (1997) for streamlining and restructuring SLPEs and to initiate privatisation process. The Committee recommended setting up of a Tamil Nadu Public Sector Disinvestment Commission. A three pronged approach was suggested for restructuring of public sector., Retention, Disinvestment and Winding up. Tamil Nadu News Print and Papers Ltd., was privatised by reducing the Government stake to 35 per cent.

4.13 West Bengal

West Bengal is contemplating to close down loss making SLPEs and welcomes private participation in state run enterprises. However, it intends to make the entire process a low key affair. A phased programme is being evolved wherein long term viability of all the SLPEs is being ascertained. The profit making SLPEs are to be retained, loss making SLPEs (large units) to be restructured and loss making SLPEs (small units) to be privatised. As on today, out of 84 SLPEs, 52 are manufacturing enterprises. 18 manufacturing SLPEs are profit making whereas 63 SLPEs are loss making. The focus of the privatisation process would be on small sized loss making manufacturing SLPEs. The government intends to turnaround 14 manufacturing SLPEs through capital infusion, organisational and manpower restructuring and divest them after turnaround, keeping 24 percent of the equity stake with itself. Prominent among these 18 enterprises are National Iron & Steel Company Limited, Shalimar Works Limited, Greater Calcutta Gas Supply, State Fisheries Development Corporation Limited and West Bengal Mineral Development and Trading Corporation Limited. At present, the state government is trying to build up a consensus to push through a minimum core programme. The restructuring exercise envisages carrying out optimisation studies of the business of these 14 enterprises keeping the existing and forseeable market demand trends. The entire exercise will be carried out in two parts. Part 1 will concern itself with evolving business optimisation plans for 4 of these enterprises, identifying necessary business, financial and administrative measures for their achieving long term viability under government ownership. Part 2 will be devoted to identifying earning potential of the remaining 10 enterprises and market the investment opportunities to secure investment of up to 74 percent in their equity, as joint venture entities.

5. Privatisation in SLPEs: Commonalities and Distinguishing Features

This section brings out the commonalities and distinguishing features of the SLPEs privatisation in the various states. It provides a comparative view of privatisation of the CPEs and the SLPEs. Finally, the chapter points to the lessons to be learnt for the SLPEs privatisation from the CPE experience.

5.1 Commonalities

In main, the following are the commonalities in the privatisation practices of the SLPEs in the various states:

(i) Most of the states explicitly or implicitly realized the need for privatisation of the SLPEs. The fiscal crunch pressed them hard to go in for privatisation.

(ii) Many states formulated a public enterprise policy to consider afresh the retention of their SLPE portfolio.
(iii) Some states set up a mechanism to deal with privatisation of the SLPEs whereas many others were in the process of imparting a thinking to this issue.
(iv) Manufacturing SLPEs found a greater appeal for privatisation.
(v) Social Safety Net emerged as an important issue in privatisation exercise.
(vi) Trade Sale was the preferred modality for the transfer of ownership.

5.2 Distinguishing Features

The following were the main distinguishing features:

(i) Whereas states such as Andhra Pradesh, Karnataka, Punjab, Maharashtra Orissa, Uttar Pradesh, Manipur and Assam showed a clear preference for privatisation, states like West Bengal, Kerala, Tamil Nadu, Madhya Pradesh and Meghalaya preferred restructuring.
(ii) Punjab, Maharashtra, Karnataka and Kerala set up the privatisation mechanism through independent enactments. Rajasthan, Haryana, Madhya Pradesh, Orissa, Andhra Pradesh, Assam and Tamil Nadu have either set up separate departments or used the existing mechanisms to handle the issues related to privatisation.
(iii) Andhra Pradesh, Orissa, Kerala and Karnataka prepared phase wise programme for privatisation of their SLPEs.
(iv) The privatisation programmes of Andhra Pradesh, Orissa and Uttar Pradesh received the support of DFID and were carried out with the support of foreign consultant. The Madhya Pradesh and Gujarat programmes received the support of Asian Development Bank and were also carried out with the support of foreign consultants.

5.3 Comparative View : Centre versus States

The following are the chief comparative features of privatisation relating to CPEs and SLPEs.

(i) The disinvestment/privatisation of CPEs began since the launching of New Economic Policy in July 1991 where as privatisation of SLPEs was resorted to much before in the case of the states e.g., Allwyn Nissan, in Andhra Pradesh, U.P Auto Tractors Limited in Uttar Pradesh and Charge Chrome Plant in Orissa.

(ii) The States preferred Trade Sale as the modality of privatisation as compared to the partial disinvestment and strategic sale by the Central Government.

(iii) There was a trend in the States to prefer an independent legislation to execute privatisation programmes as compared to the executive action in the case of the central government.

(iv) The privatisation exercise in the state governments was not target based whereas the Central Government laid down the targets of money to be mobilized through disinvestment/ privatisation.

(v) The Central Government preferred to use the term disinvestment to ward off any ideological/political problem whereas the State Governments did not refrain themselves from revealing their preference for privatisation. However, some states such as West Bengal, Kerala and Tripura rejected the use of both the terms viz., privatisation and disinvestment.

(vi) The privatisation of SLPEs, barring the State Electricity Boards (SEBs) turned out to be an easier exercise as compared to the central PEs because of their size and appeal.

(vii) The privatisation of both the CPEs and the SLPEs was confounded by the problem of transparency and valuation.

5.4 Lessons to be Learnt

The privatisation experiences of the various State Governments revealed the following lessons.

(i) It is easier to privatise the smaller enterprises.

(ii) The manufacturing enterprises possess a greater appeal for privatisation.

(iii) Effective due diligence expedites privatisation.

(iv) The SLPEs organized under companies act could be taken to market with a greater ease and comfort as compared to the SLPEs organized as public corporations.

(v) Valuation should be considered as an important element of the privatisation process. The entire valuation exercise should be made transparent.

(vi) In the case of loss making enterprises with multiple subsidiaries and product groups/SBUs (Strategic Business Units), restructuring should precede privatisation.

(vii) It is always helpful to establish a dialogue with the employees before any action is initiated to privatise an enterprise.

(viii) Sole reliance should not be placed on any particular method of privatisation. Depending on the nature of the SLPE and market conditions, a combination of methods of divesting the SLPEs should be employed to achieve the objectives of privatisation.

5.5 Problems of SLPEs and Action points

The problems of the SLPEs are galore. However, some of the dominant problems facing these enterprises and the action points to be initiated by the state governments, top level managements, SLPEs themselves, the central government/ planning commission, financial institutions and academic institutions are mentioned here below:

5.5.1 Action points for State government

Nodal agency

There should be a nodal agency to deal with issues of common interest to all SLPEs, with functions as discussed below:

(a) This can be either a specific department or agency, or part of an existing department, or other professional agency, with specific responsibility to attend to this work

(b) The nodal agency should undertake or arrange to make a review of all investments made in public enterprise, sector-wise, with reference to their financial viability and performance, as well as the achievement of the objectives set for them, and the direct and indirect benefits following to the state.

(c) The nodal agency should have the responsibility of assisting the administrative departments in setting out the objectives of new enterprises with reference to state development priorities, and in respect of existing enterprises with reference to their corporate plans and the departmental policies to set such objectives. All proposals for new investment in existing SLPEs and for launching new enterprises should be closely scrutinized by the nodal agency with reference to their financial viability and social objectives.

(d) The nodal agency in order to fulfil these responsibilities should build up a core of competent professional staff, but not necessarily by recruiting full-time employees. It should also be free to avail of the services of external consultants on a part-time or short-tenure basis, or to take the assistance of any professional agencies, to undertake the tasks. It should be an expert body and not become a regulatory agency.

(e) The institutional arrangements once set up should be fully honoured and public investment proposals carefully examined by the nodal agencies, and their recommendations give due weight.

Top level management

(a) The state governments should have institutional arrangements and well thought out procedures for selecting suitable persons for the posts of chief executive and full-time directors of SLPEs. Once a person is selected, he should be allowed to continue for a long term to enable him to implement the programmes envisaged.

(b) In the case of SLPEs which are welfare and trade and service enterprises, it may be practical to select the chief executive from among the civil servants in the general administrative or technical departments. Such persons should be nominated in advance and given suitable training in enterprise management.

(c) In the case of larger SLPEs, the selection should be based on a wider area of consideration, with a view to choose the best among the possible candidates.

(d) In all the states there are several SLPEs in manufacturing and trading sectors which produce goods and services that are also made by the private sector. In such SLPEs commercial objectives dominate. And, even if there were social objectives such as stimulation of industrial growth in backward areas, these objectives are achieved by the very act of setting up such SLPEs and only the commercial objectives have to be continued. In all such cases, it is necessary to have the leadership of the enterprise vested in a single person who can be the chairman and managing director (CMD). The CMD of such enterprises should be selected on the basis of their background and competency, and the field of choice should be as wide as possible. However, in respect of promotional and welfare enterprises, where the social objectives are significant, one could have a separate chairman in addition to the managing director. Such chairman should be involved only in strategic management issues. In consultation with the board, they should be involved in providing the directions of growth and policy guidance for the organization. The operational issues should be entirely the responsibility of the managing directors.

(e) The appointment of full-time chairman in addition to full-time chief executives has led in several cases to creation of dual poles of leadership within the enterprise, which do not function harmoniously. This should be avoided.

(f) The state governments should ensure that the boards of management are compact bodies consisting of persons with the requisite experience to guide the strategic management of the SLPEs. The boards should be decision-making and not deliberative bodies. The government officials on the board should be limited to a maximum of three.

Memorandum of understanding (MoU)

(a) The state governments should set up a procedure by which the administrative ministries have periodic discussions on the programme of each SLPE and arrive at an action plan / MoU. Such action plan / MoU should contain at least the agreed the agreed views on physical production target, financial targets, manpower targets and some targets in key results areas. The nodal agency would help in finalizing the MoU / action plan.

(b) The nodal agency would undertake annual evaluation of the performance of SLPEs with reference to the agreed targets in the MoUs.

Decision on restructuring

As most of the states have a number of loss-making SLPEs, and such enterprise would come up with rehabilitation or even restructuring proposals like merger, closure, divestiture or capital restructuring, the sate governments should set up suitable in situational arrangements to take speedy and effective decisions.

5.5.2 Action points for SLPEs

(a) All enterprises in the state sector should prepare a corporate plan for an appropriate time period based on an analysis of their strengths and weaknesses, and a realistic assessment of resources which could be mobilized. These long-term plans should examine the original objectives set for them and the current environmental conditions, and set out some specific objectives to be achieved by the enterprise, say, in five years. Such corporate plans and objectives should be harmonized with the state plans by the nodal agencies and the administrative departments of the government.

(b) In the case of SLPEs which are financially successful, their corporate plan should indicate the extend to which preferences and concessions given to them by the government could be reduced and suggested ways for minimizing their dependencies on the state budget. Such plans can also include suggestions for disinvesting government investments in favour of managers and worker, and if necessary to the public

(c) The SLEPs which are continuously making losses have to work out in detail programmes of restructuring the physical and financial areas so as to come to a position of 'no loss' within a period of, say, five years. When the restructuring involves disinvestments of certain units or activities, or mergers with other organizations, this should be worked out in consultation with the nodal agency and administrative ministries.

(d) Where an enterprise is involved in some commercial activity like manufacturing, and is also given the responsibility for certain developmental or welfare activities as a matter of public policy, the enterprise may work out the element of subsidy involved in fulfilling these non-commercial objectives. The state governments should give the SLPEs credit for meeting these objectives by direct compensation or by clear mention in the annual accounts.

(e) In working out different strategies for restructuring or for taking up appropriate expansion / diversification proposals, SLPEs which do not have internal expertise should make use of consultants.

(f) Whenever a SLPE has surplus manpower at the executive or worker level, a well –conceived programme of rationalization should be evolved. This may involve either diversification or expansion of the enterprise, or operating a voluntary retirement programme, or retraining a group of workers to take up certain activities like ancillary production, transport or marketing of the enterprise. Such proposals should be considered by the nodal agency and the admi9nistrative ministry to work out an appropriate time bound programme for utilization of surplus manpower.

5.5.3 Action points for Central Government, Department of Public Enterprises and Planning Commission

(a) The Department of Public Enterprises and Planning Commission should arrange for a periodic exchange of views and information to get an overview of the working of SLPEs. Seminars like this are a good forum. An annual conference of SLPEs may be arranged by the Planning Commission with the assistance of a research institute.

(b) Whenever the state government or state nodal agency requires technical assistance from the center for improving the quality of project appraisal or performance evaluation, this could be arranged by the Planning Commission, project appraisal division, or the Department of Public Enterprises, Government of India, New Delhi. Arrangements should also be made to provide the state nodal agencies and SLPEs with requisite information and guidance, as and when they sought. As there are a number of experts in each area of specialization, it may be useful to have a panel of experts and make them available to enterprise, which need their services.

(c) One of the major problems experienced by the SLPEs relates to the finalization of audited accounts in time. No doubt the existing provisions of Company Law and the procedure prescribed by the Comptroller and Auditor General (CAG) would work well in the case of SLPEs who finalize their accounts regularly on time. However, there are a large number of SLPEs whose accounts have fallen into arrears for a number of year. In such cases also, under the present procedures, taking up once year at a time does the finalization of accounts sequentially. There are also delays in appointment of statutory auditor s for each year. There are also delays in appointment of statutory auditors for each year. After the audit is finalized, the audited accounts have to be approved by the board and the annual meeting and only then the appointment of the auditor for the second year is made. At the request of some state nodal agencies, the CAG has approved the appointment of auditors for tow to three years at a time in certain cases, even in such cases, the approval of the audited accounts with the replies for the audit paragraphs has to be done sequentially. This leads to further delays in the finalization of the audited accounts. It is imperative that some innovative measures should be taken to bring up to date the finalization of accounts of all SLPEs. In respect f some small SLPEs, such as welfare corporation, the CAG can walve the finalization of accounts for some past periods. In the case of others, the appointment of auditors for three years at a time and revision the procedures for approval of the audited accounts would help. These suggestions could be pursued with the CAG.

5.5.4 Action points for financial institutions

(a) In many of the SLPEs especially in the manufacturing sector, funds come from the public financial institutions (PFIs). Many governments see the investment appraisal of PFIs as more efficient than their own appraisal. It becomes necessary, therefore, for the PFIs to have a much more thorough appraisal of the technical, economic and managerial aspects.

(b) The PFIs have a distinct preference to extend financial assistance to companies which are incorporated under the Companies A/c. Many of the SLPEs have activities which could be appropriately managed if the legal form of the company is a cooperative with limited liability registered under the Cooperatives Act. In order to encourage them to have appropriate forms, PFIs should revise their principles and procedures of extending financial assistance to SLPEs to make it easy and convenient for cooperatives to get financial assistance from them.

5.5.5 Action points for academic institutions

(a) There are examples of SLPEs, which have overcome many of the 'environmental' problems and are functioning very successfully. There is a need for documentation of their experience to analyze the source of their success. It would be useful to nominate a particular agency which could take up this responsibility on behalf of the planning commission. It was noted that the Department of personal, training division, has already initiated action to prepare case studies of successful enterprises. This effort could be further strengthened and the material prepared should be circulated to the SLPEs and nodal agencies.

(b) Management training institutions could also take up action based consultancy to work with specific SLPEs to assist them in corporate planning and implementing their turnaround strategies.

(c) It would be advisable for the state governments to set apart some funds for sponsoring through nodal agencies studies / training programmes relevant to SLPEs in academic institutions within or outside the state.

5.6 Conclusion

A dissection of the macro-economic performance of the SLPEs clearly reveals that their financial performance continued to caused a great deal of concern. According to the Study Group Report on the Reforms in State Public Sector Undertakings (Planning Commission, 2002), instead of earning a 10 per cent rate of return, these enterprises registered a compound annual growth of 17.36 per cent in their net losses. The fiscal impact of the viable working of the SLPEs has become a cause of concern as the total impact on state finances to total revenue of states ratio and the gross fiscal impact on state finances ratio have been found very adverse. The policy makers are left with no choice but to rethink about the retention of the SLPEs portfolio in the various states and decide what to divest and what to retain.

The state governments overtly or covertly acknowledged the need for privatisation of the non-core, continuously loss making and manufacturing SLPEs. The financial performance of the SLPEs was such that it did not leave the policy makers with choice other than redefining the respective SLPEs portfolios. Some states took the lead by putting in place a mechanism for privatisation and creating an environment conducive for the acceleration of the tempo of privatisation. However, there is no denying the fact that the states continue to face certain impediments in the successful implementation of their privatisation programmes.

Most of the states explicitly or implicitly realized the need for privatisation of the SLPEs. The fiscal crunch pressed them hard to go in for privatisation. However, whereas states such as Andhra Pradesh, Karnataka, Punjab and Orissa showed a clear preference for privatisation, the states like West Bengal, Tripura and Kerala showed their disenchantment with the term 'Privatisation' and opted for restructuring. The privatisation pattern of the central and the state governments differed in many regards especially in relation to the method of sale. The central government preferred partial disinvestment and strategic sale as compared to the trade sale modality popularly adopted by the state governments. The privatisation experiences of the state governments point to a number of lessons to be learnt for the future. Instead of depending on a specific modality, it would be beneficial to depend on a mix of methods.

The SLPEs are beset with serious problems and there is a need to initiate a series of measures to resolve these problems which basically relate to the setting up and effecting functioning of the nodal agency, revamping their top level management, introducing MoU as an instrument of performance evaluation, restructuring, performance review by central government, reformulating their investment appraisal policies and systems, finalization of audit accounts, funding from public financial institutions, improving environmental interface, preparation of corporate plans, management development and training, and legal framework governing these enterprises. This calls for a concerted action by the state governments, top level management in the SLPEs, SLPEs themselves, central government / planning commission, public financial institutions, academic institutions and legal luminaries.

2

State Level Public Enterprises in India: State-wise Analysis

Introduction

There are 28 states and 7 union territories. It is proposed to discuss the state-wise dimensions of the SLPEs in India pertaining to the various states and the union territories. The dimensions relate to the profile, classification, financial performance and budgetary support.

1. Andhra Pradesh

1.1 Financial Profile

The profile of SLPEs in Andhra Pradesh is given in the following table:

1.2 Sectoral Classification

Table 1.2 shows the classification of the SLPEs of Andhra Pradesh:

1.3 Budgetary Support

Table1.3shows that, the Government had guaranteed loans aggregating Rs.2,466.53 crore obtained by five working Government companies (Rs. 2,2,91.53 crore) and two Statutory corporations (Rs.175 crore). At the end of the year, guarantees of Rs. 20,564.66 crore against 13 working Government companies (Rs. 20,120.47) and two working Statutory corporations (Rs. 444.19

Table 1.1
Financial Profile of SLPEs in A.P.

(Rs.in.crore)

Items / Years	2002-03	2003-04	2004-05
1.Total no.of SLPEs	52	51	54
2.No.of Working SLPEs	34	34	36
3.No.of Non-Working SLPEs	18	17	18
I. Under liquidation	9	9	10
II. Under Closure	5	4	4
III. Under Merger	1	1	1
IV. Others	3	3	3
4. Total Equity	7486	8162	8346
5. Total Debt	19754	22679	25567
6.Total Investment	27240	30841	33914
7 .No.of Profit making enterprises	13	23	24
8.No.of Loss making enterprises	21	21	20
9.Net Profit/Loss	-187	-346	-393
10. Accumulated Loss(-)/Profit	-1758	-2872	-2215

(Source: Reports of the Comptroller and Auditor General of India(Commercial),on Andhra Pradesh for 2002-03 to 2004-05)

Table 1.2
Classification of SLPEs in Andhra Pradesh

Sl.No	*Category*	*No.of Enterprises*
1	Manufacturing	28
2	Financial	5
3	Trade&Service	5
4	Promotional	13
5	Welfare	1
6	Utility	8
	Total	54

(Source: Classified from the list of enterprises given in reports of the Comptroller and Auditor General of India(Commercial),on Andhra Pradesh for 2001-02)

Table 1.3
Budgetary Support to SLPEs in Andhra Pradesh

(Rs.in crore)

Particulars	*2002-03*				*2003-04*				*2004-05*			
	Companies		*Corp*		*Companies*		*Corp*		*Companies*		*Corp*	
	No.	*Amt*	*No*	*Amt*	*No*	*Amt*	*No*	*Amt*	*No*	*Amt*	*No*	*Amt*
Equity Capital Support from budget	4	18.80	--	--	5	44.76	1	2.00	8	189.61	1	2.50
Loans given from budget	14	2165.62	--	--	11	2006.19	--	--	9	927.81	1	106.00
Grants	0	0	--	--	12	633.07	--	--	--	--	--	--
Subsidy towards (i) project/programmes /Schemes	11	247.15	--	--					10	981.94	--	--
(ii) Other Subsidy	10	2093.81	2	100.55	11	2208.00	1	252.00	7	2581.81	1	167.50
Total Subsidy	16	2340.96	2	100.55	19	2841.07	1	252.00	15	3563.75	1	167.50
Total Support		4525.38		100.55	23	4892.02	2	254.00	19	4681.17	2	276.00

(Source: Reports of the Comptroller and Auditor General of India(Commercial),on Andhra Pradesh for 2002-03 to 2004-05)

crore) were outstanding. The Government had forgone Rs.5.25 crore by way of interest waiver in respect of two companies and allowed moratorium on loan repayment of Rs.728.42 crore to six companies during the year.

1.4 Social Safety Net Programme (SSNP)

SSNP has two distinct components:

Voluntary Retirement Scheme (VRS), which is essentially aimed at easing the impact of job loss by providing a severance package.

Counselling and retraining for redeployment of the displaced workers so that over a period they can be reintegrated into the emerging labour market, or become self-employed.

Voluntary Retirement Scheme (VRS)

According to the scheme, an employee of a SLPE with 10 or more years of service or 40 or more years of age and who has been identified by management as surplus is eligible for VRS @ 45 days Ex-gratia for every completed year of service, besides the terminal benefits as admissible to him/her. Employees who do not qualify for VRS are being given minimum compensation of Rs.30,000/-. Those who qualify but do not opt for VRS will be compensated under the Industrial Disputes Act, 1947 (equivalent to 15 days average pay for very completed year of continuous service plus other terminal / statutory benefits).

Under the Andhra Pradesh Economic Restructuring Programme (APERP), supported by the World Bank, the Government is providing benefits under VRS/ SCP to the job displaced employees and workers. The VRS/ SCP package is far better, compared to compensation available under Industrial Dispute Act. The package was originally envisaged for those who had completed 10 years of service. However, the Government have since removed these restrictions and now all regular employees are eligible to receive VRS/SCP.

Counselling, Retraining and Redeployment Program

Besides the monetary compensation to overcome financial loss, social safety net provides the much needed assistance and guidance to negotiate the changing market scenario for alternative livelihoods.

SSNP facilitates and empowers the affected sections to reintegrate into changing labour market by equipping them with new or improved skills that are in demand. The Department for International Development (DFID) U.K. is funding this programme, and a special wing of the Implementation Secretariat in the Department of Public Enterprises implements the programme.

Major components of the Program are:

- Survey of the employees availing VRS/SCP
- Counselling of the employees
- Retraining/Re-skilling programmes
- Limited follow-up services for redeployment or alternative livelihoods
- Integration of SSNP with other safety nets
- Labour Market Survey

Survey and Counselling

Survey and Counselling are essential inputs in the Safety Net Program for the displaced workers. Sometimes, Survey and Counselling go on simultaneously. However, counselling is not a one shot job. It is carried out in several phases.

Survey helps to understand the status of job displaced employees and workers and build exhaustive database about the enterprises covered under the reform programme. Survey covers the employee's details pertaining to the education, family background, social status, assets, and nature of job, skills; and the amount received/receivable under VRS/SCP, the way the money was spent or proposed to be utilised.

Based on the age, education, aptitude, interest, the employees are counseled to opt for retraining programmes. Retraining is essential as their skills have become obsolete and need upgradation. Counselling also helps the job displaced workers to overcome difficulties encountered with regard to utilisation of VRS amounts, meaningful choices for retraining in relevant skills and related aspects. Counselling is a process and identification of relevant skill area for retraining is one important element.

Retraining/Re-skilling programmes

Advanced age, outdated job skill, lack of awareness of opportunities and lack of education are some of the characteristics of the displaced workers in Andhra Pradesh. They are re-trained/ re-skilled in order to upgrade their skills or trained in new areas according to their aptitude and requirements of the prevailing labour market. An appropriate training institute is identified and the employers are enrolled in the programmes. Regular monitoring of the training programme helps to motivate the trainees and to sort out any difficulties faced in the retraining programme.

Skill upgradation through vocational training in new or existing skills is customized. There are a veriety of training programs of varying duration and of varying size of the batches from one to forty. Training course syllabus is specially designed to suit the requirements of trainees and conducted on timings of convenience to the learners.

Follow-up services for redeployment

Limited follow-up services are provided for self-employment and wage employment. Displaced workers are assisted through follow up services like tracking vacancies advertised in the media and other sources. Follow-up services include identifying suitable organisation, preparing the employee's bio-data and arranging interviews etc. Liaison with placement agencies facilitates retrained persons to get timely information about vacancies in the areas they are trained and to explore employment opportunities. SSNP keeps displaced employees of the employment opportunities. It also assists those interested in self employment through entrepreneurship development. Accessing the resources from experts and financial institutions helps displaced employees interested in self-employment.

Integration of SSNP with other safety nets

Displaced workers are assisted in availing the safety nets implemented by various departments of the government. It also includes livelihoods promotion activities of NGOs and the government. Linkages with the financial institutions for disadvantaged communities, employment generation programmes

(CMEY/ PMRY etc), DRDA and several departments. Facilitating displaced workers to avail the benefits of DRDA and DWCRA to mobilise sewing machines and a stall in the DWCRA bazaar for a group of displaced women workers formed into a self help group is one example. Accessing vocational educational programmes of a community polytechnic for providing retraining programme agro-based vocations in rural areas is another example.

Labour Market Survey

Keeping in view the broad parameters of the Social Safety Net Programme, and to give a practical dimension to the implementation process, a Labour Market Survey is undertaken to assess the employment opportunities with reference to the profile of the job displaced workforce. The Labour market is basically a concept where current availability of skills and requirements of skills in the near future are determined in respect of a given geographical area depending on the location of the unit, which is likely to be restructured or privatised.

Present status of SSNP in Andhra Pradesh

Social Safety Net Programme as on 31-08-2005

SNo	*Enterprise*	*Surveyed*	*Counseled*	*Trained*	*Under Training*	*Re-Deployed*
1	Adilabad Spg Mills	481	444	282	0	124
2	Allwyn watches Limited	1486	1234	1106	0	320
3	AP Agro IDC Limited	225	192	123	0	36
4	AP Fisheries Corp. Limited	146	82	59	0	0
5	AP Handicrafts Dev Corp.	10	10	3	0	2
6	AP Industrial Dev Corp.	19	16	10	0	2
7	AP Irrigation Dev Corp.	483	405	234	0	113
8	AP Meat & P Dev Corp.	118	113	29	0	17

(Contd.)

(Contd.)

SNo	*Enterprise*	*Surveyed*	*Counseled*	*Trained*	*Under Training*	*Re-Deployed*
9	AP Small Scale Inds Dev Corp.	317	283	136	0	61
10	AP Textile Dev Corp.	47	44	28	0	11
11	AP Electronics Dev Corp.	28	20	9	0	6
12	FEDCON Limited	33	31	16	0	2
13	AP Handloom weavers CSL	209	176	114	0	22
14	ASM Coop. Sugar, Palakole	149	135	110	0	8
15	Chilakaluripet Spg Mills	383	374	189	0	56
16	Chirala Spg Mills	359	354	208	0	56
17	Chittoor Diary, Chittoor	265	243	150	0	62
18	Girijan Coop Corp. (GCC)	108	33	15	0	0
19	Karimnagar Spg Mills	240	199	167	0	63
20	Leather Inds Dev Corp of AP	26	21	10	0	2
21	Nagarjuna Sugar Factory	229	229	216	0	126
22	Nandyal Spg Mills	342	331	235	0	92
23	Nandyal Sugar Factory	193	88	57	0	20
24	Nizam Sugars Limited	2823	2459	1785	0	537
25	Nellore Spg Mills	595	583	358	0	152
26	Parchur Spg Mills	332	329	201	0	69
27	Rajahmundry Spg Mills	422	389	156	0	111

(Contd.)

(Contd.)

SNo	*Enterprise*	*Surveyed*	*Counseled*	*Trained*	*Under Training*	*Re-Deployed*
28	Sri Hanuman Sugar Factory	56	55	32	0	12
29	Rajarajeshwari Spg Mills	190	178	165	0	111
30	Palair Coop Sugars Ltd.	367	324	211	0	109
31	West Godavari Coop Sugars	27	26	0	0	0
32	Other enterprises	31	26	10	0	3
	Total	**10739**	**9422**	**6424**	**0**	**2305**

(Source : Database on SLPEs, IPE, Hyderabad)

1.5 Problems / Issues

The SLPEs face both the internal and external problems. The former included unresolved issues in the areas of functional management. The basic elements of human resource management viz., manpower planning, training, improvement of personnel productivity and conflict management continued to demand serious attention. The capital structuring, budgeting, financial information systems and profit improvement efforts need to be looked into on a case by case basis. The capacity utilization in the manufacturing enterprises had stabilized at a low operational level. The 4 Ps (product, price, promotion, positioning) of marketing had a great potential to further improve the performance of the SLPEs. Externally, the short tenures of chiefs and board members of these enterprises emerged as an important impediment in their successful operation. The state government despite its good intentions has not been able to evolve a satisfactory performance evaluation system for the SLPEs.

2. Assam

2.1 Financial Profile:

The profile of SLPEs in Assam is given in the following table:

Table 2.1

Financial Profile of SLPEs in Assam

(Rs.in.crore)

Items / Years	2002-03	2003-04	2004-05
1. Total no.of SLPEs	42	42	42
2. No.of Working SLPEs	32	32	32
3. No.of Non-Working SLPEs I. Under liquidation II. Under Closure III. Under Merger IV. iv. Others	10	10	10
4. Total Equity	1828	1829	1816
5. Total Debt	2351	625	2599
6. Total Investment	4179	2454	4415
7. No.of Profit making enterprises	6	6	7
8. No.of Loss making enterprises	33	34	32
9. Net Profit/Loss	-692	-727	-671
10. Accumulated Loss(-)/Profit	-4944	-4503	-5268

(Source: Reports of the Comptroller and Auditor General of India(Commercial),on Assam for 2002-03 to 2004-05)

2.2 Sectoral Classification

Table 2.2 shows the classification of the SLPEs of Assam:

Table 2.2
Classification of SLPEs in Assam

Sl.No	*Category*	*No.of Enterprises*
1.	Manufacturing	28
2.	Financial	2
3.	Trade&Service	2
4.	Promotional	6
5.	Welfare	2
6.	Utility	2
	Total	42

(Source: Classified from the list of enterprises given in reports of the Comptroller and Auditor General of India (Commercial), on Assam for 2001-02)

2.3 Budgetary Support

The budgetary Support in the form of equity capital, loans and grants/subsidies from the State Government to 29 working Government companies and four working statutory corporations for three years up to 31 March 2005 are given below:

During the year 2004-05, the Government had guaranteed loans aggregating Rs.130 crore obtained by one working Government company (Rupees five crore) and one Statutory corporation (Rs.125 crore). At the end of the year guarantees amounting to Rs. 417.01 crore obtained by six working Government companies (Rs.102.18 crore) and two working Statutory corporations (Rs. 314.83 crore) were outstanding. There was no default in repayment of guaranteed loans during the year.

2.4 Social Safety Net Programme

The Administrative Departments of the State Public Sector Undertakings (SPSUs) will identify and decide the SPSUs to be closed or revived in State Public Sector including through merger/ improvement or to be revived in the private sector through disinvestments/lease, taking all relevant factors into consideration and submit proposals for closure/revival with all details separately

Table 2.3
Budgetary Support to SLPEs in Assam

(Rs.in.crore)

Particulars	*2002-03*				*2003-04*				*2004-05*			
	Companies		*Corp*		*Companies*		*Corp*		*Companies*		*Corp*	
	No.	*Amt*	*No*	*Amt*	*No*	*Amt*	*No*	*Amt*	*No*	*Amt*	*No*	*Amt*
Equity Capital Support from budget	3	0.54	--	--	--	--	--	--	3	0.35	--	--
Loans given from budget	4	6.24	2	52.71	1	0.10	--	--	3	8.99	3	149.64
Grants/Subsidy towards (i) project/programmes /Schemes (ii) Other Subsidy	6	9.20	--	--	9	9.97	2	194.48	8	12.25	2	583.69
Total Subsidy												
Total Support	10	15.98	2	52.71	10	10.07	2	194.48	11	21.59	3	733.33

(Source: Reports of the Comptroller and Auditor General of India(Commercial),on Assam for 2002-03 to 2004-05)

for each SPSU to the Department of Public Enterprises (DPE), for placing the same before the Public Investment Board (PIB). The Assam Governance and Public Resource Management Programme (AGPRMP) provided for an amount of $ 30 million towards settlement of outstanding liabilities of closed SLPEs and another amount of $ 5 million towards One Time Settlement (OTS) – closed SLPEs institutional loan up to 2006-07 under Sub-Programme-1, which was likely to be followed by Sub-Programme-2 through which another amount of $ 80 million may flow to the State during 2007-08 & 2008-09 for settlement of outstanding liabilities of closed SPSUs. The State Government has released Rs.9.78 crore to 22 SLPEs for payment to 23627 employees[1].

2.5 Problems / Issues

An in depth study of the working of the SLPEs in Assam suggests the following as the major problem areas:

Incidence of Sickness: About half of the SLPEs have been incurring cash losses. Of these the major losses have been incurred by the Assam Tea Corporation, Kachar Sugar Mills, Fertichem Ltd., Assam Seeds Corporation, Assam Cooperative Sugar Mills and Assam Fertilizers and Chemicals Ltd. A decision will have to be taken to attempt the restructuring and revitalization of these enterprises.

Ineffective Management: The improper selection of top level executives, their frequent transfers and lack of management expertise in the areas of Finance and Marketing have emerged as the major handicaps confronting these enterprises. The surplus manpower has compounded the problem. To add, these enterprises have not been able to keep pace with their production schedules. The administrative side is overstaffed in these enterprises whereas there has been inadequate staffing of the shop floors.

Operational Snags: These include unscientific inventory management, raw materials and marketing problems and power shortages. The power problems have badly affected these during the last 10 years. Frequent load shedding and breakdowns have resulted in heavy losses. The inventory problems are of dual nature. On the one hand, there have been excess holdings of unrequited material, components and stores and, on the other; there has been an acute shortage of certain critical spare parts. Transport costs have inflated the prices for the products have not been obtained in the absence of aggressive marketing management. It is interesting to not that same materials were procured by different enterprises at different prices.

Absence of Professionalism: The reflection of the general backwardness of Assam may be traced to the management systems of the SLPEs. The businesslike work is yet to penetrate into most of the SLPEs. This situation is epitomized in the fact that professionalisation of management is still a distant goal in Assam. Most of the managing directors are deputationists who may not have any previous experience in management of enterprises and they are frequently transferred. Distinction between financial management and book keeping is yet to be recognized in most of the SLPEs. Management Information Systems is still an unknown development. None of the SLPEs has a Cost Accountant on its rolls. Only a couple of SLPEs have availed of the services of cost accountants for as hoc purposes. The job of personnel manager in most of SLPEs is performed by the concerned administrative officer who generally happens to be a generalist of junior rank. It needs to emphasized that while absence of professionalisation and business-like work-culture have hindered adoption of modern ands effective management practices and control systems, it is equally true that professionally qualified personnel are not easily available in Assam. The SLPEs have not prepared training plans to enhance human resource potential.

Boards of Management: The power of appointing the Boards of Management in statutory corporations and government companies vests in the Government. This power as regards the SLPEs in the Co-operative sector has also been taken over by the Government. The number of the boards in case of each SLPEs is determines as per provisions of the Articles of Association or relevant rules of the SLPEs. In other cases, broadly speaking, around 11 members constitute the boards. There has been no fixed tenures for the boards. There is no fixed norm about the frequency of holding meeting of the Boards.

Monitoring and Evaluation: A negotiated performance evaluation system does not exist for the SLPEs in the state. The objectives of the SLPEs, their corporate mission, and their annual plans and targets have not been spelt out. Corporate plans have not been formulated by these enterprises. The targets for different stages of the project implementation are not quantified in terms of time and cost. All these combined have made the problem of monitoring and evaluation very complex.

3. ARUNACHAL PRADESH

3.1 Financial Profile

The profile of SLPEs of Arunachal Pradesh is given in the following table:

Table 3.1
Profile of SLPEs in Arunachal Pradesh

(Rs.in crore)

Items / *Years*	*2002-03*	*2003-04*	*2004-05*
1.Total no.of SLPEs	-	5	5
2.No.of Working SLPEs	-	3	3
3.No.of Non-Working SLPEs	-	2	2
(i) Under liquidation			
(ii) Under Closure			
(iii) Under Merger			
(iv) Others			
4. Total Equity	-	9	9
5. Total Debt	-	14	11
6.Total Investment	-	23	20
7 .No. of Profit making enterprises	-	-	-
8.No.of Loss making enterprises	-	04	04
9.Net Profit/Loss	-	-4	-6
10. Accumulated Loss(-/Profit	-	5	0.59

Source: Reports of the Comptroller and Auditor General of India (Com*mercial), on Arunachal Pradesh for 2003-04 to 2004-05.*

The financial performance of SLPEs in Arunachal Pradesh was below the mark. There are four loss making enterprises in the state during 2004-05.

3.2 Sectoral Classification of SLPEs in Arunachal Pradesh

Table 3.2 shows the classification of the SLPEs in Arunachal Pradesh

Table 3.2
Classification of SLPEs in Arunachal Pradesh

Sl.No	Category	No. of Enterprises
1	Manufacturing	2
2	Financial	1
3	Trade&Service	-
4	Promotional	2
5	Welfare	-
6	Utility	-
	Total	5

Source: Classified from the list of enterprises given in reports of the Comptroller and Auditor General of India (Commercial), on Arunachal Pradesh for 2004-05.

3.3 Budgetary Support

The budgetary outgo in the form of equity capital and loans and grants/subsidies from the State Government to working Government companies for the three years upto 2003-04 was nil, Rs. 22 lakh and nil respectively. During the year 2003-04, the Government had guaranteed the loans aggregating Rs.12 crore obtained by one working Government company. At the end of the year guarantees amounting to Rs.11.20 crore against two Government companies were outstanding. There was one case of default in repayment of guaranteed loans during the year.

3.4 Social Safety Net Programme

The Government of Arunachal Pradesh has introduced VRS in Arunachal Pradesh Forest Corporation Limited.

3.5 Problems / Issues

The State Government's favorable attitude has been the major factor which contributed to the growth of the SLPEs in the state. However, by effecting improvements in technology and developing human resources, these SLPEs could do even better.

4. Andaman Nicobar Island

The UT as two enterprise. They are ANIIDCO and AN Forest Plantation and Dev. Corp.

5. Bihar

5.1 Financial Profile

The profile of SLPEs of Bihar is given in the following table:

5.2 Sectoral Classification

Table 5.2 shows the classification of SLPEs in Bihar.

5.3 Budgetary Support

The table 5.3 below shows the budgetary support received by the working Government companies and Statutory corporations for the three years up to March 2005, in the form of equity capital and loans and grants/subsidies from the State Government.

During the year 2004-05, the Government did not guarantee any loan. At the end of the year, guarantees of loans for Rs. 267.56 crore against two working Government companies (Rs. 31.27 crore) and two working Statutory corporations (Rs. 236.29 crore) were outstanding. There was one case of default in repayment of the guaranteed loans to the extent of Rs. 43.78 crore during the year 2004-05 in respect of the Bihar State Electricity Board. The guarantee commission paid/payable to Government by Government companies was nil, however, Rs. 28.75 lakh were outstanding as guarantee fee payable to Government by Bihar State Road Transport Corporation.

5.4 Problems / Issues

The management audit of the SLPEs in Bihar indicates that there is no clear definition of objectives or privatization of objectives which enterprises are expected to fulfill. There is lack of motivation of both managerial personnel and workers. There is need to improve the work culture. The SLPEs are plugged with over-staffing. There is no well laid out policy regarding either the appointment or the terms of chief executives. The problem of

Table 5.1
Financial Profile of SLPEs in Bihar

(Rs. in crore)

Years / Items	2002-03	2003-04	2004-05
1. Total no. of SLPEs	54	54	54
2. No.of Working SLPEs	21	20	20
3. No.of Non-Working SLPEs Under liquidation Under Closure Under Merger / Others	33	34	34
4. Total Equity	623	614	614
5. Total Debt	8664	6517	4793
6. Total Investment	9287	7132	5407
7. No. of Profit making enterprises	7	9	9
8. No.of Loss making enterprises	42	40	40
9. Net Profit/Loss	-1127	-1032	-748
10. Accumulated Loss(-)/Profit	-9669	-9610	-5163

(*Source:* Reports of the Comptroller and Auditor General of India (Commercial), on Bihar for 2002-03 to 2005-06.

Table 5.2

Classification of SLPEs in Bihar

Sl. No.	*Category*	*No. of Enterprises*
1.	Manufacturing	40
2.	Financial	2
3.	Trade &Service	2
4.	Promotional	4
5.	Welfare	2
6.	Utility	4
	Total	54

Source: Classified from the list of enterprises given in reports of the Comptroller and Auditor General of India (Commercial) ,on Bihar for 2004-05.

Table 5.3
Budgetary Support to SLPEs of Bihar

(Rs. in crore)

Particulars	2002-03				2003-04				2004-05			
	Companies		Corp.		Companies		Corp.		Companies		Corp.	
	No.	Amt	No	Amt	No	Amt	No	Amt	No	Amt	No	Amt
Equity Capital Support from budget	-	-	-	-	-	-	-	-	-	-	-	-
Loans given from budget	1	5.00	3	513.04	2	23.38	3	701.39	1	3.02	3	775.23
Grant/Subsidy towards project/programmes /Schemes (ii) Other Subsidy	-	-	-	-	-	-	-	-	-	-	-	-
Total Subsidy	-	-	-	-	-	-	-	-	-	-	-	-
Total Support	1	5.00	3	513.04	2	23.38	4	701.49	1	3.02	3	775.23

Source: Reports of the Comptroller and Auditor General of India (Commercial) ,on Bihar for 2002-03 to 2004-05.

continuous supply of raw material and shortage of power has become a recurring phenomenon.

6. Chhattisgarh

Consequent on enactment of Madhya Pradesh Reorganization Act 2000, the Madhya Pradesh State was bifurcated and Chhattisgarh State was formed on 1 November 2000. Three companies and one statutory corporation were bifurcated on reorganization of MP State and transferred to Chhattisgarh State. The process of distribution of assets and liabilities of these companies and the corporation was not complete (December 2002). The Chhattisgarh State also set up two new companies. One company viz. *Audyogik Kendra Vikas Nigam Limited (*AKVN), Raipur Limited, existing in Chhattisgarh was renamed after fresh incorporation in April 2001 as Chhattisgarh State Industrial Development Corporation Limited.

6.1 Financial Profile

The profile of SLPEs in Chhattisgarh is given in the following table:

The Total Investment of SLPEs in Chhattisgarh showed a positive growth, i.e., from Rs.113.38 crore to Rs.1059.46 crore during 2002-03 to 2004-05.

6.2 Sectoral Classification

Table 6.2shows the classification of SLPEs of Chhattisgarh

6.3 Budgetary Support

The table below shows the budgetary outgo (in the form of equity capital and loans) and grants/subsidies from the State Government to Government companies and statutory corporations for the three years up to 2004-05 are given below:

During the year 2004-05, Government had guaranteed loans aggregating Rs. 429.30 crore obtained by one working Statutory corporation. At the end of the year, guarantees aggregating Rs. 354.07 crore were outstanding.

7. National Capital Territory of Delhi

7.1 Financial Profile

Table 6.1
Financial Profile of SLPEs Chhattisgarh

(Rs. in crore)

Items / *Years*	*2002-03*	*2003-04*	*2004-05*
1. Total no. of SLPEs	-	10	10
2. No. of Working SLPEs	-	10	10
3. No. of Non-Working SLPEs (I). Under liquidation (II). Under Closure (III). Under Merger (IV). Others	-	-	-
4. Total Equity	-	77	39
5. Total Debt	-	37	1020
6. Total Investment	-	113	1059
7. No. of Profit making enterprises	-	4	3
8. No. of Loss making enterprises	-	1	4
9. Net Profit/Loss	-	4	6
10. Accumulated Loss(-)/Profit	-	4	11

Source: Reports of the Comptroller and Auditor General of India (Commercial) ,on Chhattisgarh for 2003-04 to 2004-05.

Table 6.2
Classification of SLPEs in Chhattisgarh

Sl. No.	*Category*	*No. of Enterprises*
1.	Manufacturing	2
2.	Financial	1
3.	Trade&Service	2
4.	Promotional	1
5.	Welfare	-
6.	Utility	4
	Total	10

Source: Classified from the list of enterprises given in reports of the Comptroller and Auditor General of India (Commercial) ,on Chhattisgarh for 2004-05.

Table 6.1
Budgetary Support to SLPEs in Chhattisgarh

(Rs. in crore)

Particulars	2002-03				2003-04				2004-05			
	Companies		Corp		Companies		Corp		Companies		Corp	
	No.	Amt	No	Amt	No	Amt	No	Amt	No	Amount	No	Amt
Equity Capital Support from budget					2	2.45			1	1.00		
Loans given from budget	1	27.00					1	0.85			1	47.28
Grants												
Subsidy towards (i) project/programmes /Schemes												
(ii) Other Subsidy	2	258.19	1	62.87	2	153.66	2	78.11	2	40.84	1	75.86
Total Support	3	258.19	1	62.87	4	156.11	2	78.96	3	41.87	1	122.74

(*Source:* Reports of the Comptroller and Auditor General of India (Commercial) ,on Chhattisgarh for 2002-03 to 2004-05.

Table 7.1
Profile of SLPEs in National Capital Territory of Delhi

(Rs. in crore)

Items / Years	2002-03	2003-04	2004-05
1. Total no. of SLPEs	11	11	15
2. No. of Working SLPEs	11	11	11
3. No. of Non-Working SLPEs (I). Under Liquidation (II). Under Closure (III). Under Merger (IV). Others			4
4. Total Equity	3790	3790	837
5. Total Debt	4558	6194	8844
6. Total Investment	8348	9984	9681
7. No. of Profit making enterprises	6	---	7
8. No. of Loss making enterprises	2	---	4
9. Net Profit/Loss	-768	---	-1693
10. Accumulated Loss(-)/Profit	-184	---	-7143

(*Source:* Reports of the Comptroller and Auditor General of India (Commercial) ,on Delhi for 2002-03 to 2004-05.

The profile of SLPEs of National Capital Territory of Delhi is given in the following table:

The SLPEs in Delhi have showed a positive progress in their investment during the period 2002-03 to 2004-05, but incurred losses all through. The debt-equity ratio was almost infinity.

7.2 Sectoral Classification

Table 7.2 shows the classification of the SLPEs in National Capital Territory of Delhi.

Table 7.2

Classification of SLPEs in Government of National Capital Territory of Delhi

Sl.No	*Category*	*No.of Enterprises*
1	Manufacturing	1
2	Financial	2
3	Trade&Service	-
4	Promotional	2
5	Welfare	4
6	Utility	6
	Total	15

Source: Classified from the list of enterprises given in reports of the Comptroller and Auditor General of India (Commercial), on Delhi for 2001-02.

7.3 Budgetary Support

Table 7.3 shows that, the Government of NCT of Delhi had not given guarantees against the loans obtained by any of the Government companies or Statutory corporations. During the year, no Government dues have been waived by the Government. Loan of Rs. 323.14 crore was converted into equity in Pragati Power Corporation limited.

7.4 Social Safety Net Programme

Government of India introduced a scheme for voluntary retirement of employees of public enterprises in October 1988 with a view to reducing surplus manpower and optimizing performance. A total of 545 employees opted for VRS in IPGCL, DSIDC, DSCSC

Table 7.3

Budgetary Support to SLPEs in National Capital Territory of Delhi

(Rs. in crore)

Particulars	*2002-03*				*2003-04*				*2004-05*			
	Companies		*Corp.*		*Companies*		*Corp.*		*Companies*		*Corp*	
	No.	*Amt*	*No*	*Amt*	*No*	*Amount*	*No*	*Amt*	*No*	*Amt*	*No*	*Amt*
Equity Capital outgo from budget												
Loans given from budget	2	1438.27	1	761.49	3	2150.69	1	631.00	4	889.97	1	606.54
Grants/Subsidy towards project/programmes/ Schemes	2	5.84	-	-	3	57.14			3	4.17	-	-
Other Subsidy									1	0.16		
Total Subsidy									1	0.16		
Total outgo	4	1444.11	1	761.49	6	2207.83	1	631.00	5	894.3	1	606.54

Source: Reports of the Comptroller and Auditor General of India (Commercial) ,on Delhi for 2002-03 to 2004-05.

and DTTDC and were paid an amount of Rs. 44.85 crore towards ex-gratia and other terminal benefits. An audit appraisal of the implementation of the VRS schemes revealed that the enterprises did not adhere to the principles and guidelines prescribed by the Government of India in implementing the VRS. Three out of the four companies adopted VRS without obtaining necessary approval of the Government. The VRS was implemented without undertaking a systematic study to identify surplus manpower or redundant skills so as to ensure retention of an optimum manpower profile and without a full assessment of their financial liability and the resources required to meet them. The response to the schemes was poor and was not commensurate with the expected gains in terms of a streamlined organization despite heavy cash outflow towards payment of terminal benefits.

Problems / Issues

The National Capital Territory of Delhi enterprises suffer from the problem of subsidization, net worth erosion, sub-optimal asset utilisation and non-performing asset.

8. Gujarat

8.1 Financial Profile

The profile of SLPEs of Gujarat is given in the following table:

8.2 Sectoral Classification

Table 8.2 shows the classification of the SLPEs of Gujarat.

8.3 Budgetary Support

Table 8.3 shows that the Government had guaranteed loans aggregating Rs.1,355 crore obtained by one working Government company (Rs. 800 crore) and one working Statutory corporation (Rs. 555 crore). At the end of the year guarantees amounting to Rs.12,997.68 crore obtained by 11 working Government companies (Rs. 6,187.08 crore) and four working Statutory corporations (Rs. 6,810.60 crore) were outstanding as against outstanding guarantees of Rs.14,318.37 crore obtained by 11 working Government companies (Rs. 6,612.48 crore) and four working Statutory corporations (Rs. 7,705.89 crore) as on 31 March 2004. The State Government converted loan/ convertible debentures of Rs. 2.90 crore into equity in respect of two working Government

Table 8.1
Profile of SLPEs in Gujarat

(Rs. in crore)

Items / *Years*	*2002-03*	*2003-04*	*2004-05*
1. Total no. of SLPEs		49	50
2. No. of Working SLPEs		39	40
3. No. of Non-Working SLPEs		10	10
(I). Under Liquidation		4	4
(II). Under Closure		6	6
(III). Under Merger		-	-
(IV). Others		-	-
4. Total Equity		874	2631
5. Total Debt		17561	18564
6. Total Investment		18435	21195
7. No. of Profit making enterprises		20	22
8. No. of Loss making enterprises		27	25
9. Net Profit/Loss		-1181	-755
10. Accumulated Loss(-)/Profit		-7965	-7207

Source: Reports of the Comptroller and Auditor General of India (Commercial), onGujarat for 2002-03 to 2004-05.

Table 8.2
Classification of SLPEs in Gujarat

Sl. No	*Category*	*No. of Enterprises*
1	Manufacturing	25
2	Financial	6
3	Trade&Service	4
4	Promotional	7
5	Welfare	4
6	Utility	4
	Total	50

Source: Classified from the list of enterprises given in reports of the Comptroller and Auditor General of India (Commercial) ,on Gujarat for 2001-02.

Table 8.3
Budgetary Support to SLPEs in Gujarat

(Rs. in crore)

Particulars	*2002-03*				*2003-04*				*2004-05*			
	Companies		*Corp*		*Companies*		*Corp*		*Companies*		*Corp*	
	No.	*Amt*	*No*	*Amt*	*No*	*Amt*	*No*	*Amt*	*No*	*Amt*	*No*	*Amt*
Equity Capital outgo from budget	8	767.39	1	14.05	12	1813.38	1	20.11	9	1408.93	1	17.69
Loans given from budget	4	1.37	1	390.81	4	0.66	2	2074.18	4	1116.38	3	682.61
Grants Subsidy towards												
(i) project/programmes /Schemes	13	150.90	-	-	11	219.64	1	34.92	14	331.48	1	17.74
(ii) Other Subsidy	3	90.69	3	1345.83	4	102.65	2	1236.28	6	39.03	3	1758.18
Total Subsidy	15	241.59	3	1345.83	15	322.29	3	1271.20	17	370.51	4	1775.92
Total outgo	15	1010.35	3	1750.69	23	2136.33	4	3365.49	20	2895.82	4	2476.22

Source: Report of the Comptroller and Auditor General of India (Commercial) on Government of Gujarat, 2002-2003 to 2004-05.

companies. The guarantee commission paid/payable to Government by four Government companies and three Statutory corporations during 2004-05 was Rs. 98.04 crore and Rs.126.83 crore, respectively.

8.4 Social Safety Net Programme

Earlier, Government of Gujarat announced a VRS on 5th October 1988[2] to enable the SLPEs to rationalize their surplus manpower. Enterprises which are financially sound and can sustain a scheme of VRS on their own surplus resources may devise and implement variants of the exiting VRS. However, in no case shall the compensation exceed 60 days salary for each completed year of service or the salary for the number of months service left, whichever is less. Salary for the purpose of VRS shall consist of basic pay and DA only and no other element. Enterprises that make marginal profits or loss-making enterprises may adopt the revised scheme of VRS which is modeled on the Scheme that exists in the State of Gujarat.

The Government have decided further to modify, with immediate effect, the Revised VRS for the enterprises[3]. The Public Sector Restructuring Programme (PSRP), Government of Gujarat (GOG) has, as a part of "Social Safety Net", constituted State Renewal Fund (SRF) under direct control of the Finance Department in September, 1996. The main aim of the SRF is to provide funds for the VRS related expenses to the SLPEs covered under the PSRP. The parameters on the bais of which the VRS could be formulated by the SLPEs for their employees have been spelt out in the Department. However, there are certain points on which some more clarifications have been solicited by the SLPEs as well as the administrative Ministries / Departments. The points raised as well as the clarifications thereon are given hereunder : -

8.5 Problems / Issues

The problems of the SLPEs in Gujarat are no different from the problems of their counterparts in the other states. However, the Government-PE interface in Gujarat was notably different as compared to many other states in several regards. The state Bureau of public Enterprises in Gujarat acted more as a friend, philosopher and guide to the State units. Secondly, the administrative Ministries controlling the SLPEs kept themselves out of the day-to-day functioning of the units. Professionalisation further helped these units in operating smoothly.

9. Goa

9.1 Financial Profile

The profile of SLPEs of Goa is given in Table 9.1.

9.2 Sectoral Classification

Table 9.2 shows the classification of SLPEs of Goa.

9.3 Budgetary Support

During 2004-05, the Government had guaranteed loans aggregating Rs.115 crore obtained by two working Government companies. At the end of the year, guarantees of Rs. 495.06 crore obtained by three Government companies were outstanding as against the outstanding guarantees of Rs. 426.65 crore as on 31 March 2004. There was no case of default by the State Government companies/corporation in repayment of guaranteed loan during the year

9.4 Problems / Issues

Profesionalisation of the management cadres is the prime need. The enterprises in the manufacturing sector suffered from an acute shortage of raw materials, stores and spares. The marketing function requires to be strengthened.

10. Haryana

10.1 Financial Profile

The profile of SLPEs in Haryana is given in the following table:

10.2 Sectoral Classification

Table 10.2 shows the classification of the SLPEs in Haryana.

10. 3 Budgetary Support

Table 10.3 shows that, the Government had guaranteed loans aggregating Rs. 985.54 crore obtained by six working Government companies (Rs. 501.43 crore) and one working statutory corporation (Rs. 484.11 crore). At the end of the year,

Table 9.1
Profile of SLPEs in Goa

(Rs. in crore)

Items / *Years*	*2002-03*	*2003-04*	*2004-05*
1. Total no. of SLPEs	15	15	15
2. No. of Working SLPEs	15	15	15
3. No.of Non-Working SLPEs (i) Under Liquidation (ii) Under Closure (iii) Under Merger (iv) Others	-	-	-
4. Total Equity	120	131	144
5. Total Debt	552	448	442
6. Total Investment	672	579	586
7. No. of Profit making enterprises	4	5	4
8. No. of Loss making enterprises	11	9	10
9. Net Profit/Loss	-25	-33	-47
10. Accumulated Loss(-)/Profit	-119	-145	-189

Source: Reports of the Comptroller and Auditor General of India (Commercial) , on Goa 2002-03 to 2004-05.

Table 9.2

Classification of SLPEs in Goa

Sl.No	*Category*	*No.of Enterprises*
1.	Manufacturing	6
2.	Financial	2
3.	Trade and Service	-
4.	Promotional	4
5.	Welfare	1
6.	Utility	2
	Total	15

Source: Classified from the list of enterprises given in reports of the Comptroller and Auditor General of India (Commercial) ,on Gujarat for 2001-02.

Table 9.3
Budgetary Support to SLPEs in Goa

(Rs.in crore)

Particulars	*2002-03*				*2003-04*				*2004-05*			
	Companies		*Corp*		*Companies*		*Corp*		*Companies*		*Corp*	
	No.	*Amt*	*No*	*Amt*	*No*	*Amt*	*No*	*Amt*	*No*	*Amt*	*No*	*Amt*
Equity Capital outgo from budget	4	5.05	1	0.05	3	7.69	1	1.62	7	14.76	1	0.38
Loans given from budget												
Grants Subsidy towards (i) project/programmes/ Schemes (ii) Other Subsidy	4	11.11			5	15.63			6	14.70		
Total Subsidy												
Total outgo	7	16.16	1	0.05	7	23.32	1	1.62	8	30.3	1	0.38

Source: Report of the Comptroller and Auditor General of India (Commercial) on Government of Goa, 2002-2003 to 2004-05.

Table 10.1
Profile of SLPEs in Haryana

(Rs.in crore)

Items / Years	2002-03	2003-04	2004-05
1. Total no. of SLPEs	30	29	29
2. No. of Working SLPEs	21	21	21
3. No. of Non-Working SLPEs	9	8	8
(i) Under Liquidation	2	2	2
(ii) Under Closure			
(iii) Under Merger			
(iv) Others	7	6	6
4. Total Equity	2348	2486	2651
5. Total Debt	6607	6955	7196
6. Total Investment	8957	9441	9847
7. No. of Profit making enterprises	11	14	14
8. No. of Loss making enterprises	13	15	14
9. Net Profit/Loss	-178	19	68
10. Accumulated Loss(-)/Profit	-1201	-1211	-1028

Source: Reports of the Comptroller and Auditor General of India (Commercial) ,on Haryana for 2002-03 to 2004-05.

Table 10.2
Profile of SLPEs in Haryana

Sl.No	*Category*	*No.of Enterprises*
1.	Manufacturing	10
2.	Financial	2
3.	Trade&Service	2
4.	Promotional	5
5.	Welfare	3
6.	Utility	7
	Total	29

Source: Classified from the list of entrpreses given in reports of the Comptoller and Auditor of India Commercially , on Haryana for 2001-02.

Table 10.3
Budgetary support to SLPEs in Haryana

(Rs. in crore)

Particulars	2002-03 Companies		2003-04 Companies		2004-05 Companies	
	No.	Amount	No	Amount	No	Amount
Equity Capital outgo from budget	6	147.68	10	130.19	7	166.98
Loans given from budget	3	40.99	3	87.79	3	21.96
Grants						
Subsidy towards						
(i) project/programmes / Schemes						
(ii) Other Subsidy	2	2.84	7	77.74	5	16.10
	6	851.51	6	926.57	5	1170.74
Total Subsidy		854.35		1004.31		1186.84
Total outgo		1043.32		1222.29		1375.78

Source: Reports of the Comptroller and Auditor General of India (Commercial) ,on Haryana for 2002-03 to 2004-05.

guarantees amounting to Rs. 4,167.82 crore against 11 working Government companies (Rs. 4,069.31 crore) and one working Statutory corporation (Rs. 98.51 crore) were outstanding. The guarantee commission paid/payable to Government by six Government companies and one Statutory corporation during the year was Rs. 15.95 crore and Rs. 60.51 lakh, respectively.

10.4 Social Safety Net Programme

The available evidence points out that the Government of Haryana has resorted to the payment of retrenchment compensation in proportion to the assets as was the case with the privatisation of the Hansi Spinning Mill (2001). In this case, in accordance with the legal advise obtained, the employees were to share their payment in proportion to their total claim and each employee was entitled to 66 per cent of the dues payable to them by the mill. The retrenchment route was also adopted in the case of Haryana State Small Industries and Export Corporation and Haryana State Handloom and Handicrafts Corporation. Substantial resources were required to discharge retrenchment compensation and other dues. The State Government provided funds required for payment of retrenchment compensation and other statutory liabilities in the first instance. This was later to be offset against realizations from disposal of assets/properties etc., of the concerned organisation.

10. 5 Problems / Issues

The managerial deficiencies have been the prime factors responsible for the dismal show. Short tenure for the top level executives has become a common feature. Lack of Professionalisation of the SLPEs management cadres was another limitation. Too much of Government interference further held-up the SLPEs over shadow their good performance. The losses incurred by trading and marketing enterprises, which were operating in sensitive sector of the economy, were a case in point.

11. Himachal Pradesh

11.1 Financial Profile

The profile of SLPEs in HP given in the following table.

Table 11.1
Profile of SLPEs in Himachal Pradesh

(Rs. in crore)

Items / Years	2002-03	2003-04	2004-05
1. Total no. of SLPEs	21	21	21
2. No. of Working SLPEs	17	17	17
3. No. of Non-Working SLPEs	4	4	4
(i) Under Liquidation	1	1	1
(ii) Under Closure	3	3	3
(iii) Under Merger			
(iv) Others			
4. Total Equity	715	677	677
5. Total Debt	4391	3006	3006
6. Total Investment	5106	3683	3683
7. No. of Profit making enterprises	7	7	7
8. No. of Loss making enterprises	12	11	11
9. Net Profit/Loss	-77	-77	-773
10. Accumulated Loss(-)/Profit	-772	-762	-762

Source: Reports of the Comptroller and Auditor General of India (Commercial) ,on Delhi for 2002-03 to 2004-05.

11.2 Sectoral Classification

Table 11.2 shows the classification of SLPEs in Himachal Pradesh.

Table 11.2
Classification of SLPEs in Government of Himachal Pradesh

Sl.No	Category	No. of Enterprises
1.	Manufacturing	6
2.	Financial	1
3.	Trade & Service	0
4.	Promotional	10
5.	Welfare	2
6.	Utility	2
	Total	21

Source: Classified from the list of enterprises given in reports of the Comptroller and Auditor General of India (Commercial) , on Delhi for 2001-02.

11.3 Budgetary Support

The budgetary outgo in the form of equity and loans and grants/subsidies from the State Government to the working Government companies and Statutory corporations for the three years up to 2004-2005 is given below:

During 2004-2005, the Government guaranteed loans aggregating Rs. 243.10 crore obtained by four Government companies (Rs. 22.60 crore) and two Statutory corporations (Rs. 220.50 crore). At the end of the year guarantees amounting to Rs. 2,896.33 crore against eight Government companies (Rs. 179.04 crore) and three Statutory corporations (Rs. 2,717.29 crore) were outstanding. There was no case of default in repayment of guaranteed loans during the year. The Government had not forgone any amount by way of loans written off or interest waived or given moratorium on loan repayment during the year.

11.4 Problems / Issues

Many SLPEs are duplicating certain functions. In the field of industrial promotion two enterprises are competing for the same ends. The operational systems have become outdated. The sales turnover is very low. The debt- eqity misx in many SLPEs needs to be restructured.

Table 11.3

Budgetary Support to SLPEs Himachal Pradesh

(Rs. in crore)

Particulars	*2002-03*				*2003-04*				*2004-05*			
	Companies		*Corp*		*Companies*		*Corp*		*Companies*		*Corp*	
	No.	*Amt*	*No*	*Amt*	*No*	*Amt*	*No*	*Amt*	*No*	*Amt*	*No*	*Amt*
Equity Capital outgo from budget	3	1.42	1	11.00	3	1.90	2	30.70	3	1.70	2	14.41
Loans given from budget	-					-					1	6.76
Grants/Subsidy towards (i) project/programmes/ Schemes (ii) Other Subsidy	6	12.68	3	57.34	3	94.09	3	94.09	3	5.39	3	79.25
Total outgo	9	14.10	3	68.34	3	124.79	3	124.79	6	7.09	3	100.42

Source: Reports of the Comptroller and Auditor General of India (Commercial) ,on HP for 2002-03 to 2004-05.

12. Jharkhand

The Jarkhand State continues to jointly own most of the SLPEs with the Government of Bihar as the division of assets and liabilities of the erstwhile SLPEs in Bihar is yet to take place between Bihar and Jharkhand. The State Government has not applied its mind to the issue of retention of SLPEs Portfolio. On the contrary, the State Government has set up some new SLPEs. Jharkhand is a cash rich state. The party in power has donned upon itself the role of the Welfare State. This has given a fillip to the setting up of new SLPEs in the State. The new corporations set up in public sector include the State Mineral Development Corporation and the Jharkhand Technical Consultancy Organisation. The Government proposes to continue the three Industrial Area Development Authority i.e. to cure sickness, the Government of Jharkhand) proposes to set up a Special Purpose Vehicle (SPV) in order to nurse the weak and ailing SLPEs. The Government intends to set up a Committee for an assessment of sick/closed SLPEs and for revival of economically and technically viable SLPEs by taking appropriate measures which may include manpower rationalization, disinvestment and financial restructuring.

12.1 Sectoral Classification of SLPEs in Jharkhand

Table 12.1 shows the classification of SLPEs in Jharkhand.

Table 12.1
Classification of SLPEs in Jharkhand

Sl.No.	*Category*	*No.of Enterprises*
1.	Manufacturing	1
2.	Financial	-
3.	Trade&Service	-
4.	Promotional	4
5.	Welfare	-
6.	Utility	2
	Total	7

Source: Classified from the list of enterprises given in reports of the Comptroller and Auditor General of India (Commercial), on Jharkhand for 2004-05.

12.2 Budgetary Support

The budgetary outgo in the form of equity and loans and grants/subsidies from the State Government to the working Government companies and Statutory corporations for the three years up to 2004-2005 is given below:

13. JAMMU & KASHMIR

13.1 Financial Profile

The profile of SLPEs of Jammu & Kashmir is given in the following table:

13.2 Sectoral Classification

Table 13.2 shows the classification of SLPEs in Jammu & Kashmir.

13.3 Budgetary Support

The SLPEs in Jammu & Kashmir are supported by subventions for their continuation which is reinforced by the fact that they had accumulated losses in 1999-2000 and 2000-01. The number of loss making enterprises far exceeded the profit making enterprises. Table 12.3 shows that, the Government guaranteed loans aggregating Rs. 906.82 crore obtained by three working Government companies. At the end of the year, guarantees worth Rs. 1,592.86 crore against nine working Government companies (Rs. 1,528.61 crore) and two working Statutory corporations (Rs. 64.25 crore) were outstanding. Central/State Governments did not waive off any dues during the current year.

13.4 Social Safety Net Programme

The Government of Jammu & Kashmir has adopted a Golden Handshake Scheme for the employees of Public Enterprise. The Finance Department provides necessary budgetary support for the implementation of the Golden Handshake Scheme. The Finance Department has set up an SLPE restructuring fund. The scheme is applicable to all the employees of the SLPEs excepting deputationists, casual workers, employees on consolidated wages, employees on contract basis and employees against whom proceedings for termination of

Table 12.2
Budgetary Support to SLPEs Jharkhand

(Rs in crore)

Particulars	*2003-04*				*2004-05*			
	Companies		*Corp*		*Companies*		*Corp*	
	No.	*Amt*	*No*	*Amt*	*No*	*Amt*	*No*	*Amt*
Equity Capital outgo from budget	1	0.05						
Loans given from budget			1	103.59	1	0.25	1	295.76
Grants/Subsidy towards (i) project/ programme /Schemes (ii) Other Subsidy			1	95.39			1	348.39
Total outgo	1	0.05	1	198.98	1	0.25	1	644.15

Source: Reports of the Comptroller and Auditor General of India (Commercial) ,on Jharkhand for 2002-03 to 2004-05.

Table 13.1
Profile of SLPEs in Jammu & Kashmir

(Rs. in crore)

Items / *Years*	*2002-03*	*2003-04*	*2004-05*
1. Total no. of SLPEs	24	23	23
2. No. of Working SLPEs	23	20	20
3. No. of Non-Working SLPEs	1	3	3
(i) Under liquidation			
(ii) Under Closure			
(iii) Under Merger			
(iv) Others			
4. Total Equity	422	395	390
5. Total Debt	2467	1968	2603
6. Total Investment	2889	2363	2993
7. No. of Profit making enterprises	5	4	6
8. No. of Loss making enterprises	12	14	13
9. Net Profit/Loss	249	304	-5
10. Accumulated Loss(-)/Profit	-783	-917	-1056

Source: Reports of the Comptroller and Auditor General of India (Commercial) ,on Jammu & Kashmir for 2002-03 to 2004-05.

Table 13.2
Classification of SLPEs in Jammu & Kashmir

Sl.No	*Category*	*No.of Enterprises*
1.	Manufacturing	12
2.	Financial	5
3.	Trade&Service	
4.	Promotional	2
5.	Welfare	2
6.	Utility	2
	Total	23

Source: Classified from the list of enterprises given in reports of the Comptroller and Auditor General of India (Commercial) , on Jammu & Kashmir.

Table 13.3
Budgetary Support to SLPEs in Jammu & Kashmir

(Rs. in crore)

Particulars	*2002-03*				*2003-04*				*2004-05*			
	Companies		*Corp*		*Companies*		*Corp*		*Companies*		*Corp*	
	No.	*Amt*	*No*	*Amt*	*No*	*Amt*	*No*	*Amt*	*No*	*Amt*	*No*	*Amtt*
Equity Capital outgo from budget	5	13.29	-	-	4	2.80	-	-	5	3.23	1	0.80
Loans given from budget	5	9.94	1	20.45	6	10.04	1	25.43	6	8.51	2	68.42
Grants Subsidy towards	5	16.99	-	-	8	25.84	-	-	3	1.89	-	-
Subsidy	4	1.29	-	-	3	1.45	-	-	4	11.60	-	-
Total outgo	11	41.51	1	20.45	12	40.13	1	25.43	10	25.23	2	69.22

Source: Reports of the Comptroller and Auditor General of India (Commercial) ,on Jammu & Kashmir for 2002-03 to 2004-05.

employees on disciplinary grounds are unsatisfactory performance while in service, are in progress. The employees availing of the Golden Handshake Scheme are entitled for terminal benefits.

13.5 Problems / Issues

The SLPEs in J&K had operational problems in all the areas of management. They suffered from very low capacity utilization. The shortage of raw materials, delay in receiving orders, and shortage of labour and dearth of technical personnel obstructed higher capacity utilization. The marketing problems included lack of availability of suitable personnel and delay in decision making.

14. KARNATAKA

14.1 Financial Profile

The profile of SLPEs of Karnataka is given in the following table. The financial profile of the SLPEs in Karnataka shows that the huge investments either earned no or negligible returns.

14.2 Sectoral Classification

Table 14.2 shows the classification of SLPEs in Karnataka.

14.3 Budgetary Support:

Table 14.3 shows that, the Government had guaranteed the loans aggregating Rs.1,089.63 crore obtained by 15 working Government companies (Rs.1,082.60 crore) and two Statutory corporations (Rs. 7.03 crore). At the end of the year, guarantees amounting to Rs. 8,425.02 crore against 22 working Government companies (Rs. 7,907.31 crore) and three working Statutory corporations (Rs. 517.71 crore) were outstanding. The Government had foregone Rs. 0.36 crore by way of interest waiver in one company during the year.

14.4 Social Safety Net Programme

An important component of the process of privatisation of the SLPEs in Karnataka is regarding rationalization of employment in the enterprises. These enterprises suffer from surplus of labour. The Government of Karnataka has formulated a Voluntary Retirement Scheme (VRS) which has been so structured as to

Table 14.1
Profile of SLPEs of Karnataka

(Rs. in crores)

Items / *Years*	*2002-03*	*2003-04*	*2004-05*
1. Total no.of SLPEs	82	82	82
2. No.of Working SLPEs	65	65	65
3. No.of Non-Working SLPEs	17	17	17
(i) Under liquidation	8	8	8
(ii) Under Closure	4	4	4
(iii) Under Merger			
(iv) Others	5	5	5
4. Total Equity	8518	8518	12698
5. Total Debt	21493	21493	22499
6. Total Investment	30011	30011	35197
7. No. of Profit making enterprises	41	41	39
8. No. of Loss making enterprises	31	31	28
9. Net Profit/Loss	143	143	378
10. Accumulated Loss(-)/Profit	-843	-843	-808

Source: Reports of the Comptroller and Auditor General of India (Commercial) ,on Karnataka for 2002-03 to 2004-05.

Table 14.2
Classification of SLPEs in Karnataka

Sl. No	Category	No.of Enterprises
1.	Manufacturing	35
2.	Financial	2
3.	Trade & Service	3
4.	Promotional	20
5.	Welfare	7
6.	Utility	15
	Total	82

Source: Classified from the list of enterprises given in reports of the Comptroller and Auditor General of India (Commercial) ,on Karnataka for 2001-02.

Table 14.3
Budgetary Support to SLPEs in Karnataka

(Rs. in crore)

Particulars	*2002-03*				*2003-04*				*2004-05*			
	Companies		*Corp*		*Companies*		*Corp*		*Companies*		*Corp*	
	No.	*Amt*	*No*	*Amt*	*No*	*Amt*	*No*	*Amt*	*No*	*Amt*	*No*	*Amt*
Equity Capital outgo from budget	21	2960.10	-	-	13	1525.38	-	-	9	2787.24	3	30.00
Loans given from budget	3	14.36	1	6.38	6	89.46	-	-	9	209.64	1	42.00
Grants	10	51.83	-	-	11	108.05	-	-	14	377.27	-	-
Subsidy towards				-								
(i) project/programme/ Schemes	4	196.92	-		3	5.45	1	12.50	4	215.05		
(ii) Other Subsidy	8	737.86	4	85.45	9	1893.67	4	29.11	5	1585.00	5	141.48
Total Subsidy	12	934.78	4	85.45	11	1899.12	4	41.61	9	1800.05	5	141.48
Total outgo	32	3961.07	5	91.83	28	3622.00	4	41.61	25	5174.20	5	213.48

Source: Reports of the Comptroller and Auditor General of India (Commercial), on Karnataka for 2002-03 to 2004-05.

Table 13.6
Karnataka Economic Restructuring Programme –PE Reforms Phase –I

Sl.No	*Name of he Public Sector Undertaking*	*Total employees (identified surplus)*	*VRS offered to*	*VRS accepted to*	*VRS paid to*	*Employees on Rolls*
1.	Chamundi Machine Tools	107	107	107	107	-
2.	Mysore Cosmetics Ltd	22	22	22	22	-
3.	Karnataka Telecoms KTd	258	258	258	258	-
4.	Mysore Match Co. Ltd.	3	3	3	3	-
5.	Mysore Acetate and Chemicals Co. Ltd.	87	87	9	9	78
6.	Mysore Electricals Industries Ltd	573 (226)	226	202	202	336
7.	NGEF Ltd.	2183	2183	2183	2149	34
8.	Karnataka State Textiles Ltd	425	425	425	351	74
9.	Karnataka State Construction Crop. Ltd	319	319	90	89	230
10.	KAVIKA	388	-	52	40	236
11.	Mysore Paper Mills Ltd.	2939 (502)		-	--	2907
12.	Mysore Lamp works Ltd	1569	1569	1046	1081	540
13.	Mysore Agro Proteins Ltd	-				-

(Contd.)

(Contd.)

Sl.No	*Name of he Public Sector Undertaking*	*Total employees (identified surplus)*	*VRS offered to*	*VRS accepted to*	*VRS paid to*	*Employees on Rolls*
15.	Karnataka Soaps and Detergents Ltd.	1140 (169)	169	64	61	1075
16.	Karnataka Fisheries Dev. Corp.	228(175)	-	-	-	228
17.	Karnataka State Veneers Ltd	167	-	-	-	167
18.	Karnataka State Film Industries Dev. Ltd.	42	8	8	8	34
19.	Sree Kanteerava Studios Ltd.	32	-	-	-	32
20.	Karnataka Small Industries Marketing Corp. Ltd.	49	-	-	-	49
	Total	10753 (1096)	5598	4490	4338	6251

encourage retirement of surplus staff while ensuring reasonable quantum of compensation. The objectives of the VRS scheme include improving the performance of the SLPEs, maintain an optimum level of manpower, facilitate manpower adjustment through deployment and to compensate the surplus or redundant manpower reasonably. Any permanent employee with 15 years of service or 40 years of age and who has been identified as surplus by the management could be brought under the VRS. The scheme is not applicable to the employees who are due to retire or superannuate within one year from the date of application, deputationists, temporary or casual employees, employees on contract basis and employees in whose case proceedings for termination of employment on disciplinary grounds of unsatisfactory performance is in progress. The employees opting for VRS receive the terminal benefits, PF and gratuity benefits, cash equivalent of accumulated earned leave and ex-gratia benefits. The Government does not provide any budgetary support for VRS. Once the options for VRS are accepted the related posts are simultaneously abolished. The employees retired under VRS are not eligible for employment in any Government Department, SLPEs and Co-operative Institutions etc.

Each organisation identified for privatisation prepares its VRS scheme and sends it to the concerned Administrative Department for approval, which in turn furnishes its view and gets concurrence of Karnataka State Bureau of Public Enterprise and Finance Department. The Administrative Department in particular examines the effort of the undertaking to raise internal resources for the VRS.

Table 13.6 provides enterprise wise details of the number of employees availing VR and the money spent on the VRS.

14.4 Problems / Issues

The State Government of Karnataka is constantly reviewing the role of the public sector from various points of view-the most important being the need for the state's presence in any sector of public service or consumer need.

The State Government has impressed upon the SLPEs that they must put in the necessary effort towards raising institutional finance, both as regards funds required for capital investment as well as working capital. Such an approach to funding the public sector enterprises was in any case warranted because they often tend to opt for the easier method of seeking equity or loan assistance from the Government. One great advantage of these enterprises approaching financial institutions rather than the State Government would be that the project proposals would be subjected to more professional scrutiny. At least from now on their schemes must pass the test of bankability regardless of whether the funds ultimately come from the State Government or the financial institutions.

Another important area which is attracting serious attention from the State Government is the lack of proper and prompt feedback from Government nominee directors on the boards of SLPEs. There have been many instances where nominee directors not only failed to attend important board meetings. In some cases, patently inappropriate resolutions were passed, involving sizeable expenditure and outlays, without the State Government being aware of what was happening. While the State Government does not want to unduly interfere with the autonomy of the SLPEs, it expects its nominee directors to properly ands adequately represent the State's views, leaving it to board of directors to take an appropriate decision on the overall merits of a resolution. Carefully formulated guidelines have been issued in this behalf to all nominee directors and these are reiterated from time to time.

The State Government is also becoming increasingly aware of the importance of stability of tenure of chief executive of public sector enterprises. It is being increasingly realized that not only should the selection for the post of the chief executive of a public sector undertaking be based on proven flair and integrity, but once an appointment has been made, the executive should be allowed a reasonable spell of time of at least 3 to 4 years.

15. Kerala

15.1 Financial Profile

The profile of SLPEs in Kerala is given in Table15.1.

15.2 Sectoral Classification

Table 15.2 shows the classification of SLPEs of Kerala:

Table 15.1
Profile of SLPEs in Kerala

(Rs. in Crore)

Items / Years	2002-03	2003-04	2004-05
1. Total no. of SLPEs	113	113	109
2. No. of Working SLPEs	96	92	88
3. No. of Non-Working SLPEs	17	21	21
(i) Under Liquidation	12	10	13
(ii) Under Closure	5	11	8
(iii) Under Merger			
(iv) Others			
4. Total Equity	3370	3399	3436
5. Total Debt	7521	8501	7608
6. Total Investment	10891	11900	11044
7. No. of Profit making enterprises	36	36	38
8. No. of Loss making enterprises	72	72	70
9. Net Profit/Loss	-100	-145	-55
10. Accumulated Loss(-)/Profit	-1896	-2134	-2343

Source: Reports of the Comptroller and Audistor General of India (Commercial) ,on Kerala for 2002-03 to 2004-05.

Table 15.2
Classification of SLPEs

Sl.No	Category	No.of Enterprises
1.	Manufacturing	77
2.	Financial	3
3.	Trade & Service	4
4.	Promotional	12
5.	Welfare	10
6.	Utility	3
	Total	109

Source: Classified from the list of enterprises given in reports of the Comptroller and Auditor General of India (Commercial) ,on kerala for 2004-05.

Table 15.3

Budgetary support to SLPEs in Kerala

(Rs. in Crores)

Particulars	*2002-03*				*2003-04*				*2004-05*			
	Companies		*Corp*		*Companies*		*Corp*		*Companies*		*Corp*	
	No.	*Amt*	*No*	*Amt*	*No*	*Amt*	*No*	*Amt*	*No*	*Amt*	*No*	*Amt*
Equity Capital outgo from budget	19	45.33	4	29.90	16	38.50	3	14.50	18	25.47	1	2.00
Loans given from budget	13	51.97	2	61.16	9	32.92	2	44.15	7	48.40	3	66.21
Grants/Subsidy towards: (i) project/programmes /Schemes (ii) Other Subsidy	17	63.93	2	9.34	20	51.75	3	567.21	18	51.03	2	43.39
Total outgo	40	161.23	5	100.40	33	123.17	5	625.86	33	124.90	4	111.60

Source: Reports of the Comptroller and Auditor General of India (Commercial) ,on Kerala for 2002-03 to 2004-05.

15.3 Budgetary Support

During the year 2004-05, the Government had guaranteed loans aggregating Rs. 445.61 crore obtained by 15 working Government companies. At the end of the year, guarantees of Rs. 6,100.94 crore against 28 working Government companies (Rs. 3,277.79 crore) and four working Statutory corporations (Rs. 2,823.15 crore) were outstanding. The guarantee commission paid payable to Government by Government companies (Rs. 62.95 core) and Statutory corporation (Rs. 42.92 crore) during 2004-05 was Rs.105.87 crore.

15.4 Social Safety Net Programme

A Social Safely Net Programme that consists of a financial compensation package and a welfare and economic sustainability package for retired employees have been approved by the Government based on the approach paper of ERC in March 2002. The programme was approved by the Government in June 2003. Capacity building for reform implementation and post reform governance and development is being undertaken by RIAB under the MGP. A communication strategy is also being evolved and implemented for better knowledge management in SLPF reform domain.

The Government of Kerala constituted the Enterprise Reforms Committee[4] during 2001 November to recommend restructuring / reform options for the ailing public enterprises in the State. Since June 2002, the ERC has recommended reform measures in 45 SLPEs and the Government has taken decision on 30 of these enterprises. About 4832 employees have been paid retirement compensation under the SSNP that consists of a financial compensation package and a welfare and economic sustainability package. Capacity Building for reform implementation and post reform governance and development and Performance Monitoring of SLPEs is undertaken by the Public Sector Restructuring and Internal Audit Board (RIAB), which is the secretariat of the ERC. The Government constituted a sub-committee of Ministers to examine the approach and strategy on SLPE reform programme. Later the ERC was wound up with effect from 31-01-2005. A summary of the status of SLPEs reforms (as on December 2005).

Amount Spent on SLPEs Reforms

Sl No	Purpose	No. of Enterprises	Amount (Rs in crore)
1.	Retirement compensation under social safety net programme	6	27.22
2.	Payments to creditors / financial institutions	4	34.78
3.	Relief in defunct units	15	5.84
4.	Salary / Honorarium to essential staff	3	0.24
5.	Other purposes	1	7.00
	Total		**75.08**

Source: Bureau of Public Enterprises, Government of Kerala, 2004-05, p. XII.

A total amount of Rs. 75.08 crore has been spent for reforms in the public enterprises, including cooperatives units under Industries Department in the State during 2004-05. The following table shows a breakup is given below :

15.5 Problems / Issues

Some peculiar features in relation to the public enterprises functioning in Kerala might be worth discussing in the context of trying to improve the over all performance.

The production losses as a result of labour unrest and other reasons like power-cut and break down of machinery are fairly high in Kerala. It is well-known that multiplicity of trade unions causes losses in man-days with each one vying with the other for establishing a stranglehold on labour. There are instances of wild cat strikes being called even when disciplinary action is taken by the management on chronic cases of undisciplined. The domineering role of the unions and their nexus with the political executives results in frequent government intervention in pushing up wages even in loss-making units. A disturbing feature of the scenario is that most of the public enterprises in Kerala are today functioning almost as appendages of the State Government. The management very often consists of chosen representative of the ruling party and in some cases even the middle and lower level managers are appointees of the government. Easy access of such persons to the ministers causes friction between the chief executives and the ministers.

While the management failures are well established as a factor contributing to the lack of progress, another specific reason is the fact that many of the undertakings have tried to launch ambitious projects that have long gestation periods, which as result cause time and cost over-runs. The Projects reports look promising on paper. However, on implementation, several snags develop and the Government is forced to sanction upward revision of the final cost of the project from time to time. Employment generation being the prime objective of the State Government, there is extreme reluctance on the part of the government to lay off or retrench workers. Even the well established undertakings, are over-staffed both at the managerial and the workers level. The overhead costs are some times beyond the reach of the undertaking and when the question of payment of bonus is considered, the government are forced to step in by the grant of ad hoc special; allowance to some of the undertakings. A sluggish marketing strategy emerges as a serious issue when one considers the overall performance of the enterprises. However, this is balanced by the availability of a ready market for many of the goods produced by the SLPEs.

16. Lakshwadeep

This union territory has only one SLPE viz., Lakshadweep Development Corporation Limited.

17. Madhya Pradesh

17.1 Financial Profile

The profile of SLPEs in MP is given in Table 17.1.

17.2 Sectoral Classification of SLPEs of Madhya Pradesh

Table 17.2 shows the classification of SLPEs of Madhya Pradesh:

17.3 Budgetary Support

Table 17.3 shows that 18 enterprises received budgetary support of Rs. 561.29 crore in 1998-99. In 2000-01, 15 enterprises received budgetary support of Rs. 613.97 crore.

17.4 Social Safety Net Programme

Madhya Pradesh

Employee eligibility under VRS has been calculated by MPSRTC at the rate of two months' salary for each completed year of service subject to the condition that payment under proposed VRS does not exceed what the incumbent would have received for the remaining period of his service till superannuation, had he not opted for VRS. MPSRTC has stipulated that a minimum service of five years and a maximum service of 25 years will only be reckoned for grant of VRS to an employee. The proposed VRS is expected to be opted for by about 5000 employees in various categories.

Table 17.1
Financial Profile of SLPEs in Madhya Pradesh

(Rs. in crore)

Items / Years	2002-03	2003-04	2004-05
1. Total no. of SLPEs	34	38	40
2. No. of Working SLPEs	25	29	31
3. No. of Non-Working SLPEs	9	9	9
(I). Under Liquidation	4	5	5
(II). Under Closure	4	4	4
(III). Under Merger			
(IV). Others	1		
4. Total Equity	704	681	707
5. Total Debt	4881	4452	5154
6. Total Investment	5585.38	5133	5861
7. No. of Profit making enterprises	13	14	15
8. No. of Loss making enterprises	18	16	14
9. Net Profit/Loss	-1642	-510	59
10. Accumulated Loss(-)/Profit	-3016	-3878	-4062

Source: Reports of the Comptroller and Auditor General of India (Commercial) ,on MP 2002-03 to 2004-05.

Table 17.2
Classification of SLPEs in Madhya Pradesh

Sl. No	*Category*	*No. of Enterprises*
1.	Manufacturing	15
2.	Financial	2
3.	Trade &Service	3
4.	Promotional	7
5.	Welfare	9
6.	Utility	4
	Total	40

Source: Classified from the list of enterprises given in reports of the Comptroller and Auditor General of India (Commercial) ,on Madhya Pradesh for 2001-02.

Table 17.3

Budgetary Support to SLPEs of Madhya Pradesh

(Rs. in crore)

Particulars	*2002-03*				*2003-04*				*2004-05*			
	Companies		*Corp*		*Companies*		*Corp*		*Companies*		*Corp*	
	No.	*Amt*	*No*	*Amt*	*No*	*Amt*	*No*	*Amt*	*No*	*Amt*	*No*	*Amt*
Equity Capital outgo from budget	2	3.02	1	1.00	1	0.90	1	1.34	2	10.30	1	1.50
Loans given from budget	1	10.88	3	247.05	1	7.24			1	4.28	2	375.44
Grants/Subsidy towards (i) project/programmes /Schemes (ii) Other Subsidy	10	61.51	3	586.92	11	46.90			10	213.14	2	845.33
Total outgo	12	78.41	4	834.97	11	55.04	1	1.34	12	227.72	3	1222.27

Source: Reports of the Comptroller and Auditor General of India (Commercial) ,on Madhya Pradesh for 2002-03 to 2004.05.

Table 17.4

Category-wise Average Cost of VRS

(Rs. in lakhs)

S. No.	*Category*	*Number*	*Amount*	*Average per Employee*
1.	Conductors	3000	11550	3.85
2.	Mechanical Staff	100	450	4.50
3.	Others (Admn. Staff/ Officers)	1900	14500	7.63
	Total / Average	**5000**	**26500**	**5.30**

Source: MPSRTC's reply to Consultant's Questionnaire.

The Table 17.4 below gives the average cost of VRS for different categories of employees, which may vary depending on pay scales and scheme of VR.

It has been reported that the Government of MP has recently adopted the recommendations of the Central Fifth Pay Commission in respect of pay scales, and has extended it to the State Government and Public Sector employees. This is likely to form the basis of pay revision for MPSRTC employees. The exact figures would have to be calculated and will be dependent on pay structure, date of effect, numbers, scheme of VRS, and related factors. Depending on the outcome, calculations of VRS may undergo substantial upward revision. This will have to be done carefully in view of the financial implications.

18. Maharashtra

18.1 Financial Profile

The profile of SLPEs in Maharasthra is given in the following table:

Table 18.1
Profile of SLPEs in Maharashtra

(Rs in crore)

Years / *Items*	*2002-03*	*2003-04*	*2004-05*
1. Total no.of SLPEs	71	81	82
2. No.of Working SLPEs	53	60	61
3. No.of Non-Working SLPEs	18	21	21
(I). Under Liquidation	3	3	3
(II). Under Closure	9	11	12
(III). Under Merger			
(IV). Others	6	7	6
4. Total Equity	4798	4626	5331
5. Total Debt	13100	16190	15218
6. Total Investment	17898	20816	20549
7. No.of Profit making enterprises	18	15	21
8. No.of Loss making enterprises	45	59	54
9. Net Profit/Loss	-951	-1161	-1179
10. Accumulated Loss(-)/Profit	-2450	-3650	-4604

Source: Reports of the Comptroller and Auditor General of India (Commercial) ,on Maharashtra for 2002-03 to 2004-05.

18.2 Sectoral Classification of SLPEs of Maharasthra

Table 18.2 shows the classification of the SLPEs of Maharasthra.

Table 18.2
Classification of SLPEs in Maharashtra

Sl.No	*Category*	*No. of Enterprises*
1.	Manufacturing	34
2.	Financial	4
3.	Trade and Service	1
4.	Promotional	16
5.	Welfare	12
6.	Utility	4
	Total	71

Source: Classified from the list of enterprises given in reports of the Comptroller and Auditor General of India (Commercial), on Maharashtra for 2004-05.

18.3 Budgetary Support

The Budgetary Support to the SLPEs of Maharashtra during the period 2002-2003 to 2004-05 was as follows:

18.4 Problems / Issues

In the late eighties, the issues pertaining to improving the effectiveness of the SLPEs received attention at the highest levels of the State administration. The State Bureau of Public Enterprises was set up as a result of importance attached to these enterprises. The Bureau is engaged in revising a performance monitoring and evaluations system for the SLPEs. As a result, there is noticeable improvement in the performance of Maharashtra State Level Public Enterprises.

19. MANIPUR

The SLPEs in Manipur were established mainly to attract capital investment from private sector and financial institutions, expand the economic activities in the state, create employment opportunities and generate profits

Table 18.3
Budgetary Support to SLPEs of Maharasthra

(Rs. in crore)

Particulars	*2002-03*				*2003-04*				*2004-05*			
	Companies		*Corp*		*Companies*		*Corp*		*Companies*		*Corp*	
	No.	*Amt*	*No*	*Amt*	*No*	*Amt*	*No*	*Amt*	*No*	*Amt*	*No*	*Amt*
Equity Capital outgo from budget	5	7.09			5	10.35	1	121.29	7	70.77	1	127.80
Loans given from budget	6	115.10	1	179.64	5	7.23			3	13.38	1	179.64
Grants/Subsidy towards (i) project/programmes/ Schemes (ii) Other Subsidy	8	641.76	2	854.96	6	17.32	1	734.09	13	248.37	1	5790.40
Total outgo		763.95		1034.60		34.90		855.38		332.52		6097.84

Source: Reports of the Comptroller and Auditor General of India (Commercial), on Maharashtra for 2002-03 to 2004-05.

19.1 Financial Profile

The profile of SLPEs in Manipur is given in the following table :

Table 19.1
Profile of SLPEs in Manipur

(Rs in crore)

Items / *Years*	*2002-03*	*2003-04*	*2004-05*
1. Total no. of SLPEs	16	16	16
2. No. of Working SLPEs	14	10	8
3. No. of Non-Working SLPEs	2	6	8
(i) Under Liquidation	2	6	8
(ii) Under Closure			
(iii) Under Merger			
(iv) Others			
4. Total Equity	97	97	97
5. Total Debt	37	37	37
6. Total Investment	134	134	134
7. No. of Profit making enterprises	4	4	4
8. No. of Loss making enterprises	8	8	8
9. Net Profit/Loss	-31	-3	-3
10. Accumulated Loss(-)/Profit	-22	-22	-22

Source: Various reports of the Comptroller and Auditor General of India, New Delhi.

19.2 Sectoral Classification of SLPEs of Manipur

Table 19.2 shows the classification of SLPEs of Manipur

Table 19.2
Classification of SLPEs in Manipur

Sl.No	*Category*	*No.of Enterprises*
1.	Manufacturing	11
2.	Financial	1
3.	Trade and Service	-
4.	Promotional	2
5.	Welfare	1
6.	Utility	1
	Total	16

Source: Classified from the list of enterprises given in reports of the Comptroller and Auditor General of India (Commercial), on Manipur for 2004-05.

Table 19.3
Budgetary Support to SLPEs of Manipur

(Rs.in Crore)

Particulars	*2002-03*				*2003-04*				*2004-05*			
	Companies		*Corporations*		*Companies*		*Corporations*		*Companies*		*Corporations*	
	No.	*Amount*	*No*	*Amount*	*No*	*Amount*	*No*	*Amount*	*No*	*Amount*	*No*	*Amount*
Equity Capital outgo from budget	2	7.03	1	1.50	3	11.15			3	0.50		
Loans given from budget												
Grants/Subsidy towards (i) project/programmes/ Schemes (ii) Other Subsidy												
Total outgo	2	7.03	1	1.50	3	11.15			3	0.50		

Source: Reports of the Comptroller and Auditor General of India (Commercial), on Manipur for 2002-03 to 2004-05.

19.3 Budgetary Support

The budgetary outgo in the form of equity capital and loans and grants / subsidies from the State Government to working government companies for three years up to 2004-05 are depicted below :

19.4 Social Safety Net Programme

The winding up of SLPEs Manipur requires about Rs.10-15 crore. The number of employees in the SLPEs taken as a whole is 1524. The government incurred expenses of Rs. 9 crore per year on the continuation of these enterprises.

19.5 Problems / Issues

These enterprises face both operational and policy problems. Operationally they are very weak in the production, marketing and personnel areas. There is lack of internal control. The enterprise was characterized by lack of internal audit, proper records and verification systems. Annual Accounts were not finalized on a year to year basis. The recruitment policy in these enterprises was weak as a good number of personnel on the administrative side came from government departments and had no induction training in Business Management. On the policy front the enterprises suffered from inadequate interface with the government, inappropriate site selection and lack of support by way of funds.

20. Mizoram

20.1 Financial Profile

The SLPEs of Mizoram had more risk capital in their total investment which required the SLPEs to earn an adequate rate of return. However, the enterprises taken on a whole incurred losses during the period 2002-03 to 2004-05. The profile of SLPEs of Mizoram is given in the following table:

20.2 Sectoral Classification

Table 20.2 shows the classification of SLPEs of Mizoram

20.3 Budgetary Support

The budgetary outgo in the form of equity capital and loans and grants / subsidies from the State Government to working

Table 20.1
Profile of SLPEs of Mizoram

(Rs. in Crores)

Items / Years	2002-03	2003-04	2004-05
1. Total no. of SLPEs	5	5	6
2. No. of Working SLPEs	5	5	6
3. No. of Non-Working SLPEs (I). Under Liquidation (II). Under Closure (III). Under Merger (IV). Others	-	-	-
4. Total Equity	45	47	47
5. Total Debt	21	21	20
6. Total Investment	66	68	68
7. No. of Profit making enterprises	1	-	-
8. No. of Loss making enterprises	4	4	5
9. Net Profit/Loss	-3	-4	-4
10. Accumulated Loss(-)/Profit	-16	-21	-25

Source: Reports of the Comptroller and Auditor General of India (Commercial), on Mizoram for 2002-03 to 2004-05.

Table 20.2
Classification of SLPEs in Mizoram

Sl. No	*Category*	*No. of Enterprises*
1.	Manufacturing	3
2.	Financial	1
3.	Trade and Service	-
4.	Promotional	1
5.	Welfare	-
6.	Utility	1
	Total	6

Source: Classified from the list of enterprises given in reports of the Comptroller and Auditor General of India (Commercial), on Mizoram for 2001-02.

Table 20.3
Budgetary Support to SLPEs of Mizoram

(Rs. in Crore)

Particulars	*2002-03*				*2003-04*				*2004-05*			
	Companies		*Corporations*		*Companies*		*Corporations*		*Companies*		*Corporations*	
	No.	*Amount*	*No*	*Amount*	*No*	*Amount*	*No*	*Amount*	*No*	*Amount*	*No*	*Amount*
Equity Capital outgo from budget	4	3.38			4	1.67			4	1.67		
Loans given from budget												
Grants/Subsidy towards (i)project/programmes / Schemes (ii) Other Subsidy	3	0.80			4	2.86			3	1.12		
Total outgo	5	4.18			5	4.53			5	2.79		

Source: Reports of the Comptroller and Auditor General of India(Commercial), on Mizoram for 2002-03 to 2004-05)

government companies for three years up to 2004-05 are depicted below:

During the year 2004-05, the government did not give nay fresh guarantees for obtaining loans by the companies. At the end of the year, guarantees amounting to Rs. 19.64 crore were outstanding against Zoram Industrial Deve. Corp.

20.4 Problems / Issues

The entrepreneurship in the state is hampered by infrastructure bottlenecks, on the one hand, and lack of entrepreneurship on the other hand. The nature of projects to be promoted in the state need to be identified, keeping in view the special features of its economy. Once these have been identified, appropriate methods and procedures should be developed by the corporation to assess their viability. This will eliminate the problem of non-utilization of funds.

21. MEGHALAYA

21.1 Financial Profile

There is an increasing trend in the investment patron in the state. All the 13 SLPEs in the state are working. During 2004-05 the state made profit of Rs. 4.91 crore. The profile of SLPEs of Meghalaya is given in Table 21.1.

Table 21.1
Profile of SLPEs of Meghalaya

(Rs. in crore)

Years / *Items*	*2002-03*	*2003-04*	*2004-05*
1. Total no. of SLPEs	13	13	13
2. No. of Working SLPEs	13	13	13
3. No. of Non-Working SLPEs (i) Under liquidation (ii) Under Closure (iii) Under Merger (iv) Others			
4. Total Equity	144	155	363
5. Total Debt	557	412	484

(Contd.)

(Contd.)

Years / Items	2002-03	2003-04	2004-05
6. Total Investment	701	567	847
7. No. of Profit making enterprises	2	3	3
8. No. of Loss making enterprises	11	10	9
9. Net Profit/Loss	-35	-27	5
10. Accumulated Loss(-)/Profit	-407	-340	-346

Source: Reports of the Comptroller and Auditor General of India (Commercial), on Meghalaya for 2002-03 to 2004-05.

21.2 Sectoral Classification of SLPEs of Meghalaya

Table 21.2 shows the classification of SLPEs of Meghalaya:

Table 21.2
Classification of SLPEs of Meghalaya

Sl. No	Category	No. of Enterprises
1.	Manufacturing	5
2.	Financial	1
3.	Trade and Service	1
4.	Promotional	6
5.	Welfare	-
6.	Utility	-
	Total	13

Source: Classified from the list of enterprises given in reports of the Comptroller and Auditor General of India (Commercial), on Meghalaya for 2004-05.

21.3 Budgetary Support

The budgetary outgo in the form of equity capital and loans and grants / subsidies from the State Government to working government companies for three years up to 2004-05 are depicted below:

During the year 2004-05, the government had stood a guarantee of Rs. one crore in respect of one working company. At the end of the year, guarantees amounting to Rs. 281.90 crore against two working government companies and one working statutory corporation were outstanding.

Table 21.3
Budgetary Support to SLPEs of Meghalaya

(Rs. in crore)

Particulars	*2002-03*				*2003-04*				*2004-05*			
	Companies		*Corp*		*Companies*		*Corp*		*Companies*		*Corp*	
	No.	*Amt*	*No*	*Amt*	*No*	*Amt*	*No*	*Amt*	*No*	*Amt*	*No*	*Amt*
Equity Capital outgo from budget	2	0.41	1	2.00	2	9.15	1	2.00	2	3.10	2	2.80
Loans given from budget			1	48.49			1	48.73			1	25.56
Grants/Subsidy towards (i) project/ programmes / Schemes (ii) Other Subsidy	1	0.20	2	13.50	2	0.55	2	13.15	2	0.58	2	13.60
Total outgo	2	0.61	2	63.99	4	9.70	2	63.88	4	3.68	4	41.96

Source: Reports of the Comptroller and Auditor General of India (Commercial), on Meghalaya for 2002-03 to 2004-05.

Problems / Issues

Though the state government is favorably disposed to the SLPEs in Meghalaya, lack of professionalisation is coming in a big way in their growth in the State. Excepting the Meghalaya Industrial Development Corporation most of the top executives in the other SLPEs were on deputation.

22 Nagaland

22.1 Financial Profile

There are 15 SLPEs in the state where six are government companies and remaining nine are Departmental and quasi government enterprises. The profile of SLPEs of Nagaland is given in the following table:

Table 22.1
Profile of SLPEs in Nagaland

(Rs. in crore)

Items / *Years*	*2002-03*	*2003-04*	*2004-05*
1. Total no.of SLPEs	-	6	6
2. No.of Working SLPEs	-	6	6
3. No.of Non-Working SLPEs (i) Under Liquidation (ii) Under Closure (iii) Under Merger (iv) Others	-	-	-
4. Total Equity	-	27	27
5. Total Debt	-	25	25
6. Total Investment	-	52	52
7. No.of Profit making enterprises	-	-	-
8. No.of Loss making enterprises	-	3	3
9. Net Profit/Loss	-	-2	-2
10. Accumulated Loss(-)/Profit	-	-25	-25

Source: Reports of the Comptroller and Auditor General of India (Commercial), on Delhi for 2002-03 to 2004-05.

22.2 Sectoral Classification

Table 21.2 shows the classification of SLPEs in Nagaland

Table 22.2
Classification of SLPEs in Government of Nagaland

Sl.No	*Category*	*No.of Enterprises*
1.	Manufacturing	3
2.	Financial	1
3.	Trade and Service	0
4.	Promotional	2
5.	Welfare	0
6.	Utility	0
	Total	6

Source: Classified from the list of enterprises given in reports of the Comptroller and Auditor General of India (Commercial), on Delhi for 2001-02.

22.3 Budgetary Support

The budgetary in the form of equity and loans are grants / subsidies from the state government to working government companies for the three year upto 2004-05 are as follows:

23. ORISSA

23.1 Financial Profile

The financial profile of Orissa SLPEs shows that they had a mixed financial performance. The Debt-Equity ratio was 4.02 in 2004-05 compared to 4.48 in 2002-03. The profile of SLPEs of Orissa is given in the following table:

23.2 Sectoral Classification

Table 23.2 shows the classification of SLPEs in Orissa.

23.3 Budgetary Support

In the last three years, the Government guarantee issued on loans to working PEs has increased from Rs. 423.45 crore in 2001-02 to Rs. 816.89 crore in 2002-03 and further increased to Rs. 2,172.54 crore in 2003-04. There was no case of conversion of loan to equity and waiver of dues in 2003-04. During the year 2003-04, the Government had guaranteed loans aggregating Rs. 2,177.04 crore obtained by seven working Government companies (Rs. 2,172.54 crore) and one non-working company

Table 22.3
Budgetary Support to SLPEs Nagaland

(Rs. in crore)

Particulars	*2002-03*				*2003-04*				*2004-05*			
	Companies		*Corp*		*Companies*		*Corp*		*Companies*		*Corp*	
	No.	*Amt*	*No*	*Amt*	*No*	*Amt*	*No*	*Amt*	*No*	*Amt*	*No*	*Amt*
Equity Capital outgo from budget	3	1.87							2	0.60		
Loans given from budget												
Grants/Subsidy towards (i) project/programmes/ Schemes (ii) Other Subsidy	4	7.32			4	5.76			4	6.22		
Total Subsidy												
Total outgo	4	9.19			4	5.76			4	6.82		

Source: Reports of the Comptroller and Auditor General of India (Commercial), on Delhi for 2002-03 to 2004-05.

Table 23.1
Profile of SLPEs in Orissa

(Rs.in crore)

Items / *Years*	*2002-03*	*2003-04*	*2004-05*
1. Total no. of SLPEs	70	70	70
2. No. of Working SLPEs	36	35	35
3. No. of Non-Working SLPEs	34	35	35
(i) Under liquidation	12	13	13
(ii) Under Closure	7	22	22
(iii) Under Merger			
(iv) Others	15		
4. Total Equity	2483	2265	2265
5. Total Debt	9912	10151	10151
6. Total Investment	12395	12416	12416
7. No. of Profit making enterprises	16	14	14
8. No. of Loss making enterprises	40	42	42
9. Net Profit/Loss	-189	-571	-571
10. Accumulated Loss(-)/Profit	-2002	-2669	-2669

Source: Data collected from the Bureau of Public Enterprises, Government of Orissa.

Table 23.2
Classification of SLPEs in Orissa

Sl. No	*Category*	*No. of Enterprises*
1.	Manufacturing	47
2.	Financial	5
3.	Trade and Service	2
4.	Promotional	7
5.	Welfare	2
6.	Utility	7
	Total	70

Source : Classified from the list of enterprises given in reports of the Comptroller and Auditor General of Indian (Commercial), on Orissa for 2004-05.

Table 23.3
Budgetary Support to SLPEs of Orissa

Particulars	*2002-03*				*2003-04*				*2004-05*			
	Companies		*Corp*		*Companies*		*Corp*		*Companies*		*Corp*	
	No	*Amt*	*No*	*Amt*	*No*	*Amt*	*No*	*Amt*	*No*	*Amt*	*No*	*Amt*
Equity Capital outgo from budget	1	10.00	--	--	4	22.77	--	--	--	--	--	--
Loans given from budget		--	1	0.81	2	438.00	1	0.25	1	53.45	1	13.65
Grants/Subsidy towards (i) project/programmes/ Schemes		0.20	--	--	3	34.05	1	6.00	2	23.11	1	1.50
(ii) Other Subsidy		55.08	2		3	88.38	--	2.00	4	32.17	2	1.82
Total Subsidy				1.80			2					
Total outgo		66.18	2	2.61	10	583.20	3	8.25	6	108.73	3	17.02

Source: Reports of the Comptroller and Auditor General of India (Commercial), on Orissav for 2002-03 to 2004-05.

(Rs. 4.49 crore). At the end of the year, guarantees of Rs. 3,046.11 crore against seven working Government companies (Rs. 2,677.44 crore), two working Statutory corporations (Rs. 368.60 crore) and one non-working Government company (Rs. 0.07 crore) were outstanding. The guarantee commission paid or payable to Government by six working companies (Rs. 36.10 crore), one non-working company (Rs. 0.08 crore) and two Statutory corporations (Rs. 5.48 crore) during 2003-04 was Rs. 41.66 crore.)

23.4 Social Safety Net Programme

The target group for SSNP comprises employees of closed/ liquidated enterprise and employees opting for Voluntary Retirement. As part of the PE Reform programme, the Government has introduced 'Social Safety Net' mechanism to protect the interest of the retired/retrenched workers since December 1999. This programme is in operation with the objective to identify the needs of the Voluntary retirees of the Public Sector Enterprises (SLPEs) to take up alternative employment. It also assists the voluntary retirees to build their skill and expertise, so as to enable them to be relevant in the changing labour market conditions. The Social Safety Net Programme (SSNP) is being implemented along with Voluntary Retirement Scheme (VRS), as an important social component of the Public Enterprises reform programme of the State. The programme includes the following activities:

- Survey/Counseling for adjudging the skill set, aptitude capability and needs of individual workers and offering them vocational guidance. This also includes advising to a limited extent on the safeguard and prudent investment of the severance compensation that workers receive.
- In-depth counseling for identifying available options for workers and exploration of opportunities including adjudgment of capability and offering skill up-gradation or acquiring new skills, which could improve one's chances for alternative source of earning.
- Free vocational training orientation and guidance for alternative livelihood through either redeployment or self-employment ventures.

- Limited follow up services for redeployment by building access to institutions and subject experts for those who are interested in starting self-employment ventures. Under the SSNP the nodal agency performs the following tasks:
- Contacts the target group at the Counseling camps or at their residence to provide necessary information on new employment opportunities.
- Enlist the support of skill promotion agencies, placement agencies, trade unions, employers and development agencies to address the problem of VRS/retrenched employees.
- Surveys and identifies the job market and also assesses the demand for goods and services and then imparts training that would improve the chances of redeployment.
- Provides training to VRS employees in varied areas such as IT and computers, integrated farming, small business like beautician, electronics repairing, tailoring etc, and any other skill in demand in the market. Training is imparted by credible professional institutions.

The programme is fully funded by Department for International Development (DFID), UK Government under Technical Assistance Grant for Orissa Public Sector Reform Project. Kalinga Institute of Industrial Technology (KIIT), a NGO is selected as the nodal agency to undertake this programme on behalf of Department of Public Enterprises (DPE). Department of Public Enterprises and Adam Smith Institute (ASI), the DFID consultant, are monitoring the programme at regular intervals. Elaborate arrangements have been made to create awareness about the programme by organizing pre-VRS counseling camps in different State SLPEs.

A Center for Counseling and Redeployment has been set up at Campus-I, KIIT having a plinth area of about 10,000 sq ft. Besides the Center, 5 Regional Counseling & Redeployment Centers (RCRCs) have been set up to cover all districts of Orissa effectively.

There are 114 types of training modules developed for the Voluntary Retirees under the Programme. Each training programme is designed as per the specific requirements of the

Table 19.6
Details of Regional Counseling & Redeployment Centers RCRCs

Sl.No	Location	Distance from Bhubaneswar	Districts covered
1.	Cuttack	30	Cuttack, Kendrapara, Jagatsingpur, Dhenkanal, Angul, Khurda, Puri and Nayagarh
2.	Baripada	250	Mayurbhanj, Balesore, Bhadrak and Keonjhar
3.	Bhawanipatna	600	Kalahandi, Koraput, Malkangiri, Rayagada, Nawarangpur, Nuapada, Sonepur & Bolangir and Bijaya Nagaram (Andhra Pradesh)
4.	Berhampur	195	Ganjam, Gajapati, Phulbani and Boudh
5.	Sambalpur	305	Sambalpur, Bargarh, Jharsuguda, Sundargarh and Deogarh

Table 19.7
SSNP Performance Abstract

Sl.No	*SSNP Components*	*Phase-I (2000-2002)*	*No of Employees Extension (Mar-June 2003)*	*Total*
1.	Staff Profile Survey	10,003	561	10,564
2.	Initial Counseling	9,488	561	10,049
3.	In-Depth Counseling	5,506	561	6,067
4.	Retraining	2,876	707	3,583
5.	Redeployment	3,477	-	3,447

Voluntary Retired employees. Duration of the training programmes varies from a few weeks to six months. The achievement under the programme up to 31st March 2003 is given below:

Out of the surveyed retirees, 34 per cent have since been redeployed, 17 per cent of which are wage employment and 83 per cent are self-employed. This performance under the programme in Orissa compares favourably with other Indian States.

The phenomenal success of the Social Safety Net Programme during 1st phase of PE Reform Programme, encouraged the State Government to continue the programme for another three years with the financial assistance of DFID. Proposal to this effect is now active consideration of DFID/Government of India.

To illustrate the success of the programme, the Department in association with ASI/KIIT produced a compilation of 150 recipients "success stories". A few of them are produced below:

If you thought the fallout of the slowdown in the information technology sector could only be felt in Silicon Valley, Bangalore or Cyberabad; meet Muralidhar Patnaik of Bargarh-the business hub of western Orissa. A man of sound logic Muralidhar after quitting his secretarial job in a state owned enterprise through voluntary retirement has set up his own software unit. The slump in the IT sector has affected him as many computer professionals of Bargarh have returned from jobs outside and are setting up shop in the small township. Muralidhar has not lost out to competition and has adapted to the changing circumstances. His focus is now on computerising drawings of industrial setups and he has undergone a three month specialized training in Autocad software for this. This was almost a year after his first brush with computers, which came about during the training provided by the social safety net. He was mostly managing the pay rolls and personnel section records for fourteen rice mills, four hotels and several other business set ups in and around Bargarh.

Muralidhar makes almost one and a half times of what his last salary in the government enterprise was, has created almost a lakh of rupees worth of assets in the form of computers and peripherals and employs three people who work in shifts. With remorse and regret he however laments 'that had we been privatised at the right time, the situation would be quiet different'.

Table 19.8

Achievement of SSNP During 2000-2002 (Phase-I)

Sl.No	*PSU Name*	*Relieved Under VRS/VSS*	*Surveyed*	*Counseled*		*Trained*	*Redeployed*		
				Initial Counseling	*In-depth Counseling*		*Self Employed*	*Wage Employed*	*Total*
1.	ABS Spinning Mill-Aska	393	363	363	277	157	151	33	184
2.	ABS Spinning Mill-Baripada	608	629	629	523	338	129	9	138
3.	ABS Spinning Mill-Sonepur	666	485	485	338	233	194	50	244
4.	Barunei Powerloom, Khurda	199	152	152	33	0	50	13	63
5.	Baripada Powerloom, Baripada	61	62	62	27	37	48	2	50
6.	Berhampur Powerloom Weavers' Cooperative Ltd, Berhampur	100	70	70	49	30	36	2	38
7.	Bhaskar Textile Mill	1196	752	752	460	218	307	45	352

(Contd.)

(Contd.)

Sl.No	PSU Name	Relieved Under VRS/VSS	Surveyed	Counseled		Trained	Redeployed		Total
				Initial Counseling	In-depth Counseling		Self Employed	Wage Employed	
8.	The Co-operative Sugar Industries Ltd, Nayagarh	211	51	51	14	0	25	4	29
9.	Chhatia Weaving Mills, Chhatia	167	122	122	27	26	72	17	89
10.	Ferro Chrome Plant	106	44	44	31	1	17	1	18
11.	Hira Cables	61	66	66	54	30	10	1	11
12.	Hira Industrial Works, Hirakud	41	39	39	30	9	7	0	7
13.	IDCOL Cement	24	16	16	10	4	7	1	8
14.	IDCOL Corp.Off	14	7	7	3	1	0	0	0
15.	IDCOL Piping	16	1	1	0	0	0	0	0
16.	Kalinga Times	110	79	79		33	12	3	15
17.	Kalinga Iron Works	196	80	80	15	25	27	4	31
18.	Konark Jute	103	57	57	41	7	15	6	21

(Contd.)

(Contd.)

Sl.No	PSU Name	Relieved Under VRS/VSS	Surveyed	Counseled		Trained	Redeployed		Total
				Initial Counseling	In-depth Counseling		Self Employed	Wage Employed	
19.	Kalinga Spinning Mill	478	411	411	358	113	72	5	77
20.	Konark TV	462	234	234	139	121	111	13	124
21.	Maa Bauti Powerloom Weavers' Cooperative Society, Athagarh	49	49	49	9	0	34	5	39
22.	Mahalaxmi Powerloom Weavers' Cooperative Society, Sundargarh	67	65	65	15	0	3	0	3
23.	OAIC	113	43	43	25	8	19	2	21
24.	OFDC	114	16	16	8	8	1	1	2
25.	Oil Orissa	60	23	23	19	8	5	4	9
26.	Orichem	165	85	85	43	41	6	6	12

(Contd.)

(Contd.)

Sl.No	PSU Name	Relieved Under VRS/VSS	Surveyed	Counseled		Trained	Redeployed		Total
				Initial Counseling	In-depth Counseling		Self Employed	Wage Employed	
27.	Orissa Weavers Cooperative Society Spinning Mill	117	243	242	108	55	31	5	36
28.	OSHDC	273	105	105	52	26	59	7	66
29.	Orissa State Handloom Weavers Corporative Society	158	31	31	16	1	15	4	19
30.	OSRTC	1559	1567	1564	1047	218	153	18	171
31.	OTM	2208	1328	1302	552	598	410	79	489
32.	Rolling Mill	81	91	91	81	20	1	0	1
33.	The Ramnagar Powerloom Weavers' Coop.Society, Tora	29	61	61	21	1	0	0	0
34.	Sarala Weaving Corporation, Tirtol	256	186	186	72	53	39	8	47

(Contd.)

(Contd.)

Sl.No	PSU Name	Relieved Under VRS/VSS	Surveyed	Counseled		Trained	Redeployed		
				Initial Counseling	In-depth Counseling		Self Employed	Wage Employed	Total
35.	Shri Manikeswari Powerloom Weavers' Cooperative Society, Bhawanipatna	94	79	78	29	0	8	1	9
36.	Spinfed	25	25	25	22	4	2	0	2
37.	Utkal Spinning Mill	569	369	369	212	132	158	31	189
38.	Shri Parbati Weavers' Cooperative Society, Jagatsinghpur	0	161	161	56	0	59	7	66
39.	Gopinath Spiniing Mill, Baliapal, Balasore	0	48	48	1	0	0	0	0

(Contd.)

(Contd.)

Sl.No	*PSU Name*	*Relieved Under VRS/VSS*	*Surveyed*	*Counseled*		*Trained*	*Redeployed*		*Total*
				Initial Counseling	*In-depth Counseling*		*Self Employed*	*Wage Employed*	
40.	Shri Baladevjew Weavers' Cooperative Society-Kendrapada	0	37	37	8	0	0	0	0
41.	Elcosomos	58	23	23	10	4	9	4	13
42.	Ipitron	199	144	144	62	58	44	14	58
43.	KSR	167	147	147	122	67	55	36	91
44.	OHPC	962	473	473	326	166	336	41	377
45.	OLI	22	21	21	10	0	3	1	4
46.	OSCTC	314	253	253	89	13	74	48	122
47.	OSLC	183	126	126	49	12	44	58	102
	Total	**13054**	**10,003 (9519+484*) (100.03%)**	**9488**	**5506**	**2876**	**2858**	**589**	**3447**

** 484 are surveyed from Secondary sources (From family members, neighbours, colleagues & friends)*

Anadi Behera remembers the day the Baripada unit of the state owned ABS spinning mill was inaugurated in 1983 with nostalgia. The mill was set up barely a kilometer away from his house. The hard work that they had put in for the construction of the mill was finally bearing fruit after two years. Anadi was a traditional potter for several generations and was then employed in the mill. Most of the youth in the village were jealous of him as he earned handsomely and had a 'government job'. The mud and moulding days were over for him.

23.5 Problems / Issues

An overall survey indicates that short-tenures of the chief executives and lack appropriate systems and procedures for internal operations crippled the working of the SLPEs in Orissa.

24. PUNJAB

The CAG reports on the SLPEs of Punjab reveal that these enterprises had a mixed financial performance during 2002-03 to 2004-05 although investment therein continued to grow during this period. The number of loss making enterprises was more than profit making enterprises. It may be noted that the number of non-working enterprises showed the tendency to increase. The profile of SLPEs of Punjab is given in Table 24.1.

24.2 Sectoral Classification

Table 24.2 shows the classification of the SLPEs of Punjab:

24.3 **Budgetary Support**

Table 24.3 shows the budgetary outgo, grants / subsidies, guarantees issued, waiver of dues and conversion of loans into equity by State Government to working government companies and statutory corporations. The budgetary outgo in the form of equity capital and loans for three years upto 2004-05 is given below:

During the year 2004-05, the government had guaranteed the loans aggregating Rs. 8781.06 crore obtained by five working government companies (Rs. 6538.09) and three working statutory corporations (Rs. 2197.97 crore). At the end of the year, guarantees amounting to Rs. 5991.49 crore against eight government

Table 24.1
Profile of SLPEs of Punjab

(Rs. in Crore)

Items / Years	2002-03	2003-04	2004-05
1. Total no. of SLPEs	-	57	56
2. No. of Working SLPEs	-	26	28
3. No. of Non-Working SLPEs	-	38	28
(i) Under Liquidation		6	6
(ii) Under Closure		12	11
(iii) Under Merger			
(iv) Others		20	11
4. Total Equity		3455	3466
5. Total Debt	-	10369	10557
6. Total Investment	-	13824	14023
7. No. of Profit making enterprises	-	9	12
8. No. of Loss making enterprises	-	29	24
9. Net Profit/Loss	-	-901	72.58
10. Accumulated Loss(-)/Profit	-	-2056	-1953

Source: Classified from the list of enterprises given in reports of the Comptroller and Auditor General of India (Commercial), on Punjab for 2001-02.

Table 24.2
Classification of SLPEs

Sl.No	*Category*	*No.of Enterprises*
1.	Manufacturing	24
2.	Financial	2
3.	Trade&Service	6
4.	Promotional	17
5.	Welfare	1
6.	Utility	6
	Total	56

Source: Reports of the Comptroller and Auditor General of India (Commercial), on Punjab for 1998-99 to 2001-02.

Table 24.3
Budgetary Support to SLPEs in punjab

Particulars	*2002-03*				*2003-04*				*2004-05*			
	Companies		*Corp*		*Companies*		*Corp*		*Companies*		*Corp*	
	No.	*Amt*	*No*	*Amt*	*No*	*Amt*	*No*	*Amt*	*No*	*Amt*	*No*	*Amt*
Equity Capital outgo from budget	5	7.10			2	7.50			1	10.87		
Loans given from budget												
Grants/Subsidy towards (i) project/programmes/ Schemes	3	56.73	1	950.14	1	33.03	1	1704.25	1	31.06	1	2285.19
(ii) Other Subsidy	1	5.85										
Total Subsidy	4	62.58	1.	950.14	1	33.03	1	1704.25	1	31.06	1	2285.19
Total outgo	4	2811.04	2	2575.53	4	6623.38	2	1569.25	5	6583.09	3	2197.97

Source: Reports of the Comptroller and Auditor General of India (Commercial), on Punjab for 1998-99 to 2001-02.

companies (Rs. 2140.47 crore) and four working statutory corporations (Rs. 3851.02 crore) were outstanding. There guarantee commission paid and payable to government by government copnaies and statutory corporations during 2004-05 was 9.50 crore and Rs. 0.96 crore respectively.

24.4 Social Safety Net Programme

The Government of Punjab has approved a Voluntary Retirement Scheme for the Employees of the SLPEs broadly modeled on the Government of India scheme. The scheme is called as the Punjab State Public Sector Undertakings Voluntary Retirement Scheme (VRS). This scheme is applicable to all the SLPEs including all Co-operative Institutions. The scheme is also applicable to the subsidiaries of the SLPEs defined as entities in which SLPEs and/or Government of Punjab hold more than 50 per cent equity.

The objectives of the scheme include optimum human resource utilisation, optimum return on investment and implementation of the VRS scheme. The scheme prohibits the grant of VRS as a right to the employees to prevent denudation of talent. The employees are given 100 per cent of the amount of ex-gratia under this Scheme within 60 days from the date of relief. To avail VRS, an eligible employee is required to submit request opting for Voluntary Retirement under the scheme to the Competent Authority through proper channel in a prescribed proforma available with the concerned SLPE. The Competent Authority passes the order with in a period of three months either accepting or rejecting the request.

The Government of Punjab would provide budgetary support for the application of the VRS to the loss making enterprises or those making marginal profit and to the sick enterprises for implementing VRS only in case bank credit is not available. However, before seeking budgetary support in cases of unviable/ sick SLPEs other sources of funding should be fully explored such as asset Securitisation and bank loan against government guarantee for funding VRS. With the adoption of the VRS scheme, the State Renewal Fund ceases to exist in Punjab.

24.5 Problems / Issues

These enterprises were lacking clarity as regards their objectives structures, capital, but boards of management, and linkages with the different sectors of society.

25. PONDICHERRY

25.1 Financial Profile

The financial performance of the SLPEs in Pondicherry is depicted below:

Table 25.1
Pondicherry

(Rs. in crore)

Items \ Years	2002-03	2003-04	2004-05
1. Total no. of SLPEs*	12	11	11
2. No. of Working SLPEs	12	11	11
3. No. of Non-Working SLPEs (i) Under Liquidation (ii) Under Closure (iii) Under Merger (iv) Others			
4. Total Equity	75	428	449
5. Total Debt	66	8	3
6. Total Investment	141	436	453
7. No. of Profit making enterprises	5	5	5
8. No. of Loss making enterprises	8	4	4
9. Net Profit/Loss	-3	-5	-7
10. Accumulated Loss(-)/Profit	-57	-132	-146

Source: Reports of the Comptroller and Auditor General of India (Commercial), on Pondicherry for 2002-03 to 2004-05.

25.2 Sectoral Classification

Table 25.2 shows the classification of SLPEs in Pondicherry.

25.3 Budgetary Support

At the end of the year, guarantees of Rs. 2.70 crore against one working government company were outstanding. During the year, loan of Rs. one crore given to a government company.

Table 25.2
Classification of SLPEs in Pondicherry

Sl.No	*Category*	*No.of Enterprises*
1.	Manufacturing	5
2.	Financial	1
3.	Trade&Service	-
4.	Promotional	3
5.	Welfare	2
6.	Utility	1
	Total	11

Source: Classified from the list of enterprises given in reports of the Comptroller and Auditor General of India (Commercial), on Rajasthan for 2001-02.

Table 25.3
Budgetary Support to SLPEs in Pondicherry

(Rs. in crore)

Particulars	*2002-03*				*2003-04*				*2004-05*			
	Companies		*Corp*		*Companies*		*Corp*		*Companies*		*Corp*	
	No.	*Amt*	*No*	*Amt*	*No*	*Amt*	*No*	*Amt*	*No*	*Amt*	*No*	*Amt*
Equity Capital outgo from budget	8	22.59			8	22.92			8	22.04		
Loans given from budget	5	4.19			6	7.61			6	6.64		
Grants/Subsidy towards (i) project/programmes/ Schemes (ii) Other Subsidy	2	0.27			1	0.20			1	0.40		
Total Subsidy												
Total outgo	8	27.05			8	30.73			8	29.08		

(*Source:* Reports of the Comptroller and Auditor General of India(Commercial), on Pondicherry for 2002-03 to 2004-05.)

26. RAJASTHAN

26.1 Financial Profile

The profile of SLPEs in Rajasthan is given in the following table:

Table 26.1
Profile of SLPEs in Rajasthan

(Rs. in Crore)

Items \ Years	2002-03	2003-04	2004-05
1. Total no. of SLPEs*	27	26	29
2. No. of Working SLPEs	10	19	19
3. No. of Non-Working SLPEs	8	7	10
(i) Under Liquidation	2	1	1
(ii) Under Closure			
(iii) Under Merger			
(iv) Others	6	6	9
4. Total Equity	2959	3375	3762
5. Total Debt	9932	10702	10055
6. Total Investment	12891	14077	13817
7. No. of Profit making enterprises	9	8	11
8. No. of Loss making enterprises	13	12	8
9. Net Profit/Loss	-18	11	146
10. Accumulated Loss(-)/Profit	-288	-312	-275

Source: Reports of the Comptroller and Auditor General of India (Commercial), on Rajasthan for 2002-03 to 2004-05.

The financial performance of the SLPEs in Rajasthan transformed itself from the one of profit making to that of a loss making. The number of non-working companies increased from seven to eight. The debt-equity ratio became more adverse during the period 1998-99 to 2002-03.

26.2 Sectoral Classification

Table 26.2 shows the classification of SLPEs in Rajasthan.

26.3 Budgetary Support

Table 26.3 shows that 10 enterprises received budgetary support to the tune of Rs. 598.93 crore in 1998-99, whereas in

Table 26.2

Classification of SLPEs in Rajasthan

Sl. No	*Category*	*No. sof Enterprises*
1.	Manufacturing	12
2.	Financial	3
3.	Trade and Service	1
4.	Promotional	4
5.	Welfare	-
6.	Utility	9
	Total	29

Source: Classified from the list of enterprises given in reports of the Comptroller and Auditor General of India (Commercial), on Rajasthan for 2001-02.

Table 26.3
Budgetary Support to SLPEs in Rajasthan

(Rs. in crore)

Particulars	*2002-03*				*2003-04*				*2004-05*			
	Companies		*Corp*		*Companies*		*Corp*		*Companies*		*Corp*	
	No.	*Amt*	*No*	*Amt*	*No*	*Amt*	*No*	*Amt*	*No*	*Amt*	*No*	*Amt*
Equity Capital outgo from budget	7	333.85	-		8	305.11	1	112.11	9	372.92	1	14.00
Loans given from budget	6	143.85	-	-	4	711.57	-	-	2	52.90	-	-
Grants/Subsidy towards (i) project/programmes/ Schemes			-	-							-	-
(ii) Other Subsidy	9	432.46			10	995.81	1	4.63	10	1105.20		
Total Subsidy	9	432.46	-	-		995.81	1	4.63	10	1105.20	-	-
Total outgo		910.16	-	-		2012.49		116.74		1531.02		14.00

Source: Reports of the Comptroller and Auditor General of India (Commercial), on Rajasthan for 2002-03 to 2004-05.

2000-01, 6 enterprises received budgetary support of Rs.73.30 crore. The steep fall in budgetary support in 2000-01 was due to negligible sanction of other subsidy.

26.4 Social Safety Net Programme

As long as a formal policy is not adopted on privatisation, the Government of Rajasthan proposes to adjust the surplus labour force in the SLPEs. The Government intends to take recourse to its order of 5th July, 1989, whereby employees who have completed ten years of service or 40 years of age could opt for Voluntary Retirement through a written request. The respective managements of the SLPEs could grant the request. An ex-gratia payment equivalent to 1.5 months emoluments for each completed year of service or the monthly emolument at the time of retirement multiplied by the balance months of service left before normal date of retirement, which ever is less, is granted as the VRS offer. The management of an enterprise may make, in exceptional cases, a higher ex-gratia payment with prior approval of the State Bureau of Public Enterprise. If an enterprise has already adopted a voluntary retirement scheme on conditions different from what have been stated above, it could continue to follow its own scheme.

26.5 Problems / Issues

The SLPEs in Rajasthan are a post-independence phenomenon. During the last 3 ½ decades both their numbers and investment have multiplied phenomenally. The objectives of these enterprises have ranged from regional development and provision of basic inputs to agriculturist and small artisans to the industrialization of the economy and earning surpluses for the growth of the economy as a whole. The professionalisation of the management of these enterprises and making them stand on their won has been the two major planks of the state policy with regard to the management of these enterprises. However, the management practices and the financial performance of these enterprises have run contrary to these expectations. During the Sixth plan period in all the years all the SLPEs taken together incurred huge losses and as a result, their net worth declined rapidly. The excessive external controls, unsound internal management and un healthy management of operations were primarily responsible for the loss making by these enterprises. If the SLPEs have to turn the corner, they should design ands implement suitable turn-around strategies and the Government should help them in an efficient discharge of their functions by distancing them out to a great extent.

27. SIKKIM

The profile of SLPEs in Rajasthan is given in the following table:

Table 27.1
Profile of SLPEs in Sikkim

(Rs.in crore)

Years / *Items*	*2002-03*	*2003-04*	*2004-05*
1. Total no. of SLPEs	15	15	11
2. No. of Working SLPEs	12	12	8
3. No. of Non-Working SLPEs	3	3	3
(i) Under Liquidation			
(ii) Under Closure	2	2	2
(iii) Under Merger			
(iv) Others	1	1	1
4. Total Equity	65	73.30	75.03
5. Total Debt	65	65.66	66.18
6. Total Investment	130	139	141
7. No. of Profit making enterprises	4	4	5
8. No. of Loss making enterprises	9	8	8
9. Net Profit/Loss	-3	-22	-3
10. Accumulated Loss(-)/Profit	-34	-58	-57

Source: Reports of the Comptroller and Auditor General of India (Commercial), on Sikkim.

27.2 Sectoral Classification

Table 27.2 shows the classification of SLPEs in Sikkim.

27.3 Budgetary Support

At the end of the year, guarantees amounting to Rs. 78.07 crore against three Government companies (Rs. 78.00 crore) and one Statutory corporation (Rupees seven lakh) were outstanding.

Table 27.2

Classification of SLPEs in Government of Sikkim

Sl. No	*Category*	*No.of Enterprises*
1.	Manufacturing	4
2.	Financial	2
3.	Trade&Service	1
4.	Promotional	2
5.	Welfare	1
6.	Utility	1
	Total	11

Source: Classified from the list of enterprises given in reports of the Comptroller and Auditor General of India (Commercial), on Delhi for 2004-05.

Table 27.3
Budgetary Support to SLPEs Sikkim

(Rs. in crore)

Particulars	*2002-03*				*2003-04*				*2004-05*			
	Companies		*Corp*		*Companies*		*Corp*		*Companies*		*Corp*	
	No.	*Amt*	*No*	*Amt*	*No*	*Amt*	*No*	*Amt*	*No*	*Amt.*	*No*	*Amt*
Equity Capital outgo from budget	7	3.35	1	0.50	5	4.90	1	0.94	3	0.91	1	0.26
Loans given from budget												
Grants/Subsidy towards (i) project/programmes/ Schemes (ii) Other Subsidy												
Total Subsidy												
Total outgo	7	3.35	1	0.05	5	4.90	1	0.94	3	0.91	1	0.26

Source: Reports of the Comptroller and Auditor General of India (Commercial), on Sikkim for 2002-03 to 2004-05.

There was no case of loans written off, interest waived, moratorium on loan repayment and conversion of loans into equity capital in any company or corporation during the year.

28. TAMIL NADU

28.1 Financial Profile

The profile of SLPEs of Tamil Nadu is given in the following table:

Table 28.1
Profile of SLPEs in Tamil Nadu

(Rs. in crore)

Items / *Years*	*2002-03*	*2003-04*	*2004-05*
1. Total no. of SLPEs	80	68	85
2. No. of Working SLPEs	68	54	71
3. No. of Non-Working SLPEs	12	14	14
(i) Under liquidation	2	2	2
(ii) Under Closure	7	8	8
(iii) Under Merger	1	2	2
(iv) Others	2	2	2
4. Total Equity	1681	2138	2300
5. Total Debt	8868	11527	11877
6. Total Investment	10549	13665	14177
7. No. of Profit making enterprises	52	38	48
8. No. of Loss making enterprises	31	23	19
9. Net Profit/Loss	320	97	-1032
10. Accumulated Loss(-)/Profit	570	-4205	-5251

Source: Reports of the Comptroller and Auditor General of India (Commercial), on Tamil Nadu for 2002-03 to 2004-05.

28.2 Sectoral Classification

28.3 Budgetary Support

During 2004-05, the Government had guaranteed loans aggregating to Rs.499.01 crore obtained by 11 working Government companies. At the end of the year, guarantees

Table 28.2
Classification of SLPEs in Tamil Nadu

Sl .No	*Category*	*No. of Enterprises*
1.	Manufacturing	26
2.	Financial	5
3.	Trade and Service	3
4.	Promotional	22
5.	Welfare	4
6.	Utility	20
	Total	80

Source: Classified from the list of enterprises given in reports of the Comptroller and Auditor General of India (Commercial), on Andhra Pradesh for 2001-02.

Table 28.3
Budgetary Support to SLPEs in Tamil Nadu

(Rs. in crore)

Particulars	*2002-03*				*2003-04*				*2004-05*			
	Companies		*Corp*		*Companies*		*Corp*		*Companies*		*Corp*	
	No.	*Amt*	*No*	*Amt*	*No*	*Amt*	*No*	*Amt*	*No*	*Amt*	*No*	*Amt*
Equity Capital outgo from budget	5	34.35	1	25.00	4	33.46	1	200.00	5	71.62	1	85.00
Loans given from budget	5	19.57	1	29.47	4	223.51			5	159.02	1	0.61
Grants/Subsidy towards (i) project/programmes /Schemes	9	1373.60			10	894.86			3	85.62	1	0.05
(ii) Other Subsidy	5	21.86	1	2212.14	4	7141			4 7	1015.98 221.95	1	924.50
Total Subsidy	14	1395.46	1	2212.14	14	966.27			11	1237.93	1	924.55
Total outgo	19	149.38	1	2266.61					19	1554.19	1	1010.16

Source: Reports of the Comptroller and Auditor General of India (Commercial), on Tamil Nadu for 2002-03 and 2004-05.

amounting to Rs. 5,892.38 crore against 18 working Government companies (Rs. 2,047.42 crore) and one working Statutory corporation (Rs. 3,844.96 crore) were outstanding. The guarantee commission paid/payable to Government by Government companies and Statutory corporations during 2004-05 was Rs. 3.19 crore and Rs. 20.79 crore respectively. During the year, the Government waived interest/penal interest of Rs. 97.28 lakh in respect of Tamil Nadu Handicrafts Development Corporation Limited. The Government converted loan of Rs. 61 crore of Tamil Nadu Industrial Investment Corporation Limited into equity during 2004-05.

28.4 Problems / Issues

The financial Performance of the SLPEs in Tamil Nadu measured in terms of addition to net worth is very dismal. Profit consciousness need to be infused in these enterprises. The basic elements of a good accounting and costing system should find a place in the working of all the SLPEs. The conventional methods of a administration have to give way to the modern methods of management.

29 TRIPURA

29.1 Financial Profile

The financial performance of SLPEs in Tripura was below the mark. The number of loss making enterprises were more than twice as compared to the profit making enterprises during the period of the study. The profile of SLPEs of Tripura is given in Table 29.1.

29.2 Sectoral Classification of SLPEs in Tripura

Table 29.2 shows the classification of SLPEs in Tripura

29.3 Budgetary Support

The budgetary outgo in the form of equity capital, loans and subsidies from the State Government to working Government companies and working Statutory corporation for the three years upto 31 March 2005 is given below During the year 2004-05, no guarantee was given.

Table 29.1
Profile of SLPEs in Tripura

(Rs. in crore)

Items / Years	2002-03	2003-04	2004-05
1. Total no. of SLPEs	10	10	10
2. No. of Working SLPEs	9	9	9
3. No. of Non-Working SLPEs	1	1	1
(i) Under liquidation			
(ii) Under Closure			
(iii) Under Merger			
(iv) Others			
4. Total Equity	255.08	255.08	278.01
5. Total Debt	10.11	10.11	9.03
6. Total Investment			
7. No. of Profit making enterprises	1	1	3
8. No. of Loss making enterprises	8	8	6
9. Net Profit/Loss	-20	-20	-19
10. Accumulated Loss(-/Profit	-172	-172	-176

Source: Reports of the Comptroller and Auditor General of India (Commercial), on Tripura 2002-03 to 2004-05.

Table 29.2
Classification of SLPEs in Tripura

Sl. No	*Category*	*No. of Enterprises*
1.	Manufacturing	3
2.	Financial	3
3.	Trade and Service	--
4.	Promotional	3
5.	Welfare	-
6.	Utility	1
	Total	10

Source: Classified from the list of enterprises given in reports of the Comptroller and Auditor General of India (Commercial),on Uttar Pradesh for 2001-02.

Table 29.3
Budgetary Support to SLPEs in Tripura

(Rs.in crore)

Particulars	*2002-03*				*2003-04*				*2004-05*			
	Companies		*Corp*		*Companies*		*Corp*		*Companies*		*Corp*	
	No.	*Amt*	*No*	*Amt*	*No*	*Amt*	*No*	*Amt*	*No*	*Amt*	*No*	*Amt*
Equity Capital outgo from budget	7	15.53			4	9.11	1	9.24	7	14.19	1	8.80
Loans given from budget	-		1	9.13								
Total (1+2)	-											
Grants/Subsidy towards (i) project/programmes/ Schemes (ii) Other Subsidy					2	0.94						
Total Subsidy												
Total outgo	7	15.53	1	9.13	6	10.05	1	9.24	7	14.19	1	8.80

Source: Reports of the Comptroller and Auditor General of India(Commercial), on Tripura for 2002-03 to 2004-05.

29.4 Problems / Issues

Among the major problems, the one of supply of raw materials and related inputs was very prominent. The Tripura Jute Mill fell sick mainly on account of the outdated technology. The enterprises were generally over staffed and the time and cost overruns increased the cost of production

30 UTTARANCHAL

Uttranchal has 10 SLPEs. Most of the SLPEs are in promotional and utility areas. The Government has no policy on privatization/disinvestment. However, the Government intends to promote public-private participation for undertaking ventures in different areas of economic activity.

31 UTTAR PRADESH

31.1 Financial Profile

The profile of SLPEs of Uttar Pradesh is given in the following table:

Table 31.1
Profile of SLPEs in Uttar Pradesh

(Rs. in crore)

Items / Years	2002-03	2003-04	2004-05
1. Total no. of SLPEs	93	96	104
2. No. of Working SLPEs	53	55	65
3. No. of Non-Working SLPEs	40	41	39
(i) Under liquidation	9	11	10
(ii) Under Closure	2	2	1
(iii) Under Merger			
(iv) Others	29	28	28
4. Total Equity	8925	10445	10819
5. Total Debt	7868	9768	8133
6. Total Investment	16793	20213	18952
7. No. of Profit making enterprises	22	26	56
8. No. of Loss making enterprises	61	55	29
9. Net Profit/Loss	-2355	-1307	-1813
10. Accumulated Loss(-/Profit	-8905	-10674	-10589

Source: Reports of the Comptroller and Auditor General of India (Commercial), on Uttar Pradesh for 2002-03 to 2004-05.

31.2 Sectoral Classification of SLPEs in Uttar Pradesh

Table 31.2 shows the classification of SLPEs in Uttar Pradesh.

Table 31.2
Classification of SLPEs in Uttar Pradesh

Sl. No	*Category*	*No. of Enterprises*
1.	Manufacturing	52
2.	Financial	7
3.	Trade and Service	1
4.	Promotional	10
5.	Welfare	3
6.	Utility	9
	Total	82

Source: Classified from the list of enterprises given in reports of the Comptroller and Auditor General of India (Commercial), on Uttar Pradesh for 2001-02.

31.3 Budgetary Support

During the year 2004-05, the Government had guaranteed the loans aggregating Rs.1,634.28 crore obtained by eight working companies (Rs.1,475.78 crore) and three working Statutory corporations (Rs.158.50 crore). At the end of the year, guarantees amounting to Rs.1,464.88 crore against nine working Government companies (Rs.846.61 crore) and four working Statutory corporations (Rs. 618.27 crore) were outstanding. The guarantee commission paid/payable to Government by two 8 Government companies and by two 8 Statutory corporations during the year 2004-05 was Rs. 21.28 crore and Rs. 98.17 lakh respectively. The Government had converted loan of Rs. 3.07 crore outstanding from Shreetron India Limited into equity.

31.4 Social Safety Net Programme

A Voluntary Retirement Scheme was initiated in the year 1993 for the employees of Public Enterprises/Corporations with the object of reducing surplus man power. The VRS is to be implemented with the objective of ensuring consistency as to those employees who have availed the benefits of VRS, would not be

Table 31.3
Budgetary Support to SLPEs in Uttar Pradesh

(Rs.in crore)

Particulars	*2002-03*				*2003-04*				*2004-05*			
	Companies		*Corp*		*Companies*		*Corp*		*Companies*		*Corp*	
	No.	*Amt*	*No*	*Amt*	*No*	*Amt*	*No*	*Amt*	*No*	*Amt*	*No*	*Amt*
Equity Capital outgo from budget	4	264.23			7	1512.91			7	5575.04		
Loans given from budget	9	582.35			13	433.40	1	2.00	9	453.40	1	3.02
Total (1+2)		846.58			14	1946.31	1	2.00	13	6028.44	1	3.02
Grants/Subsidy towards (i) project/programmes/ Schemes (ii) Other Subsidy	6	445.93	1	2.07	5	1289.19	1	213.21	7	1297.26	1	76.91
	3	695.63			3	2.91	1	2.11	3	5.23		
Total Subsidy		141.56		2.07		1292.10		215.32		1302.49		76.91
Total outgo	16	1988.14	1	2.07	19	3238.41	2	217.32	17	7330.93	1	79.93

Source: Reports of the Comptroller and Auditor General of India (Commercial), on Uttar Pradesh for 2002-03 to 2004-05.

Enterprise -wise VRS Position

S.No	Name of the Corporation	Unit	Total Amount Required for VRS	Amount Received for VRS	No.of Employees paid	VRS paid	No.of Emp.left out	
1.	U.P State Sugar Corporation		146.40				Opted	Not-opted
		(i) Maholi		13.26	911	13.09	8	20
		(ii) Nawabganj		9.00	664	9.03	2	36
		(iii) Barabanki		9.67	468	6.75	2	26
		(iv) Bareilly		11.20	580	6.79	3	22
		(v) Nandganj		9.85	432	6.77	2	35
		(vi) Meerut		8.91	235	4.06	38	96
		(vii) Ghughli		11.24	710	8.79	3	21
		(viii) Chhitauni		9.83	590	8.64	0	1
		(ix) Hardoi		11.89	600	8.97	6	33
		(x) Rampur		13.69	569	6.08	8	178
		(xi) Munderwa		9.75	517	5.18	3	82
				118.29	6276	84.04	75	546 (A)

re-employed or re-deployed in the same SLPE or in other SLPE or Government Department.

For the implementation of VRS in an SLPE, the concerned enterprise evaluates its resources and a conclusion is drawn as to what extent the SLPE is able to fund the VRS from its own sources. The VRS is being implemented in case of Closure, Re-organsiation and Restructuring.

Under the World Bank SLPE reform Phase-I programme , VRS has been implemented in the following six corporations:

1. U.P State Textile Corporation (3 Units & Head office)
2. U.P State Sugar Corporation (11 closed mills)
3. U.P State Mineral Development Corporation
4. U.P State Pashudhan Udyog
5. U.P Instruments Ltd. (UPIL)

In above mentioned SLPEs, 13681 employees have so far availed the benefits under VRS and the funds to the tune of Rs.175.25 crore have been utilised. 1087 employees have been given the benefit of VRS and a utilisation of Rs.57.25 crore have been made in the following six SLPEs.

1. U.P Electronics Corporation
2. U.P Export Corporation
3. U.P Small Industries Corporation (UPSIC)
4. U.P State Handloom Corporation
5. The Indian Turpentine & Rosin CO.Ltd. (BIFR)
6. U.P State Leather Development and Marketing Corporation Ltd

31.5 Problems / Issues

There is no denying the fact that the SLPEs in U.P Have woefully failed to measure up to the expectations. Ultimately financial reporting is one of the key problems facing these enterprises. There Are enterprises in all the lines of activity having their accounts in arrears for inordinately long period. This situation has arisen owing to imperfect accounting system, absence of audit and accounts manuals. Most of the SLPEs had the accounts and finance departments in disarray. The required number of professional accountants has not been attracted. It is difficult to overcome this problem as the SLPEs such as the U.P. State

Brassware Corporation, U.P. State Tourism Development Corporation, U.P Film Development Corporation, U.P.State Electricity Generation Corporation and U.P. Tube Wells Corporations have only one officer each in their finance departments who at times also discharge the responsibility of the company secretary and the personnel manager. Another major weakness affecting the performance of SLPEs was lack of clarity of objectives which, in turn, was responsible for the absence of clearly defined performance indicators. The Area Development Corporations in U.P were set up to accelerate the industrial development of different regions by utilizing the locally available raw materials and talents. They were also expected mobilize assistance from the financial institutions. It is interesting to note that a majority of these corporations transformed themselves into trading enterprises as activities emerged as money spinners. The welfare enterprises also fell I the same trap. The top management in these enterprises was very weak. Most of them came from the parent departments and brought along with them the bureaucratic culture. Their tenures were less than 12 months. The problem got further compounded by the appointment of the secretaries of the parent departments as chairmen in these enterprises. This practice in many of the cases reduced the board meetings to the level of departmental committee meetings. The enterprises such as the U.P State Bridge Corporation, U.P. State Export Corporation, U.P./ State Cement Corporation, U.P Jal Nigam and the welfare enterprises worked as extensions to their administrative ministries. As a result these enterprises did not develop their own systems, procedures and norms for operations and maintenance. These enterprises utterly failed in fulfilling their task of mobilizing the institutional finance. The easy availability of the finances from their administrative ministries did not motivate them to approach the financial institutions which would have subjected them to a rigorous scrutiny. Some enterprises inflated their claims about the subsides and succeeded in receiving higher amounts then justified. The enterprises were excessively over-manned. No effort was made to retain and redeploy the superfluous labor force. The training and management development At all level were at discount. The SLPES could not pursue the goal of professionalisation because they could not offer salaries commensurate with the experience and qualifications to the professionals. To sum up, The investments in the SLPEs in U.P increased phenomenally reflecting the strong support extended to these enterprises by the State Government. How ever, their performance reflected clear gap between the reality and aspirations. The professionalisation of cadres coupled with the transformation of their organizational culture could possibly bridge up this gap to a large extent.

32 WEST BENGAL

32.1 Financial Profile

The profile of SLPEs of West Bengal is given in the following table:

Table 32.1
Profile of SLPEs in West Bengal

(Rs. in crore)

Items / Years	2002-03	2003-04	2004-05
1. Total no. of SLPEs	84	84	82
2. No. of Working SLPEs	75	74	72
3. No. of Non-Working SLPEs (i) Under Liquidation (ii) Under Closure (iii) Under Merger (iv) Others	9	10	10
4. Total Equity	3556	3718	3717
5. Total Debt	21998	14084	14084
6. Total Investment	25554	17802	17802
7. No. of Profit making enterprises	24	18	18
8. No. of Loss making enterprises	58	63	63
9. Net Profit/Loss	-1391	-749	-749
10. Accumulated Loss(-)/Profit	-8558	-9257	-9257

Source: Reports of the Comptroller and Auditor General of India (Commercial), on West Bengal for 2002-03 to 2004-05.

The investment in SLPEs in West Bengal declined during 2004-05. The number of non-working enterprises more than doubled only to indicate the financial mal-functioning in the SLPEs.

32.2 Sectoral Classification

Table 32.2 shows the classification of SLPEs in West Bengal.

Table 32.2
Classification of SLPEs in West Bengal

Sl. No	Category	No. of Enterprises
1.	Manufacturing	52
2.	Financial	7
3.	Trade and Service	1
4.	Promotional	10
5.	Welfare	3
6.	Utility	9
	Total	82

Source: Classified from the list of enterprises given in reports of the Comptroller and Auditor General of India (Commercial), on West Bengal for 2004-05.

32.3 Budgetary Support

During the year 2004-05 the Government had guaranteed loans aggregating Rs. 1,301.31 crore obtained by five working Government companies (Rs. 1,120.95 crore) and six working Statutory corporations (Rs. 180.36 crore). At the end of the year, the amount outstanding against guarantees aggregated Rs. 14,169.50 crore against 25 working Government companies (Rs. 12,383.96 crore) and nine working Statutory corporations (Rs. 1,785.54 crore) as compared to Rs. 12,011.40 crore in 28 working companies and Rs. 1,636.72 crore in eight working Statutory corporations at the end of the previous year. The guarantee fees paid/ payable to the Government by 17 Government companies and three Statutory corporations during 2004-05 was Rs. 70.29 crore and Rs. 119.68 crore respectively.

32.4 Social Safety Net Programme

As a prelude phase to the pilot project, PE Department suggested the closure of the 2 PE Department enterprises requiring no restructuring intervention. The DFID and the Government of India accepted the suggestion and the former agreed to pro £ 2.6 million (Rs.19.5 crore) as a 100 per cent grant, towards the full

Table 32.3
Budgetary Support to SLPEs in West Bengal

(Rs. in crore)

Particulars	*2001-02*				*2002-03*				*2003-04*			
	Companies		*Corp*		*Companies*		*Corp*		*Companies*		*Corp*	
	No.	*Amt*	*No*	*Amt*	*No*	*Amt*	*No*	*Amt*	*No*	*Amt*	*No*	*Amt*
Equity Capital outgo from budget	21	48.33	3	15.57	17	47.91	2	6.60	11	11.10	3	5.87
Loans given from budget	31	480.94	6	1,212.22	33	846.57	6	392.35	31	820.85	4	2257.28
Grants/Subsidy towards (i) project/programmes/ Schemes	14	151.41	4	4.10	13	17.87	4	5.90	12	15.25	4	8.93
(ii) Other Subsidy	4	72.97	4	391.80	6	76.20	3	156.43	4	89.70	4	155.73
Total Subsidy												
Total outgo	48	753.65	9	1,623.69	47	988.55	9	561.28	44	936.90	9	2427.81

Source: Reports of the Comptroller and Auditor General of India (Commercial), on West Bengal for 2002-03 to 2004-05.

VRS compensation to be disbursed to the 738 employees (including 52 casual employee) of IPP ltd and Sundarban Sugarbeet processing company Ltd. All the employees of both the enterprises submitted applications seeking Early Retirement Scheme (ERS) compensation. The GOI and DFID placed Rs.1636.70 lakh at the hands of the PE Department for ERS compensation. The Early Retirement took place from 31st December 2003 and the employees received their compensation cheques in the first week of January 2004. The programme aims at unlocking the potential of job-displaced employees so as to be relevant in the changing business environment. Employees facing displacement through restructuring measures are counseled and offered re-skilling for alternate livelihood - earning under this programme to facilitate their reintegration into the labour market through self employment. An important innovation to reinforce the effectiveness of this programme is in its availability as an option, to the dependent nominees of displaced employees.

The Social Safety Net focused on two aspects:

(a) providing financial security including ERS money, health and accident/disability coverage for workers and spouses and counseling for using the money;

(b) developing self-confidence and esteem through skill training, psychological and rehabilitation counseling.

The SSNP was made available to all workers (including casual workers) and had four components

- The first one would provide group health and accident/ disability coverage to the displaced workers and their spouses until retirement.
- The second is financial (how best to use the ERS money),psychological (support at a time of major life change) and rehabilitation counseling
- The third one provided training that was open to all displaced workers. If a worker did not wish to take advantage of this possibility, he/she could designate an unemployed dependent son/daughter to take his/her place. This innovation has allowed a larger participation in training than has been observed in other States.

· The last component was a Poverty and Social Impact Assessment (PSIA) using baseline socio-economic data concerning the workers' families collected at the time of applying for ERS. The PSIA was to be carried out for each enterprise about six months after completion of the training. It would identify mitigation measures and propose action plans for implementation. The social staff of the PE Cell/ PED would manage the SSNP.

Features of Social Safety Net Programme

Against the backdrop of Government of West Bengal's labour - friendly policy in industrial restructuring, the SSNP has been designed with sensitivity and provides a 'human face'.

Counseling activities covered:

- Psychological counseling to overcome trauma of job loss and develop positive attitude in life and re-build self-confidence
- Awareness on available avenues for training, skill development, self-employment.
- Information on institutions providing vocational training and job prospects
- Financial counseling for investment of compensation money.

The approach to counseling included:

- In house focused group meetings
- Gained common consensus for implementation of the programme amongst trade union members and workers
- Used available videocassettes on counseling

Other steps covered:

(a) Counseling undertaken in affected PSE premises.

(b) ERS Application Form designed and made available.

(c) Rama Krishna Mission that runs a strong vocational training programme, drawn into the programme.

(d) Record generated of number and profile of affected workers on the basis of available information – age, education, skill.

(e) Inventory of training institutions, training / reskilling programmes and selection based on workers needs, track record of organisations and assessment of growing opportunities for successful redeployment in the labour market.

(f) Identification of SSNP training agencies:

- Rama Krishna Mission Shilpamandir, Community Polytechnic, Belur Math
- Rama Krishna Mission Shilpamandir, Computer Center, Belur Math
- Sree Sarada Math, Daksheneswar
- Rama Krishna Mission Jan Shiksha Sansthan, Narendrapur
- Rama Krishna Ashram Krishi Bigyan Kendrya, Nimpith
- Indian Council of Small Industries
- ZEE Interactive Learning Systems, Kolkata
- Center for Electronics Test Engineering, Kolkata
- Society for School of Medical Technology, Kolkata

The design also suggested undertaking business optimisation studies for the remaining 14 units to be restructured. The business optimization studies were undertaken for 14 enterprises and were parallely carried out in two parts. The first was for the 4 enterprises that had potential for achieving viability with the restructuring of their businesses and were to be retained under the ownership of Government with necessary measures for optimizing their businesses. The second focused on 'earning potential' of the 10 enterprises, which were assessed to havepotential for achieving viability with investments. The services of professional consultants PricewaterhouseCoopers (PWC) were retained to carry out these studies and advise the restructuring transactions.

Extensive consultations between PED and all major stakeholders

An extensive consultation process was carried out by PED with all major stakeholders at different levels. The PED could impress on the employees the need of restructuring and closure, and their possible impacts, the constituents of ERS, SSNP, and Government's commitment to employees welfare and the training and counseling of workers. The MIC and the Principal Secretary, PED focused on workers concerns, safety issues and their expectations from the Government. PED also held open discussions with the trade unions to enlist their support in the restructuring programme. PED made significant efforts to inform unions and workers about restructuring and involve them in the process at every stage. Principal Secretary, PED addressed several letters to the employees of enterprises under pilot project through their respective unions/associations starting from inception stage to implementation stage explaining:

- Rationale, costs and benefits of restructuring were explained and publicized in the interest of transparency and wider visibility.
- Unions and workers were both constantly kept in loop and given complete information about the method and process of restructuring.
- Incentives and social safety net measures that were put in place, including details about ERS package, insurance, training and redeployment options.
- Regulatory and other arrangements being designed to protect their interests. The communication strategy involved information on criteria for selection of JV partner, and checks inbuilt into the contract to protect their interests.

Implementation Mechanism

SBEG began with submitting study reports and recommendation in respect of the loss-making PSUs under PED as they had built upon an extensive data base in in their respect over 1998- 2001. CPR determined the necessity of making a measured beginning in this sensitive area and on their recommendation, SCCI approved the design and implementation of a Pilot project comprising the restructuring of 16 PED PSUs . The objective of this measured approach was to gain popular acceptance in the complexities of restructuring PSUs and to evolve a structural framework in this respect that would be replicable in designing restructuring of the remaining PSUs in the next phase. Through the design phase, the restructuring of subsidiaries (seven) of the WBEIDC and the strategic transfer of the Great Eastern Hotel under the IT Department (earlier under the Commerce & Industries Department) and Tourism Department respectively, were added to the scope of the Pilot project. Further during the implementation phase, one PSU under Commerce & Industries (C&I) Department, six PSUs under Cottage & Small Scale

Industries (C&SSI) Department and one PSU under the direct control of PED has been added to the project, totaling the scope of the Pilot project to 26 PSUs

Closure of 2 units

The first step in the reform process was the closure of two non-viable units - Indian Paper & Pulp Ltd. and Sundarban Sugarbeet Processing Company Ltd. The two enterprises had been defunct for the previous six years and their closure would secure cessation of recurring budgetary expenditure of almost nine crores. All assets and liabilities of these two companies invested in Government.

Prior to announcing ERS, PED held consultations with trade unions and workers to explain:

- The overall economic/financial situation of the PSE including the drain it was causing on the budgetary resources,
- Nature and extent of protective measures adopted by the Government.

Counseling and implementation of ERS in 2 units

As earlier stated, counseling activities covered financial counseling, psychological counseling, training and general counseling. Financial counseling was undertaken by SSNP group under PE Cell, PED and invitees from financial institutions and started before announcement of ERS. Invitees and select NGOs working in the area undertook psychological counseling, which continued all through. Ramakrishna Mission also undertook counseling in respect of their re-skilling programs. The counseling was delivered individually or in-group sessions on the PSE premises, wherein spouses were also invited to attend. Comprehensive ERS forms including Application Forms, ER schemes, Hand out of information, Nomination Form, acknowledgement Form and Bench - marking Proformas were designed and given to workers along with information on schemes for investment. A SSNP Committee designated at the enterprise level, worked full time on explaining procedures and requirements to employees. After the applications were received, they were quickly processed to ensure full disbursement of compensation entitlements and dues if any, at one time, within one week of the retirement taking effect.

32.5 Problems / Issues

The manufacturing enterprises contributed the most important segment of the SLPEs in West Bengal. The financial performance of these enterprises shows that out of 35 manufacturing SLPEs more than 30 had been incurring cash losses. Almost all the enterprises in this category had a sales lower than their expenses on raw materials, salaries and wages which together accounted in many cases for more than 200 percent of the turnover. The expenses incurred on maintenance of plant and machinery were a very small portion and were less than 1.5 % of the cost of sales indicating that this function was not given due importance. The profit after taxes ran in to negative because of high interest and indirect overhead incidence. This told upon the SLPEs heavily as they had very low capacity utilization. For Example, Durgapur project Ltd., was utilizing 33.3 percent of its installed capacity. Its spun-pipe factory registered production of a meager 6000 tones of pipes as against the projected 50,000 tones in 1985-86. Its efficiency with regard to power generation was also low. Its consumption of operating raw materials such as furnace oil was on the high side. i.e., RS. 40 crores as against an income of Rs. 50 crores in the year 1985-86. In the same year, the capacity utilization in Lily Biscuit and Dr. Paul Lohman Eastern Distilleries was as low as 8.8 and 21 percent, respectively. The trady management of working capital watered down the profit earnings as working capital for all the enterprises taken together was to the tune of 9 months turn over in 1985-86. The laxity in the area of inventory and receivables management was mainly responsible for this situation. These enterprises stocked inventory to the tune of 7 months turn over requirements and extended credit to the tune of 240 days turn over. It is pertinent to note that in in the case of a large number of SLPEs the working capital was negative. The problem was further accentuated by the refusal of commercial banks to operate the cash limits. The Westinghouse Saxby Ltd., Kalyan Spinning Mills and National Iron and Steel Company Ltd. Were cases in point.

The Study brings out the fact that the problems responsible for the sub-optimal physical and financial performance of SLPEs in the state were commercial, financial, technical, and managerial in nature. Commercially, these enterprises were characterized by low capacity utilization, did not have the commercial freedom to adjust their could not import to the desired extent the raw materials for production schedules, suffered from an inappropriate product mix and had mechanistic organizations devoid of any flavor for marketing. The economic liberalization policies pursued by the Central Government also had a negative impact on some of these enterprises. The Durgapur Chemicals Ltd. Could not push through its product because of periodic imports of anhydride. The Westinghouse Saxby Ltd. Depends totally on railways for market which provided a very thin margin for them. The company used to operate in a monopolistic market and could not adjust itself to a competitive market when the situation so demanded. The West Bengal tea development Corporation did not take up new plantation and other development work. The West Bengal Ceramic Development Corporation utilized its capacity to the tune of 35%. It was distributing its out put to entrepreneurs at a subsidized rate of Rs. 400 per MT against a production cost of Rs. 1400/-MT. The West Bengal Handicrafts Development Corporation was not effectively marketing its product and that markets had not been identified and developed. The financial problems included blocking of funds in working capital, absence of timely release of funds by the state Government, Suspension of Working Capital financing by the commercial banks and lack of cost control. The Durgapur Project Ltd had blocked huge money with sundry debtors including state undertakings. In view of its dismal performance, the company could not generate its working finance. It had to solely depend on the State Government for working capital support but such support did not come at the right time. The West Durgapur Spinning Mill had huge losses and was not in a position to even pay interest to the financial institutions. The wages and salaries were 25% of the total turnover. In many companies wages constituted more than 55% of the total cost of production. In the case of the Kalyan Spinning Mills Ltd. And West Dinaajpore Spinning ills Ltd. Material consumption was more then 56% of the total cost of production.

The technical problems varied from inapt site selection, in appropriate technology provided by the various suppliers, and worn out machinery to lack of quality and wastage control, and absence of balancing equipment., The technology provided by the foreign suppliers for the phenol plant was defective from the very beginning and it never operated anywhere near the rated capacity in the case of the Durgapur Chemicals Project Ltdf. The Kalyani Spinning Mills Ltd. Suffered from low spindle capacity, lack of plant equipment, and wastage and quality control. Most of the gardens were old and their yield was too low in the case of the West Bengal Tea Development Corporation. The sites of the gardens were also uneconomic. The managerial problems affected the SLPEs in more than one way. The enterprises could not professionalize their cadres as the salaries offered. were ridiculously low. The component managers and technical personnel left the organizations with in short period of the time. The enterprises introduced frequent changes in the operational strategies with lout any justification. The manufacturing SLPEs were characterized by soft shop floor management, lack of supervision, low productivity, lack of proper maintenance and absence of work norm. This is corroborated by the fact the some units had considerable assets in the form of vacant land, they still ran short of working capital which they mobilized only through the government. The appointments of the officers of the Indian Administrative Service added fuel to the fire as they went on shifting very frequently and did not commit themselves to the development of organization specific culture and result-oriented performance. Training and management development were at bay.

References

1. Extract from the minutes of the meeting held on 17-03-2005 under the chairmanship of honaroble Chief Minister.
2. Government Order no. OM No. 2 (36) / 86 – BPE (WC) dated 5th October 1988.
3. Government order OM dated 5th May 2000.
4. G O (MS) No 134/2W4/ ID dated 26-11-2004.

Annexure-1

State-wise List of SLPEs in India

Andhra Pradesh

1.	Andhra Pradesh Industrial Development Corporation Limited
2.	Andhra Pradesh Industrial Infrastructure Corporation Limited
3.	Andhra Pradesh Urban Finance and Infrastructure Development Corporation Limited
4.	Andhra Pradesh Power Finance Corporation Limited
5.	Andhra Pradesh State Financial Corporation
6.	Andhra Pradesh State Agro Industries Development Corporation Limited
7.	Andhra Pradesh Meat Development Corporation Limited
8.	Leather Industries Development Corporation of Andhra Pradesh Limited
9.	Andhra Pradesh Beverages Corporation Limited
10.	Andhra Pradesh Heavy Machinery and Engineering Limited (S)
11.	Andhra Pradesh Electronics Development Corporation Limited
12.	Andhra Pradesh State Textile Development Corporation Limited
13.	Andhra Pradesh Handicrafts Development Corporation Limited
14.	Andhra Pradesh Mineral Development Corporation Limited
15.	The Nizam Sugars Limited
16.	Non Conventional Energy Development Corporation of Andhra Pradesh Limited
17.	Andhra Pradesh Wind Farms Limited (S)
18.	Andhra Pradesh Technology Services Limited
19.	Andhra Pradesh State Irrigation Development Corporation Limited
20.	Andhra Pradesh Forest Development Corporation Limited
21.	The Singareni Collieries Company Limited
22.	Andhra Pradesh State Police Housing Corporation Limited
23.	Andhra Pradesh State Housing Corporation Limited

(Contd.)

(Contd. Annexure-1)

24.	Andhra Pradesh Tourism Development Corporation Limited
25.	Andhra Pradesh State Film Television and Theatre Development Corporation Limited
26.	Andhra Pradesh State Civil Supplies Corporation Limited
27.	Andhra Pradesh State Trading Corporation Limited
28.	Andhra Pradesh State Warehousing Corporation
29.	Andhra Pradesh Power Generation Corporation Limited
30.	Transmission Corporation of Andhra Pradesh Limited
31.	Eastern Power Distribution Company of Andhra Pradesh Limited (S)
32.	Southern Power Distribution Company of Andhra Pradesh Limited (S)
33.	Central Power Distribution Company of Andhra Pradesh Limited (S)
34.	Northern Power Distribution Company of Andhra Pradesh Limited (S)
35.	Andhra Pradesh State Road Transport Corporation
36.	Andhra Pradesh State Minorities Finance Corporation Limited
37.	Andhra Pradesh Fisheries Corporation Ltd
38.	Prodduture Milk Foods Ltd
39.	Andhra Pradesh Diary Development Corporation Ltd
40.	Andhra Pradesh Small Scale Industrial Development Corporation Ltd
41.	Southern Transformers and Electricals Limited
42.	Allwyn Watches Limited
43.	Allwyn Auto Limited
44.	Republic Forge Company Limited
45.	Andhra Pradesh Steels Limited
46.	Andhra Pradesh Scooters Limited
47.	Marine and Communications Electronics Development Corporation Limited
48.	Aptronix Communication Limited
49.	Andhra Pradesh Essential Commodities Corporation Ltd
50.	Hyderabad Chemicals and Fertiliers Limited
51.	Andhra Pradesh Tourism Finance Limited
52.	Andhra Pradesh State Non Resident Indian Investment Corporation Limited

(Contd.)

(Contd. Annexure-1)

53.	Damodar Minerals Private Limited
54.	Wolkman Andhra Mining Private Limited

Arunachal Pradesh

1.	Arunachal Pradesh Industrial Development and Financial Corporation Limited
2.	Arunachal Pradesh Mineral Development and Trading Corporation Limited
4.	Parasuram Cements Limited
3.	Arunachal Pradesh Forest Corporation Limited
5.	Arunachal Horticulture Processing Industries Limited

Assam

1.	Assam Financial Corporation
2.	Assam Industrial Development Corporation Limited
3.	Assam Seeds Corporation Limited
4.	Assam Agro-Industries Development Corporation Limited
5.	Assam Livestock and Poultry Corporation Limited
6.	Assam Tea Corporation Limited
7.	Assam Gas Company Limited
8.	Assam Petrochemicals Limited (Subsidiary of AIDC Ltd)
9.	Ashok Paper Mills (Assam) Limited
10.	Assam Conductor & Tubes Limited
11.	Assam Electronics Development Corporation Limited
12.	Assam State textile Corporation Limited
13.	Assam Mineral Development Corporation Limited
14.	Assam Police Housing Corporation Limited
15.	Assam Government Construction Corporation Limited
16.	Assam State Fertilizers and Chemicals limited (Subsidiary of AIDC Limited)
17.	Assam State Text Book Production and Publication Limited
18.	Industrial Papers (Assam) Limited (Subsidiary of AIDC Limited)
19.	Amtron Sen Electronics Limited
20.	Assam Spun Silk Mills Limited
21.	Assam Polytex Limited (Subsidiary of AIDC Ltd)

(Contd.)

(Contd. Annexure-1)

22.	Assam Syntex Limited (Subsidiary of AIDC Limited)
23.	Assam State Weaving and Manufacturing Company Limited (Subsidiary of AIDC Ltd)
24.	Assam & Meghalaya Mineral Development Corporation Limited
25.	Cachar Sugar Mills Limited
26.	Fertichem Limited
27.	Assam Power loom Development Corporation Limited
28.	Assam Plantation Crop Development Corporation Limited
29.	Assam Plains Tribes Development Corporation Limited
30.	Assam Tanneries Limited
31.	Assam State Minor Irrigation Development Corporation Limited
32.	Assam Fisheries Development Corporation Limited
33.	Assam Hills Small Industries Development Corporation Limited
34.	Assam Small Industries Development Corporation, Limited
35.	Assam Tourism Development Corporation Limited
36.	Assam State Film (Finance and Development) Corporation Limited
37.	Assam Government Marketing Corporation Limited
38.	Assam State Warehousing Corporation
39.	Assam State Electricity Board
40.	Assam State Transport Corporation
41.	Assam State Development Corporation for Other Backward Classes Limited
42.	Assam State Development Corporation for Scheduled Cases Limited.

Andaman and Nicobar

1.	ANIIDC
2.	AN Forest Plantation Dev. Corp. Ltd

Bihar

1.	Bihar Panchayat Raj Fianancial Corp. Ltd.
2.	Bihar State Financial Corp.
3.	Bihar State Diary Corporation Ltd.
4.	Bihar State Agro Industries Dev. Corp. Ltd.
5.	Bihar Rajya Beej Nigam Ltd.

(Contd.)

(Contd. Annexure-1)

6.	Bihar Fruits and Vegetables Dev. Corp. Ltd.
7.	Bihar Insecticides Ltd.
8.	Bihar Rajya Matsya Vikas Nigam Ltd.
9.	Bihar State Small Industries Corp. Ltd.
10.	Bihar State Industrial Dev. Corp. Ltd.
11.	Bihar State Leather Industries Dev. Corp. Ltd.
12.	Bihar Scooters Ltd.
13.	Bihar Paper Mills Ltd.
14.	Bihar State Finished Leather Corp. Ltd
15.	Bihar State Glazed Tiles and Ceramic Industries Ltd.
16.	Vishwamithra Paper Industries Ltd
17.	Jhanjharpur Paper Industries Ltd.
18.	Bihar State Tannin Extracts Ltd.
19.	Bihar Solvent and Chemicals Ltd.
20.	Synthetic Resins (Eastern) Ltd.
21.	Magadha Minerals Ltd.
22.	Bhawani Active Carbon Ltd.
23.	Kumardhubi Metal Casting and Engineering Ltd.
24.	Bihar State Electronics Development Corp.
25.	Beltron Video System Ltd .
26.	Beltron Mining Systems
27.	Beltron Informatics Ltd.
28.	Bihar State Textiles Corp. Ltd.
29.	Bihar State Handloom and Handicrafts Corp. Ltd.
30.	Bihar State Mineral Development Corp. Ltd.
31.	Bihar Police Building Construction Corp. Ltd.
32.	Bihar State Construction Corp. Ltd.
33.	Bihar Rajya Pul Nirman Nigam Ltd.
34.	Bihar State Sugar Corp. Ltd.
35.	Bihar State Cement Corp. Ltd.
36.	Bihar State Pharmaceuticals and Chemicals Dev. Corp. Ltd.
37.	Bihar Maize Products Ltd.
38.	Bihar Drugs and Chemicals Ltd.

(Contd.)

(Contd. Annexure-1)

39.	Bihar State Hydro Electric Power Corp. Ltd.
40.	Tenughat Vidyut Nigam Ltd.
41.	Bihar State Text Book Publishing Corp. Ltd.
42.	Bihar State Film Dev. Finance Corp.Ltd.
43.	Bihar State Forest Development Corp. Ltd.
44.	Bihar State Tourism Dev. Corp. Ltd.
45.	Bihar State Credit and Investment Corp. Ltd
46.	Bihar State Exports Corp. Ltd.
47.	Bihar State Food and Civil Supplies Ltd.
48.	Bihar State Warehousing Corp.
49.	Bihar State Water Development Corp. Ltd.
50.	Bihar Hill Area Lift Irrigation Corp.
51.	Bihar State Electricity Board.
52.	Bihar State Road Transport Corp.
53.	Bihar State Minorities Finance Corp. Ltd.
54.	Bihar State Backward Classes Finance and Dev. Corp. Ltd.

Chattisgarh

1.	Chattisgarh State Beverages Corp. Ltd
2.	Chhattisgarh Mineral Dev. Corp. Ltd
3.	Chhattisgarh Infrastructure Dev. Corp. Ltd
4.	Chhattisgarh State Power Gen Corp Ltd
5.	Chhattisgarh State Power Transmission Co. Ltd
6.	Chhattisgarh State Power Distribution Co. Ltd
7.	Chhattisgarh State Electricity Board
8.	Chhattisgarh Rajya Van Vikas Nigam Ltd
9.	Chhattisgarh State Civil Supplies Corp. Ltd
10.	Chhattisgarh State Warehousing Corp.

Delhi

1.	Delhi State Industrial Development Corporation Limited
2.	Delhi Financial Corporation
3.	Delhi State Mineral Development Corporation Limited
4.	Delhi Tourism and Transportation Development Corporation Limited

(Contd.)

(Contd. Annexure-1)

5.	Delhi State Civil Supplies Corporation Limited
6.	Pragti Power Corporation Limited
7.	Delhi Power Company Limited
8.	Indraprastha Power Generation Company Limited
9.	Delhi Power Supply Company Limited
10.	Central-East Delhi Electricity Distribution Company Limited
11.	South-West Delhi Electricity Distribution Company Limited
12.	North North-West Delhi Distribution Company Limited
13.	Delhi Vidyut Board
14.	Delhi Transport Corporation
15.	Delhi Scheduled Caste Financial and Development Corporation Limited

Goa

1.	Goa Construction, Housing and Finance Corp. Ltd.
2.	Goa Financial and Leasing Services Limited
3.	Goa Meat Complex Limited
4.	Goa Auto Accessories Limited
5.	Goa Handicrafts, Rural and Small Scale Industries Development Corporation Limited
6.	Goa Electronics Limited
7.	Electronics Corporation of Goa Limited *
8.	Goa Antibiotics and Pharmaceuticals Limited
9.	Goa State Horticulture Corporation Limited
10.	Goa Forest Development Corporation Limited
11.	Economic Development Corporation of Goa, Daman & Diu Limited
12.	Goa Tourism Development Corporation Limted
13.	Kadamba Transport Corporation Limited
14.	Kadamba Suburban Transport Corporation Limited
15.	Goa State Scheduled Caste and Other Backward Classes Development Corporation Ltd

Gujarat

1.	Gujarat Industrial Investment Corporation Limited (GIIC)
2.	Gujarat State Investments Limited

(Contd.)

(Contd. Annexure-1)

3.	Gujarat State Financial Services Limited (GSFS Ltd.)
4.	GSFS Capital and Securities Ltd.(Subsidiary of GSFS Ltd.)
5.	Gujarat State Road Transport Corporation
6.	Gujarat State Financial Corporation
7.	Gujarat Industrial Development Corporation
8.	Gujarat Agro-Industries Corporation Limited
9.	Gujarat Sheep and Wool Development Corporation Limited
10.	Gujarat State Seeds Corporation Limited
11.	Gujarat State Land Development Corporation Limited
12.	Gujarat State Petroleum Corporation Limited (GSPC Ltd.)
13.	Gujarat State Handicrafts Development Corporation Limited
14.	Gujarat State Handloom Development Corporation Limited (B)
15.	Gujarat Mineral Development Corporation Limited
16.	Gujarat State Petronet Limited (Subsidiary of GSPC Ltd.)
17.	Gujarat State Police Housing Corporation Limited
18.	Gujarat Growth Centres Development Corporation Ltd.
19.	Alcock Ashdown (Gujarat) Limited
20.	Gujarat National Highways Limited
21.	Gujarat Informatics Limited
22.	Gujarat Fisheries Development Corporation Limited
23.	Gujarat Dairy Development Corporation Limited@@
24.	Gujarat Small Industries Corporation Limited
25.	Gujarat Communications and Electronics Limited
26.	Gujarat Trans-Receivers Limited (Subsidiary of GIIC)
27.	Gujarat State Textile Corporation Limited(GSTC)@
28	Gujarat Fintex Limited (Subsidiary of GSTC)@
29.	Gujarat Siltex Limited (Subsidiary of GSTC)@
30.	Gujarat Texfab Limited (Subsidiary of GSTC)@
31.	Gujarat State Construction Corporation Limited
32.	Gujarat State Forest Development Corporation Limited
33.	Gujarat State Rural Development Corporation Limited
34.	Gujarat Urban Development Company Limited
35.	Tourism Corporation of Gujarat Limited

(Contd.)

(Contd. Annexure-1)

36.	Gujarat Water Resources Development Corporation Limited
37.	Sardar Sarovar Narmada Nigam Limited
38.	The Film Development Corporation of Gujarat Limited
39.	Gujarat State Civil Supplies Corporation Limited
40.	Gujarat State Export Corporation Limited
41.	Gujarat Rural Industries Marketing Corporation Limited
42.	Gujarat State Warehousing Corporation
43.	Gujarat StateRoad Dev. Corp. LTd
44.	Gujarat Power Corporation Limited
45.	Gujarat Water Infrastructure Ltd.
46.	Gujarat Electricity Board
47.	Gujarat Scheduled Castes Economic Development Corporation Limited
48.	Gujarat Women Economic Development Corporation Limited
49.	Gujarat Minorities Finance and Development Corporation Limited
50.	Gujarat Safai Kamdar Vikas Nigam Limited

Haryana

1.	Haryana State Industrial Development Corporation Limited
2.	Haryana Financial Corporation
3.	Haryana Agro Industries Corporation Limited
4.	Haryana Seeds Development Corporation Limited
5.	Hartron Informatics Limited@
6.	Haryana Minerals Limited@
7.	Haryana Police Housing Corporation Limited
8.	Haryana State Roads and Bridges Development Corporation Limited.
9.	Haryana Dairy Development Corporation Limited
10.	Haryana Tanneries Limited
11.	Punjab State Irons Limited
12.	Haryana Concast Limited
13.	Haryana Land Reclamation and Development Corporation Limited
14.	Hyraya State Housing Finance Corp. Ltd

(Contd.)

(Contd. Annexure-1)

15.	Haryana State Handloom and Handicrafts Corporation Limited
16.	Haryana Forest Development Corporation Limited
17.	Haryana Tourism Corporation Limited
18.	Haryana State Small Industries and Export Corporation Limited
19.	Haryana Warehousing Corporation
20.	Haryana State Minor Irrigation and Tubewells Corporation Limited
21.	Haryana Roadways Engineering Corporation Limited
22.	Haryana State Electronics Development Corporation Limited
23.	Haryana Power Generation Corporation Limited
24.	Haryana Vidyut Prasaran Nigam Limited
25.	Uttar Haryana Bijli Vitran Nigam Limited
26.	Dakshin Haryana Bijli Vitran Nigam Limited
27.	Haryana Scheduled Castes Finance and Development Corporation Limited
28.	Haryana Backward Classes and Economically Weaker Section Kalyan Nigam Limited
29.	Haryana Women Development Corporation Limited

Himachal Pradesh

1.	Himachal Pradesh State Industrial Development Corporation Limited
2.	Himachal Pradesh Financial Corporation
3.	Himachal Pradesh Agro Industries Corporation Limited
4.	Himachal Pradesh Horticultural Produce Marketing and Processing Corp Ltd
5.	Agro Industrial Packaging India Limited
6.	Himachal Pradesh General Industries Corporation Limited
7.	Himachal Pradesh State Electronics Development Corporation Limited
8.	Himachal Worsted Mills Limited
9.	Nahan Foundry Limited
10.	Himachal Pradesh State Handicrafts and Handloom Corporation Limited
11.	Himachal Pradesh State Forest Corporation Limited
12.	Himachal Pradesh Tourism Development Corporation Limited

(Contd.)

(Contd. Annexure-1)

13.	Himachal Pradesh State Small Industries and Export Corporation Limited
14.	Himachal Pradesh State Civil Supplies Corporation Limited
15.	Himachal Pradesh Road and Other Infrastructure Development Corporation Limited
16.	Himachal Pradesh State Electricity Board
17.	Himachal Road Transport Corporation
18.	Himachal Pradesh Mahila Vikas Nigam
19.	Himachal Backward Classes Finance and Development Corporation
20.	Himachal Pradesh Minorities Finance and Development Corporation
21.	Himachal Pradesh Health Systems Corporation Limited

Jammu & Kashmir

1.	Jammu and Kashmir State Agro Industries Development Corporation Limited
2.	Jammu and Kashmir Small Scale Industries Development Corporation Limited
3.	Jammu and Kashmir State Industrial Development Corporation Limited
4.	Jammu and Kashmir Bank Limited
5.	Jammu and Kashmir State Financial Corporation Limited
6.	Jammu and Kashmir State Horticultural Produce Marketing and Processing Corporation Limited
7.	Jammu and Kashmir Industries Limited
8.	Himalayan Wool Combers Limited
9.	Jammu and Kashmir State Handloom Development Corporation Limited
10.	Jammu and Kashmir Handicrafts (Sales and Export) Development Corporation Limited
11.	Jammu and Kashmir State Handloom Handicrafts Raw Material Supplies Organisation Limited (a Subsidiary of Himalayan Wool Combers Limited)**
12.	Jammu and Kashmir Minerals Limited
13.	Jammu and Kashmir Projects Construction Corporation Limited
14.	Jammu and Kashmir Police Housing Corporation Limited
15.	Jammu and Kashmir Cements Limited

(Contd.)

(Contd. Annexure-1)

16.	Jammu and Kashmir State Cable Car Corporation Limited***
17.	Tawi Scooters Limited
18.	Jammu and Kashmir State Tourism Development Corporation Limited
19.	Jammu and Kashmir State Forest Corporation Limited
20.	Jammu and Kashmir State Power Development Corporation Limited#
21.	Jammu and Kashmir State Road Transport Corporation
22.	Jammu and Kashmir Scheduled Castes, Scheduled Tribes and Other Backward Classes Development Corporation Limited
23.	Jammu and Kashmir State Women's Development Corporation Limited **

Jharkhand

1.	Jharkhand State Mineral Dev. Corp. Ltd
2.	Jharkhand Hill Arad Lift Irrigation Corp. Ltd
3.	Jharkhand Police Housing Corp. Ltd
4.	jharkhand Tourism Dev. Corp. Ltd
5.	Jharkahand State Forest Dev Corp. Ltd
6.	Jharkhand State Electricity Board
7.	Jharkhand State Electricity Regulatory Commission

Karnataka

1.	Karnataka Sate Financial Corp.
2.	Karnataka State Industrial Investment & Dev. Corp.
3.	Karnataka State Police Housing Corp.
4.	Karnataka Agro Industries Corp. Ltd.
5.	Karnataka Compost Dev. Corp. Ltd.
6.	Karnataka State Electronics Dev. Corp. Ltd.
7.	Karnataka Cashew Dev. Corp. Ltd.
8.	Karnataka State Coir Dev. Corp. Ltd.
9.	Shree Kanteerava Studios Ltd.
10.	Karnataka State Construction Corp. Ltd.
11.	Karnataka State Beverages Ltd
12.	Karnataka Urban Infra Development Corp. Ltd.

(Contd.)

(Contd. Annexure-1)

13.	Mysore Sugar Co. Ltd.
14.	Mysore Paper Mills Ltd.
15.	Mysore Lamps Ltd.
16.	Mysore Tobacco Co. Ltd.
17.	Mysore Paints Varnish Ltd.
18.	Mysore Match Co. Ltd.
19.	Mysore Chrome Tanning Co. Ltd.
20.	Mysore Electrical Industries Ltd.
21.	Hutti Gold Mines.
22.	Mysore Acetate and Chemicals Co. Ltd.
23.	Mysore Cosmetics
24.	Mysore Minerals
25.	Karnataka State Agro Corn Products Ltd.
26.	Karnataka State Veeners Ltd.
27.	Chamundi Machine Tools
28.	Karnataka Argo Protiens Ltd.
29.	Karnataka Soaps And Detergents Ltd.
30.	Karnataka State Textiles Ltd.
31.	Karnataka Telecom Ltd.
32.	Karnataka Pulp Wood Ltd.
33.	Karnataka Tungsten Molly ltd.
34.	Vidhya Nagar Steel Ltd.
35.	Mysore Sales International Ltd.
36.	Karnataka Forest Dev. Corp.
37.	Karnataka State Agricultural Produce Procession & Export.
38.	Karnataka Film Industries Dev. Corp.
39.	Karnataka Fisheries Dev. Corp.
40.	Karnataka Handloom Dev. Corp. Ltd.
41.	Karnataka Leather Dev. Corp. Ltd.
42.	Karnataka Inland Fisheries Dev. Corp. Ltd.
43.	Karnataka State Small Industries Dev. Corp.
44.	Karnataka Land Army Corp. Ltd.
45.	Jungles and Lodges and Resorts Ltd
46.	Krishna Bhagya Jala Nigam LTd.

(Contd.)

(Contd. Annexure-1)

47.	Karnataka Neeravri Nigam LTd.
48.	NGEF Ltd.
49.	NGEF (Hubli)
50.	Karnataka State Forest Industries Corp. Ltd.
51.	Karnataka Silk Industries Corp Ltd.
52.	Marketing Consultants And Agencies Ltd.
53.	Karnataka Silk Marketing Board Ltd.
54.	Karnataka small Industries Marketing Corp.
55.	Karnataka Sheep Wool Dev. Corp. Ltd
56.	Karnataka State Khadi & Villages Industries Board.
57.	Karnataka State Food and Civil Supplies Corp. Ltd.
58.	Karnataka State Warehousing Corp.
59.	D.Devraj URs Truck Terminals Ltd.
60.	Karnataka Power Transmission Corp Ltd
61.	Karnataka State Road Transport Corp.
62.	North East Karnataka State Road Transport Corp.
63.	Karnataka Power Corp. Ltd.
64.	Karnataka State Tourism Dev. Corp. Ltd.
65.	Bangalore Mass Rapid Transit Ltd.
66.	Karnataka Renewable Energy Dev. Corp. Ltd.
67.	Karnataka Road Dev. Corp. Ltd.
68.	Karnataka Vidyuth Karnatakakhane Ltd.
69.	Karnataka State Powerloom Development Corp Ltd.
70.	Bangalore Metropolitan Transport Corporation
71.	Bangalore Electricity Supply Co. Ltd
72.	Hublic Electricity Supply Co. Ltd
73.	Mangalore Electricity Supply Co. Ltd
74.	Gulbarga Electricity Supply Co. Ltd
75.	North Western Karnataka Road Transprot Corp.
76.	Karnataka SC /ST Development Corp.
77.	Karnataka Backward Classes Development corp.
78.	Karnataka State Minorities Dev. Corp.
79.	Karnataka State Women's Dev. Corp.

(Contd.)

(Contd. Annexure-1)

81.	Karnataka Tagori Abhivridhi Manddali Nigam Ltd
82.	Rajiv Gandhi Rural Housing Corp.

Kerala

1.	The Kerala State Financial Enterprises Limited
2.	Kerala Urban Development Finance Corporation Limited
3.	Kerala Financial Corporation
4.	Oil Palm India Limited
5.	The Kerala Agro -Industries Corporation Limited
6.	The Kerala State Coir Corporation Limited
7.	The Kerala State Cashew Development Corporation Limited
8.	Kerala Agro-Machinery Corporation Limited
9.	Foam Mattings (India) Limited
10.	Kerala Feeds Limited
11.	United Electrical Industries Limited
12.	Traco Cable Company Limited
13.	Transformers and Electricals Kerala Limited
14.	Kerala Electrical and Allied Engineering Company Limited
15.	Trivandrum Rubber Works Limited (Subsidiary of SFCK)
16.	The Kerala Ceramics Limited
17.	Kerala Construction Components Limited
18.	Kerala Small Industries Development Corporation Limited (SIDCO)
19.	The Metal Industries Limited
20.	The Metropolitan Engineering Company Limited
21.	Steel Complex Limited (SCL) (Subsidiary of KSIDC)
22.	Steel Industrials Kerala Limited (SILK)
23.	Scooters Kerala Limited
24.	Kerala Automobiles Limited
25.	Steel and Industrial Forgings Limited (Subsidiary of SILK)
26.	Autokast Limited (Subsidiary of SILK)
27.	Kerala Hitech Industries Limited
28.	Keltron Counters Limited (Subsidiary of KELTRON)

(Contd.)

(Contd. Annexure-1)

29.	Kerala State Electronics Development Corporation Limited(KELTRON)
30.	Keltron Electro-Ceramics Limited (Subsidiary of KELTRON)
31.	Keltron Crystals Limited (Subsidiary of KELTRON)
32.	Keltron Component Complex Limited (Subsidiary of KELTRON)
33.	Keltron Magnetics Limited (Subsidiary of KELTRON)
34.	Keltron Resistors Limited (Subsidiary of KELTRON)
35.	Keltron Rectifiers Limited (Subsidiary of KELTRON)
36.	Astral Watches Limited (Susidiary of KSIDC)
37.	Trivandrum Spinning Mills Limited
38.	Kerala State Textile Corporation Limited
39.	Kerala Garments Limited (Subsidiary of KSHDC)
40.	Sitaram Textiles Limited
41.	Kerala State Handloom Development Corporation Limited (KSHDC)
42.	Handicrafts Development Corporation of Kerala Limited
43.	Travancore Plywood Industries Limited
44.	Kerala State Bamboo Corporation Limited
45.	Kerala State Mineral Development Corporation Limited
46.	Kerala Clays and Ceramic Products Limited
47.	Kerala State Construction Corporation Limited
48.	Kerala Police Housing and Construction Corporation Limited
49.	Roads and Bridges Development Corporation of Kerala Limited
50.	The Kerala Land Development Corporation Limited
51.	The Travancore Cements Limited
52.	Malabar Cements Limited
53.	The Travancore-Cochin Chemicals Limited
54.	Kerala Soaps and Oils Limited
55.	Kerala State Drugs and Pharmaceuticals Limited
56.	The Pharmaceutical Corporation(Indian Medicines) Kerala Limited
57.	Kerala State Detergents and Chemicals Limited
58.	Kerala State Salicylates and Chemicals Limited

(Contd.)

(Contd. Annexure-1)

59.	Travancore Titanium Products Limited
60.	The Kerala Minerals and Metals Limited
61.	The Travancore Sugars and Chemicals Limited
62.	Kerala State Industrial Development Corporation Limited (KSIDC)
63.	Kerala State Industrial Products Trading Corporation Limited
64.	Kerala State Beverages (Manufacturing and Marketing) Corporation Limited
65.	Kerala State Industrial Enterprises Limited (KSIE)
66.	Kerala State Maritime Development Corporation Limited
67.	Meat Products of India Limited
68.	Kerala Shipping and Inland Navigation Corporation Limited
69.	Kerala State Coconut Development Corporation Limited
70.	The Kerala Fisheries Corporation Limited
71.	Kerala Inland Fisheries Development Corporation Limited
72.	The Kerala Premo Pipe Factory Limited
73.	The Chalakudy Refractories Limited
74.	Kerala Special Refractories Limited
75.	The Kerala Asbestos Cement Pipe Factory Limited
76.	Kerala State Engineering Works Limited
77.	SIDECO Mohan Kerala Limited (Subsidiary of SIDCO)
78.	Keltron Power Devices Limited (Subsidiary of KELTRON)
79.	SIDKEL Televisions Limited (Subsidiary of SIDCO)
80.	Kerala State Wood Industries Limited (Subsidiary of KFDC)
81.	The Plantation Corporation of Kerala Limited
82.	The State Farming Corporation of Kerala Limited
83.	Kerala State Horticultural Products Development Corporation Limited
84.	Kerala Livestock Development Board Limited
85.	Kerala State Poultry Development Corporation Limited
86.	Kerala State Film Development Corporation Limited
87.	Kerala Forest Development Corporation Limited (KFDC)
88.	Forest Industries (Travancore) Limited
89.	Kerala Tourism Development Corporation Limited (KTDC)

(Contd.)

(Contd. Annexure-1)

90.	Kerala Transport Development Finance Corporation Limited
91.	Overseas Development and Employment Promotion Consultants Limited.
92.	Kerala Industrial Infrastructure Development Corporation
93.	The Kerala State Civil Supplies Corporation Limited
94.	Tourist Resorts (Kerala) Limited (Subsidiary of KTDC)
95.	Bekal Resorts Development Corporation Limited
96.	Kerala State Ware-housing Corporation
97.	Kerala Power Finance Corporation Limited
98.	Kerala State Electricity Board
99.	Kerala State Road Transport Corporation
100.	The Rehabilitation Plantations Limited
101.	Kerala State Development Corporation for Scheduled Castes and Scheduled Tribes Limited
102.	The Kerala State Backward Classes Development Corporation Limited
103.	Kerala State Handicapped Persons' Welfare Corporation Limited
104.	Kerala State Development Corporation for Christian Converts from Scheduled Castes & the Recommended Communities Limited
105.	Kerala Artisans' Development Corporation Limited
106.	Kerala State Palmyrah Products Development and Workers' Welfare Corporation Limited
107.	Kerala School Teachers and Non-teaching Staff Welfare Corporation Limited
108.	Kerala State Women's Development Corporation Limited
109.	Kerala Fishermen's Welfare Corporation Limited

Madhya Pradesh

1.	Madhya Pradesh Financial Corporation
2.	Industrial Infrastructure Development Corp. Ltd
3.	M.P.State Agro Industrial Dev Corpn. Ltd.
4.	M.P.State Industries Corporation Ltd.
5.	M.P. Laghu Udyog Nigam Ltd.
6.	M.P.State electronics Development Corporation Ltd.
7.	Optel Telecommunications Ltd.

(Contd.)

(Contd. Annexure-1)

8.	M.P. State Textile Corporation Ltd.
9.	M.P. State Mining Corporation Ltd.
10.	M.P. Police Housing Corporation Ltd.
11.	M.P. State Industrial Development Corporation Ltd.
12.	Pithampur Auto Cluster Pvt. Ltd
13.	M.P.State Dairy Dev. Corpn. Ltd.
14.	M.P. Leather Development Corporation Ltd.
15.	M.P. Rajya Setu Nirman Nigam Ltd.
16.	M.P. Panchayati Raj Vitta Avam Gramin Vikas Nigam Ltd.
17.	M.P.Export Corporation Ltd.
18.	M.P. Rajya Van Vikas Nigam ltd.
19.	M.P. State Tourism Development Corporation Ltd.
20.	The Provident Investment Company Ltd.
21.	MP Trade Investment Facilitation Corp Ltd
22.	SEZ Indore Ltd
23.	M.P.Lift Irrigation Corporation Ltd.
24.	M.P.Film Development Corporation Ltd.
25.	M.P. State Civil Supplies Corporation ltd.
26.	Madhya Pradesh State Warehousing Corporation
27.	MP Warehousing and Logistics Corp.
28.	M.P. Urja Vikas Nigam Ltd.
29.	Madhya Pradesh State Electricity Board
30.	MP Raod Development Corp. Ltd
31.	M.P. State Road Transport Corporation
32.	M.P. Hasthshilp Avam Hath Kargha Vikas Nigam Ltd.
33.	M.P.A.K.V.N. (Bhopal) Ltd.,
34.	M.P.A.K.V.N. (Raipur) Ltd.
35.	M.P.A.K.V.N. (Indore) Ltd.
36.	M.P.A.K.V.N. (Jabalpur) Ltd.
37.	M.P.A.K.V.N. (Rewa) Ltd.
38.	M.P.A.K.V.N. (Gwalior) Ltd.
39.	M.P. Pichhda Varg Tatha Alpsankhyak Vitta avam Vikas Nigam ltd.
40.	M.P. Adivasi Vitta Avam Vikas Nigam Ltd.

(Contd.)

(Contd. Annexure-1)

Maharashtra	
1.	Maharashtra Small Scale Industries Development Corporation Limited
2.	City and Industrial Development Corporation of Maharashtra Limited
3.	Maharashtra State Financial Corporation
4.	Maharashtra Urban Infrastructure Fund Trustee Co. Ltd
5.	Maharashtra Urban Infrastructure Development Trustee Co. Ltd
6.	Maharashtra Industrial Development Corporation
7.	Maharashtra State Handicapped Finance And Development Corp
8.	Maharashtra Agro Industries Development Corporation Limited
9.	Maharashtra Insecticides Limited
10.	MAFCO Limited
11.	Leather Industries Corporation of Marathwada Limited
12.	Satara Kagal Highway Construction Co. Ltd
13.	Maharashtra Petrochemical Corporation Limited
14.	Maharashtra Electronics Corporation Limited
15.	Godavari Garments Limited
16.	Maharashtra State Textile Corporation Limited
17.	Maharashtra State Powerlooms Corporation Limited
18.	Maharashtra State Handlooms Corporation Limited
19.	Maharashtra State Mining Corporation Limited
20.	Haffkine Bio-Pharmaceuticals Corporation Limited
21.	Haffkine Ajintha Pharmaceuticals Limited
22.	Krupanidhi Limited
23.	Kolhapur Chitranagri Mahamandal Limited
24.	Dairy Development Corporation of Marathwada Limited
25.	Ellora Milk Products Limited
26.	Konkan Sea Foods Limited
27.	Vidarbha Quality Seeds Limited
28.	Kinwat Roofing Tiles Limited
29.	Marathwada Ceramic Complex Limited
30.	Shahyadri Glass Works Limited

(Contd.)

(Contd. Annexure-1)

31.	The Gondwana Paints and Minerals Limited
32.	Vidarbha Tanneries Limited
33.	Meltron Instrumentation Limited
34.	Textile Corporation of Marathwada Limited
35.	The Pratap Spinning, Weaving and Manufacturing Company Limited
36.	The Maharashtra Fisheries Development Corporation Limited
37.	Maharashtra Land Development Corporation Limited
38.	Maharashtra State Farming Corporation Limited
39.	Maharashtra Co-operative Development Corporation Limited (New Company w.e.f. 28-8-2000)
40.	Leather Industries and Charmakar Community Development Corporation of Maharashtra Limited
41.	Forest Development Corporation of Maharashtra Limited
42.	Development Corporation of Konkan Limited
43.	Development Corporation of Vidarbha Limited
44.	Marathwada Development Corporation Limited
45.	Western Maharashtra Development Corporation Limited
46.	Maharashtra Tourism Development Corporation Limited
47.	Maharashtra Film, Stage and Cultural Development Corporation Limited
48.	Abhijat Samayadarshika (Maharashtra) Limited
49.	Maharashtra State Housing Corporation Limited
50.	Maharashtra Rural Development Corporation Limited
51.	Maharashtra Patbandhare Vittiya Company Ltd
52.	The Overseas Employment and Export Promotion Corporation of Maharashtra Limited
53.	Maharashtra State Warehousing Corporation
54.	Maharashtra State Road Development Corporation Limited
55.	Maharashtra State Electricity Board
56.	Maharashtra State Road Transport Corporation
57.	Solapur City Intigrated Road Devlopment Ltd
58.	Pune City Integrated Road Dev. Ltd
59.	Irrigation Development Corporation of Maharashtra Limited
60.	Maharashtra Mendhi Va Sheli Vikas Mahamandal Limited

(Contd.)

(Contd. Annexure-1)

61.	Maharashtra State Police Housing and Welfare Corporation Limited
62.	Shivshahi Punarvasan Prakalp Limited
63.	Lokshahir Annabhau Sathe Development Corporation Limited
64.	Mahatma Phule Backward Class Development Corporation Limited
65.	Vasantrao Naik Vimukta Jatis and Nomadic Tribes Development Corporation Limited
66.	Maharashtra Rajya Itar Magas Vargiya Vitta Ani Vikas Mahamandal Limited
67.	Anna Saheb Patil Arthik Magas Vikas Mahamandal Limited (New Company w.e.f. 27-11-98)
68.	Shabri Adivasi Vitta Va Vikas Mahamandal Limited
69.	Mahila Arthik Vikas Mahamandal Limited
70.	Parbhani Krishi Gosamvardhan Limited
71.	Punyashloka Ahalyadevi Maharashtra Mendhi Va Sehil Vikas Mahanmandal Ltd

Manipur

1.	Manipur Industrial Development Corporation Ltd.
2.	Manipur Agro Industries Corporation Ltd.
3.	Manipur Plantation Crops Corporation Ltd.
4.	Manipur Cycle Corporation Ltd.
5.	Manipur Pulp and Allied Products Ltd.
6.	Manipur Electronics Development Corporation Ltd.
7.	Manipur Spinning Mills Corporation Ltd.
8.	Manipur Handloom and Handicrafts Development Corporation Ltd.
9.	Manipur Food Industries Corporation Ltd.
10.	Manipur Cement Ltd.
11.	Manipur State Drugs and Pharmaceuticals Ltd.
12.	Manipur State Power Development Corporation Ltd.
13.	Manipur Police Housing Corporation Ltd.
14.	Manipur Film Development Corporation Ltd.
15.	Manipur State Road Transport Corporation
16.	Manipur Tribal Development Corporation Ltd.

(Contd.)

(Contd. Annexure-1)

Meghalaya

1.	Meghalaya Industrial Development Corporation Ltd.
2.	Meghalaya Bamboo Chips Ltd.
3.	Mawmluh Cherra Cements Ltd.
4.	.Meghalaya Government Construction Corporation Ltd.
5.	Meghalaya Watches Ltd.
6.	Meghalaya Electronic Development Corp.
7.	Meghalaya Tourism Development Corporation Ltd.
8.	Meghalaya Handloom and Handicrafts Development Corporation
9.	Meghalaya Mineral Development Corporation Ltd.
10.	Meghalaya Apex Handloom Weavers & Handicrafts Cooperative
11.	Meghalaya State Cooperative Marketing & Consumers
12.	Forest Dev. Corp. of Meghalaya Ltd.
13.	Meghalaya State Warehousing Corporation

Mizoram

1.	Mizoram Industrial Development Corporation Ltd.
2.	Mizoram Food And Allied Industries Corporation Ltd.
3.	Mizoram State Cooperative Fruit Forestry and Vegetable
4.	Mizoram Electronics Development Corporation Limited
5.	Mizoram Agricultural Marketing Devp.Corpn.Ltd.
6.	Mizoram Handloom & Handicraft Development Corpn.Ltd.

Nagaland

1.	Nagaland Industrial Development Corporation Ltd.
2.	Nagaland Industrial and Raw Material Supply Corpn.
3.	Nagaland Sugar Mills Co.Ltd.
4.	Nagaland Mineral Development Corpn.
5.	Nagaland Handloom & Handicrafts Devp.Corpn.Ltd.
6.	Nagaland Hotels Ltd.

Orissa

1.	Agricultural Promotion and Investment Corporation of Orissa Limited

(Contd.)

(Contd. Annexure-1)

2.	Industrial Promotion and Investment Corporation of Orissa Limited
3.	Industrial Development Corporation of Orissa Limited
4.	Orissa Small Industries Corporation Limited
5.	Orissa State Financial Corporation
6.	Orissa Agro Industries Corporation Limited
7.	Orissa State Seeds Corporation Limited
.	Orissa StateBewarages Ltd
8.	Orissa State Cashew Development Corporation Limited
9.	Neelachal Ispat Nigam Limited
10.	Hirakud Industrial Works Limited (Subsidiary of Sl.No.23 of WC)
11.	Orissa State Electronics Development Corporation Limited
12.	ELMARC Limited (Subsidiary of Sl.No.7 WC)
13.	IDCOL Software Limited(Subsidiary of Company at Sl. No. 23 of WC)
14.	ABS Spinning Orissa Limited (Subsidiary of Sl.No.23 of WC)
15.	Orissa Mining Corporation Limited
16.	Orissa Construction Corporation Limited
17.	Orissa Bridge & Construction Corporation Limited
18.	IDCOL Cement Limited (Subsidiary of Sl.No.23 of WC)
19.	Kalinga Studios Limited(subsidiary of company at Sl. No. 25 of WC)
20.	Orissa Timber and Engineering Works Limited (subsidiary of company at Sl. No. 24 of WC)
21.	Konark Jute Limited (subsidiary of Company at Sl. No. 23 of WC)
22.	ORICHEM Limited (Subsidiary of Sl.No.23 of WC)
23.	Konark Detergent and Soaps Limited (Subsidiary of Sl.No.24 of WC)
24.	Kalinga Steel (India) Limited (Subsidiary of Sl.No.21 of WC)
25.	Orissa Electrical Manufacturing Company Limited (Company closed since 1968; under voluntary liquidation since 30.08.1976)
26.	Gajapati Steel Industries Limited (Company closed since 1969-70; under voluntary liquidation since 01.03.1974)
27.	Premiere Bolts and Nuts Limited (Company closed)

(Contd.)

(Contd. Annexure-1)

28.	Modern Malleable Casting Company Limited (Closed since 1968 Under voluntary liquidation since 09.03.1976)
29.	Orissa Rolling Mills Ltd
30.	Orissa Instruments Company Limited
31.	Hira Steel and Alloys Limited (Subsidiary of Sl.No.23 of WC)
32.	IDCOL Piping & Engineering Works Limited (Subsidiary of Sl.No.23 of WC)
33.	General Engineering & Scientific Works Limited (Subsidiary of Sl.No.24 of WC)
34.	Manufacture Electro Limited (Assets have been sold)
35.	Modern Electronics Limited
36.	IPITRON Times Limited (Subsidiary of Sl.No.7 of WC)
37.	Konark Television Limited
38.	ELCOSMOS Electronics Limited (Subsidiary of Sl.No.7 of WC)
39.	ELCOPHONES Limited (Subsidiary of Sl.No.7 of WC)
40.	ELCO Communication &Systems Limited (Subsidiary of Sl.No. 7 of WC)
41.	Mayurbhanj Textiles Limited
42.	New Mayurbhanj Textiles Limited
43.	Orissa Textile Mills Limited
44.	Orissa State Textile Corporation Limited
45.	Orissa Handloom Development Corporation Limited
46.	Eastern Aquatic Products Limited
47.	Orissa Boat Builders Limited (Company closed since 1987)
48.	Orissa Board Mills Limited (Closed. Decided for liquidation)
49.	Orissa State Leather Corporation Limited
50.	Orissa Leather Industries Limited (Subsidiary of Company at Sl.No.32 of NWC)
51.	Kanti Sharma Refractories Limited (Subsidiary of company at Sl.No.24 of WC)
52.	Orissa Forest Development Corporation Limited
53.	Orissa Tourism Development Corporation Limited
54.	Orissa Film Development Corporation Limited
55.	Orissa Rural Housing and Development Corporation Limited
56.	Orissa Fisheries Development Corporation Limited

(Contd.)

(Contd. Annexure-1)

57.	Orissa Fish Seed Development Corporation Limited
58.	Orissa Pisciculture Development Corp. Ltd
59.	Orissa State Export Development Corporation Limited
60.	Orissa State Civil Supplies Corporation Limited
61.	Orissa State Warehousing Corporation
62.	Orissa Power Generation Corporation Limited
63.	Orissa Hydro Power Corporation Limited
64.	Grid Corporation of Orissa Limited
65.	Orissa Lift Irrigation Corporation Limited
66.	Orissa State Road Transport Corporation
67.	Orissa Power Transmission Corp.
68.	Orissa State Commercial Transport Corporation Limited
69.	Orissa State Police Housing & Welfare Corporation Limited
70.	Orissa Maritime & Chilka Area Development Corporation Limited

Pondicherry

1.	Pondicherry Agro Service and Industries Corporation Limited
2.	Pondicherry Agro Products, Food and Civil Supplies Corporation Limited
3.	Pondicherry Distilleries Limited
4.	Pondicherry Electronics Limited (Subsidiary of PIPDIC)
5.	Pondicherry Textile Corporation Limited
6.	Pondicherry Industrial Promotion Development and Investment Corporation Limited (PIPDIC)
7.	Pondicherry Adi-dravidar Development Corporation Limited
8.	Pondicherry Tourism and Transport Development Corporation Limited
9	Pondicherry Power Corporation Limited
10.	Pondicherry Corporation for Development of Women and Handicapped persons Limited
11.	Pondicherry Backward Classes & Minorities Development Corporation Limited

Punjab

1.	Punjab State Industrial Development Corporation Limited
2.	Punjab Financial Corporation
3.	Punjab Agro Industries Corporation Limited

(Contd.)

(Contd. Annexure-1)

4.	Punjab State Tubewell Corporation Limited
5.	Punjab State Seeds Corporation Limited
6	Punjab Recorders Limited
7.	Punjab State Electronics Development and Production Corporation Ltd.
8.	Punjab Digital Industrial Systems Limited
9.	Consumer Electronics (Punjab) Limited
10.	Electronic Systems Punjab Limited
11.	Punjab Communications Limited
12.	Punjab Police Housing Corporation Limited
13.	Punjab Dairy Development Corporation Limited
14.	Punjab Micro Nutrients Limited
15.	Punjab Bio Medical Equipments Limited
16.	Punjab Electro Optics Systems Limited
17.	Intermagnetic India Limited
18.	Zimag India Limited
19.	PCL Telecom Limited
20.	Punjab Housing Finance Corporation Limited
21.	Punjab State Hosiery and Knitwear Development Corporation Limited
22.	Sutlej Shoddy Spinners Limited
23.	Punjab Export Corporation Limited
24.	Punjba Agro Food Grains Corp. Ltd
25.	Punjba Grains Procuremetn Corp
26.	Punjab Poultry Development Corporation Limited
27.	Punjab Land Development and Reclamation Corporation Limited
28.	Punjab Renewable Energy Development and Power Generation Company Ltd
29.	Punjab State Forest Development Corporation Limited
30.	Punjab Film and News Corporation Limited
31.	Punjab Information and Communication Technology Corp. Ltd
32.	Amristhsar Hotels Pvt Ltd
33.	Gulmohar Tourist Complex Private Ltd
34.	Neem Chameli Toursit Complex Private Ltd

(Contd.)

(Contd. Annexure-1)

35.	Sukhchain Toursit Complex Pvt Ltd
36.	Shangol toursit Complex Pvt Ltd
37.	Surajmukhi Tourist Complext Pvt Ltd
38.	Aamkhas Bhag Toursit complex Pvt Ltd
39.	Pukacassia Tourist Complex Pvt Ltd
40.	Kapurthala Tourist complex Pvt LTd
41.	Faridokot Tourist Complex Pvt Ltd
42.	Pathankot Toursit Complex Pvt Ltd
43.	Punjab State Handloom and Textiles Development Corporation Limited
44.	Punjab State Container and Warehousing Corporation Ltd
45.	Punjab State Civil Supplies Corporation Limited
46.	Punjab State Warehousing Corp.
47.	Punjab Small Industries and Export Corporation Limited
48.	Punjab Tourism Development Corporation Limited
49.	Punjab State Warehousing Corporation
50.	Punjab State Electricity Board
51.	PEPSU Road Transport Corporation
52.	Punjab Power Products Limited
53.	Punjab Power Packs Limited
54	Punjab Genco Ltd
55.	Pubjab State Electricity baord
56.	Punjab Scheduled Castes Land Development and Finance Corporation

Rajasthan

1.	Rajasthan State Industrial Development and Investment Corporation Limited
2.	Rajasthan Small Industries Corporation Limited
3.	Rajasthan Financial Corporation
4.	Rajasthan State Seeds Corporation Limited
5.	Rajasthan State Mines & Minerals Limited
6.	Rajasthan State Mineral Development Corporation Limited
7.	Rajasthan State Ganganagar Sugar Mills Limited
8.	Rajasthan State Hotels Corporation Limited

(Contd.)

(Contd. Annexure-1)

9.	Rajasthan State Power Corporation Limited
10.	Rajasthan State Agro Industries Corporation Limited
11.	Rajasthan State Dairy Development Corporation Limited
12.	Hi-Tech Precision Glass Limited
13.	Rajasthan Electronics Ltd. {Subsidiary of SI No.A(3)}
14.	Rajasthan State Granites & Marbles Limited {Subsidiary of S. No.A(7)
15.	Rajasthan State Tungstem Development Corporation Limited {Subsidiary of S No. A(7)}
16.	Rajasthan Jal Vikas Nigam Limited
17.	Rajasthan State Handloom Development Corporation Limited
18.	Rajasthan Paryatan Vikas Nigam Limited
19.	Rajasthan Rajya Van Vikas Nigam Limited
20.	Rajasthan State Warehousing Corporation
21.	Rajasthan State Road Development and Construction Corporation Limited
22.	Rajasthan Rajya Vidyut Utpadan Nigam Limited
23.	Rajasthan Rajya Vidyut Prasaran Nigam Limited
24.	Jaipur Vidyut Vitran Nigam Limited
25.	Jodhpur Vidyut Vitran Nigam Limited
26.	Ajmer Vidyut Vitran Nigam Limited
27.	Rajasthan State Electricity Board*
28.	Rajasthan State Road Transport Corporation
29.	Rajasthan State Electricity Corporation Limited

Sikkim

1.	Sikkim Industrial Development and Investment Corporation Limited (SIDICO)
2.	State Bank of Sikkim (SBS)
3.	Sikkim Jewels Limited (SJL)
4.	Sikkim Time Corporation Limited (SITCO)
5.	Sikkim Mining Corporation (SMC)
6.	Sikkim Flour Mills Limited (SFML)
7.	Sikkim Tourism Development Corporation

(Contd.)

(Contd. Annexure-1)

8.	Sikkim Livestock Processing and Development Corporation Limited (SLPDC)
9.	State Trading Corporation of Sikkim (STCS)
10.	Transport Department (SNT) Chanmari Workshop and Auto Mobiles Ltd.
11.	Scheduled Caste, Scheduled Tribe, Other Backward Class Development Corporation Limited (SABCO)

Tamil Nadu

1.	Tamil Nadu Small Industries Development Corporation Limited (SIDCO)
2.	Tamil Nadu Industrial Invest-ment Corporation Limited (TIIC)
3.	Tamil Nadu Urban Finance and Infrastructure Development Corporation Limited
4.	Tamil Nadu Power Finance and Infrastructure Development Corporation Limited
5.	Tamil Nadu Corporation for Industrial Infrastructure Deve-lopment Limited
6.	Tamil Nadu Transport Develo-pment Finance Corporation Limited
7.	Tamil Nadu Poultry Develop-ment Corporation Limited
8.	Tamil Nadu Sugarcane Farm Corporation Limited
9.	Tamil Nadu Tea Plantation Corporation Limited
10.	Tamil Nadu State Tube wells Corporation Limited
11.	Tamil Nadu Dairy Development Corporation Limited
12.	Tamil Nadu Agro Industries Development Corporation Limited
13.	Tamil Nadu Industrial Develop-ment Corporation Limited (TIDCO)
14.	Tamil Nadu Industrial Explosives Limited (Subsidiary of TIDCO)
15.	Tamil Nadu Magnesium and Marine Chemicals Limited (Subsidiary of TIDCO)
16.	Tamil Nadu Paints and Allied Products Limited (Subsidiary of TANSI)
17.	Tamil Nadu Small Industries Corporation Limited (TANSI)
18.	Tamil Nadu Ceramics Limited
19.	Tamil Nadu Salt Corporation Limited
20.	Tamil Nadu Magnesite Limited
21.	Tamil Nadu Leather Develo-pment Corporation Limited

(Contd.)

(Contd. Annexure-1)

22.	Arasu Rubber Corporation Limited
23.	Tamil Nadu Graphites Limited
24.	State Engineering and Servicing Company of Tamil Nadu Limited (SESCOT) (Subsidiary of TANSI)
25.	Southern Structural Limited
26.	Tamil Nadu Steels Limited
27.	Electronics Corporation of
28.	Tamil Nadu Limited (ELCOT)
29.	Tanitec Limited
30.	Tamil Nadu Textile Corporation Limited
31.	Tamil Nadu Zari Limited
32.	Tamil Nadu Minerals Limited (TAMIN)
33.	Tamil Nadu Medicinal Plant Farms and Herbal Medicine Corporation Limited
34.	Tamil Nadu Sugar Corporation Limited (TASCO)
35.	Perambalur Sugar Mills Limited (Subsidiary of TASCO)
36.	Tamil Nadu Cements Corpo-ration Limited
37.	Tamil Nadu Spirit Corporation Limited (Subsidiary of TASMAC)
38.	Tamil Nadu Handloom Development Corporation Limited
39.	Tamil Nadu Fisheries Develo-pment Corporation Limited
40.	Tamil Nadu State Farms Corporation Limited
41.	State Industries Promotion Cor-poration of Tamil Nadu Limited (SIPCOT)
42.	Tamil Nadu Handicrafts Development Corporation Limited
43.	Tamil Nadu Forest Plantation Corporation Limited
44.	Tamil Nadu State Construction Corporation Limited
45.	Tamil Nadu Police Housing Corporation Limited
46.	Tamil Nadu Medical Services Corporation Limited
47.	Dharmapuri District Development Corporation Limited
48.	Tamil Nadu Tourism Development Corporation Limited
49.	The Chit Corporation of Tamil Nadu Limited
50.	Overseas Manpower Corpo-ration Limited
51.	Tamil Nadu State Sports Development Corporation Limited
52.	Tamil Nadu Film Development Corporation Limited

(Contd.)

(Contd. Annexure-1)

53.	Tamil Nadu Civil Supplies Cor-poration Limited
54.	Tamil Nadu State Marketing Corporation Limited (TASMAC)
55.	Tamil Nadu Warehousing Corporation
56.	Metropolitan Transport Cor-poration (Chennai Division I) Limited
57.	Tamil Nadu State Transport Corporation (Madurai Division I) Limited
58.	Tamil Nadu State Transport Corporation (Coimbatore Division I) Limited
59.	Tamil Nadu State Transport Corporation (Kumbakonam Division I) Limited
60.	Tamil Nadu State Transport Corporation (Salem Division I) Limited
61.	Tamil Nadu State Transport Corporation (Madurai Division II) Limited
62.	Poompuhar Shipping Corpora-tion Limited
63.	Tamil Nadu State Transport Corporation (Villupuram Division I) Limited
64	Tamil Nadu Goods Transport Corporation Limited
65.	State Express Transport Cor-poration (Tamil Nadu Division I) Limited
66.	Tamil Nadu State Transport Corporation (Kumbakonam Division III) Limited
67.	Tamil Nadu State Transport Corporation (Villupuram Division II) Limited
68.	Tamil Nadu State Transport Corporation (Coimbatore Division II) Limited
69.	Tamil Nadu State Transport Corporation (Madurai Division III) Limited
70.	Pallavan Transport Consultancy Services Limited
71.	Tamil Nadu State Transport Corporation (Kumbakonam Division II) Limited
72.	Tamil Nadu State Transport Corporation (Madurai Division IV) Limited
73.	Tamil Nadu State Transport Corporation (Salem Division II) Limited
74.	Tamil Nadu State Transport Corporation (Villupuram Division III) Limited
75.	State Express Transport Corpo-ration (Tamil Nadu Division II) Limited
76.	Metropolitan Transport Cor-poration (Chennai Division II) Limited

(Contd.)

(Contd. Annexure-1)

77.	Tamil Nadu State Transport Corporation (Coimbatore Division III) Limited
78.	Tamil Nadu State Transport Corporation (Madurai Division V) Limited
79.	Tamil Nadu State Transport Corporation (Kumbakonam Division IV) Limited
80.	Tamil Nadu Electricity Board
81.	Tamil Nadu Adi Dravidar Housing and Development Cor-poration Limited
82.	Tamil Nadu Backward Classes Economic Development Corporation Limited
83.	Tamil Nadu Minorities Economic Development Corporation Limited
84.	Tamil Nadu Corporation for Development of Women Limited
85.	Tamil Nadu Ex-servicemen's Corporation Limited

Tripura

1.	Tripura Small Industries Corporation Ltd.
2.	Tripura Industrial Development Corporation Ltd.
3.	Tripura State Bank
4.	Tripura Handloom and Handicrafts Development Corporation Ltd.
5.	Tripura Jute Mills Ltd.
6.	Tripura Tea Development Corporation Ltd.
7.	Tripura Horticulture Corporation Ltd.
8.	Tripura Forest Development and Plantation Corporation Ltd.
9.	Tripura Rehabilitation Plantation Corporation Ltd.
10.	Tripura Road Transport Corporation

Uttar Pradesh

1.	Uttar Pradesh Small Industries Corporation
2.	Uttar pradesh State Industrial Development Corporation Limited
3.	The Pradeshiya Industrial and Investment Corporation of Uttar Pradesh Limited
4.	Uplease Financial Services Limited (Subsidiary of Uttar Pradesh Electronics Corporation Limited)
5.	Uttar Pradesh Financial Corporation
6.	Uttar Pradesh State Agro Industrial Corporation Limited

(Contd.)

(Contd. Annexure-1)

7.	Uttar Pradesh Poultry and Live-stocks Special-ties Limited
8.	Uttar Pradesh Projects and Tubewells Corporation Limited
9.	Trans Cables Limited (Subsidiary of Kumaon Mandal Vikas Nigam Limited)
10.	Uttar Pradesh State Leather Development and Marketing Corporation Limited
11.	UPSIC Potteries Limited (Subsidiary of Uttar Pradesh Small Industries Corporation Limited)
12.	Uttar Pradesh Digitals Limited (Subsidiary of Uttar Pradesh State Industrial Corporation Limited)
13.	Uttar Pradesh Electronics Corporation Limited
14.	Uptron Powertronics Limited (Subsidiary of Uttar Pradesh Electronics Corporation Limited)
15.	Shreetron India Limited (Subsidiary of Uttar Pradesh Electronics Corporation Limited)
16.	Uptron India Limited (Subsidiary of Uttar Pradesh Electronics Corporation Limited)
17.	Uttar Pradesh Hill Electronics Corporation Limited
18.	Uttar Pradesh State Spinning Company Limited
19.	Uttar Pradesh State Handloom Development Corporation Limited
20.	Uttar Pradesh State Bridge Corporation Limited
21.	Uttar Pradesh Rajkiya Nirman Nigam Limited
22.	Uttar Pradesh Police Avas Nigam Limited
23.	Uttar Pradesh Food and Essential Commodities Corporation Limited
24.	Uttar Pradesh State Sugar Corporation Limited
25.	Kichha Sugar Company Limited (Subsidiary of Uttar Pradesh State Sugar Corporation Limited)
26.	Chhata Sugar Company Limited (Subsidiary of Uttar Pradesh State Sugar Corporation Limited)
27.	Nandganj Sihori Sugar Company Limited (Subsidiary of Uttar Pradesh State Sugar Corporation Limited)
28.	Ghatampur Sugar Company Limited (Subsidiary of Uttar Pradesh State Sugar Corporation Limited)
29.	The Indian Turpentine and Rosin Company Limited

(Contd.)

(Contd. Annexure-1)

30.	Uttar Pradesh Development Systems Corporation Limited
31.	Uttar Pradesh Avas Evam Vikas Parishad
32.	Mohammadabad Peoples Tannery Limited
33.	Uttar Pradesh Plant Protection Appliances (Private) Limited (Subsidiary of Uttar Pradesh Small Industries Corporation Limited)
34.	Auto Tractors Limited
35.	Uttar Pradesh Instruments Limited (Subsidiary of Uttar Pradesh State Industrial Development Corporation Limited)
36.	Uttar Pradesh State Brassware Corporation Limited
37.	Continental Float Glass Limited (Subsidiary of Uttar Pradesh State Mineral Development Corporation Limited)
38.	The Turpentine Subsidiary Industries Limited (Subsidiary of The Indian Turpentine and Rosin Company Limited)
39.	Indian Bobbin Company Limited
40.	Uttar Pradesh Abscott Private Limited (Subsidiary of Uttar Pradesh Small Industries Corporation Limited)
41.	Uttar Pradesh Tyre and Tubes Limited (Subsidiary of Uttar Pradesh State Industrial Development Corporation Limited)
42.	UPAI Limited
43.	Kumtron Limited (Subsidiary of Uttar Pradesh Hill Electronics Corporation Limited)
44.	Uttar Pradesh Hill Phones Limited (Subsidiary of Uttar Pradesh Hill Electronics Corporation Limited)
45.	Uttar Pradesh Hill Quartz Limited (Subsidiary of Uttar Pradesh Hill Electronics Corporation Limited)
46.	Teletronix Limited (Subsidiary of Kumaon Mandal Vikas Nigam Limited)
47.	Uptron Sempack Limited (Subsidiary of Uttar Pradesh Electronics Corporation Limited)
48.	Kumaon Television Limited (Subsidiary of Kumaon Mandal Vikas Nigam Limited)
49.	Kanpur Components Limited (Subsidiary of Uttar Pradesh Electronics Corporation Limited)
50.	Uttar Pradesh State Textile Corporation Limited

(Contd.)

(Contd. Annexure-1)

51.	Uttar Pradesh Textile Printing Corporation Limited (Subsidiary of Uttar Pradesh State Handloom Development Corporation Limited)
52.	Bhadohi Woollens Limited (Subsidiary of Uttar Pradesh State Textile Corporation Limited)
53.	Handloom Intensive Development Project (Bijnore) Limited (Subsidiary of Uttar Pradesh State Handloom Development Corporation Limited)
54.	Uttar Pradesh State Mineral Development Corporation Limited
55.	Vindhyachal Abrasives Limited (Subsidiary of Uttar Pradesh State Mineral Development Corporation Limited)
56.	Uttar Pradesh State Cement Corporation Limited
57.	Uttar Pradesh Carbon and Chemicals Limited (Subsidiary of Uttar Pradesh State Industrial Development Corporation Limited)
58.	Uttar Pradesh Carbide and Chemicals Limited (Subsidiary of Uttar Pradesh State Mineral Development Corporation Limited)
59.	Uttar Pradesh Bhumi Sudhar Nigam
60.	Uttar Pradesh Matsya Vikas Nigam Limited
61.	Uttar Pradesh State Tourism Development Corporation Limited
62.	Uttar Pradesh Panchayati Raj Vitta Evam Vikas Nigam Limited
63.	Uttar Pradesh Export Corporation Limited
64.	Uttar Pradesh Forest Corporation
65.	Uttar Pradesh Pashudhan Udyog Nigam Limited
66.	Uttar Pradesh Bundelkhand Vikas Nigam Limited
67.	Uttar Pradesh Poorvanchal Vikas Nigam Limited
68.	Bundelkhand Concrete Structurals Limited (Subsidiary of Uttar Pradesh Bundelkhand Vikas Nigam Limited)
69.	Allahabad Mandal Vikas Nigam Limited
70.	Bareilly Mandal Vikas Nigam Limited
71.	Lucknow Mandaliya Vikas Nigam Limited
72.	Agra Mandal Vikas Nigam Limited
73	Gorakhpur Mandal Vikas Nigam Limited
74	Meerut Mandal Vikas Nigam Limited
75	Varanasi Mandal Vikas Nigam Limited
76	Moradabad Mandal Vikas Nigam Limited

(Contd.)

(Contd. Annexure-1)

77.	Gandak Samadesh Kshetriya Vikas Nigam Limited
78.	Tarai Anusuchit Janjati Vikas Nigam Limited
79.	Uttar Pradesh Chalchitra Nigam Limited
80.	Uttar Pradesh State Warehousing Corporation
81.	Uttar Pradesh Horticultural Produce Marketing and Processing Corporation Limited
82.	Uttar Pradesh Rajya Vidyut Utpadan Nigam Limited
83.	Uttar Pradesh Jal Vidyut Nigam Limited
84.	Uttar Pradeh Power Corporation Limited
85.	Kanpur Electric Supply (Subsidiary of Uttar Pradesh Power Corporation Limited)
86.	Uttar Pradesh State Road Transport Corporation
87.	Uttar Pradesh Jal Nigam
88.	Northern Electrical Equipment Industries Limited (Subsidiary of Kumaon Mandal Vikas Nigam Limited)
89.	Uttar Pradesh (Rohelkhand-Tarai) Ganna Beej Evam Vikas Nigam Limited
90.	Uttar Pradesh (Paschim) Ganna Beej Evam Vikas Nigam Limited
91.	Uttar Pradesh (Poorva) Ganna Beej Evam Vikas Nigam Limited
92.	Uttar Pradesh (Madhya) Ganna Beej Evam Vikas Nigam Limited
93.	Kumaon Mandal Vikas Nigam Limited
94.	Garhwal Mandal Vikas Nigam Limited
95.	Uttar Pradesh Scheduled Castes Finance and Development Corporation Limited
96.	Garhwal Anusuchit Janjati Vikas Nigam Limited (Subsidiary of Garhwal Mandal Vikas Nigam Limited)
97.	Kumaon Anusuchit Janjati Vikas Nigam Limited (Subsidiary of Kumaon Mandal Vikas Nigam Limited)
98.	Uttar Pradesh Samaj Kalyan Nirman Nigam Limited
99.	Uttar Pradesh Pichhara Varg Vitta Evam Vikas Nigam Limited (Formerly Uttar Pradesh Pichhari Jati Vitta Evam Vikas Nigam Limited)
100.	Uttar Pradesh Alpsankhyak Vittya Evam Vikas Nigam Limited
101.	Uttar pradesh Waqf Vikas Nigam Limited
102.	Uttar Pradesh Mahila Kalyan Nigam Limited

(Contd.)

(Contd. Annexure-1)

103.	Uttar Pradesh Bhutpurva Sainik Kalyan Nigam Limited
104.	Uttar Pradesh State Employees Welfare Corporation[44]

West Bengal

1.	Pulver Ash Projects Limited (subsidiary of WBSIDC Limited)
2.	The West Bengal Small Industries Development Corporation Limited
3.	The West Bengal Projects Limited (subsidiary of WBSIDC Limited)
4.	West Bengal Housing Infrastructure Development Corporation Limited
5.	West Bengal Infrastructure Development Finance Corporation Limited
6.	West Bengal Financial Corporation
7.	West Bengal Industrial Infrastructure Development Corporation
8.	West Bengal State Seed Corporation Limited
9.	West Bengal Tea Development Corporation Limited
10.	West Bengal Plywood and Allied Products Limited
11.	West Bengal Agro Industries Corporation Limited
12.	West Bengal State Food Processing and Horticulture Development Corporation Limited
13.	West Bengal Dairy and Poultry Development Corporation Limited
14.	Krishna Silicate and Glass (1987) Limited
15.	West Bengal Ceramic Development Corporation Limited
16.	Greater Calcutta Gas Supply Corporation Limited
17.	The West Bengal State Leather Industries Development Corporation Limited
18.	Neo Pipes and Tubes Company Limited
19.	Britannia Engineering Limited
20.	National Iron and Steel Company(1984) Limited
21.	The Carter Pooler Engineering Company Limited
22.	The Shalimar Works(1980) Limited
23.	The Electro Medical and Allied Industries Limited
24.	Westinghouse Sax by Farmer Limited
25.	Engel India Machines & Tools (1987) Limited

(Contd.)

(Contd. Annexure-1)

26.	West Bengal Electronics Industry Development Corporation Limited
27.	Webel Electronic Communication Systems Limited (subsidiary of WBEIDC Limited)
28.	Webel Crystals Limited (subsidiary of WBEIDC Limited)
29.	Webel Power Electronics Limited (subsidiary of WBEIDC Limited)
30.	Webel Mediatronics Limited (subsidiary of WBEIDC Limited)
31.	Webel Informatics Limited (subsidiary of WBEIDC Limited)
32.	Webel Multimedia Limited (subsidiary of WBEIDC Limited)
33.	Webel Consumer Electronics Limited (subsidiary of WBEIDC Limited)
34.	Webel Capacitors Limited (subsidiary of WBEIDC Limited)
35.	The Kalyani Spinning Mills Limited
36.	Mayurakshi Cotton Mills (1990) Limited
37.	West Bengal Agro-Textiles Corporation Limited
38.	The West Dinajpur Spinning Mills Limited
39.	West Bengal Handloom and Powerloom Development Corporation Limited
40.	West Bengal Handicraft Development Corporation Limited (subsidiary of WBSIC Limited)
41.	West Bengal Mineral Development and Trading Corporation Limited
42.	West Bengal Essential Commodities Supply Corporation Limited
43.	West Bengal Sugar Industries Development Corporation Limited
44.	Durgapur Chemicals Limited
45.	West Bengal Pharmaceutical and Phytochemical Development Corporation Limited
46.	Eastern Distilleries and Chemicals Limited
47.	West Bengal Chemical Industries Limited
48.	The Infusions (India) Ltd.
49.	The Durgapur Projects Limited
50.	Silpabarta Printing Press Limited (subsidiary of WBSIC Limited)
51.	Basumati Corporation Limited
52.	Saraswaty Press Limited
53.	Great Eastern Hotel Authority

(Contd.)

(Contd. Annexure-1)

54.	The West Bengal Livestock Processing Development Corporation Limited
55.	Webel Video Devices Limited (subsidiary of WBEIDC Limited)
56.	Webel Carbon and Metal Film Resistors Limited (subsidiary of WBEIDC Ltd)
57.	Sundarban Sugarbeet Processing Company Limited
58.	I.P.P. Limited
59.	Lime Light Industries (Private) Limited (subsidiary of WBSIC Limited)
60.	The State Fisheries Development Corporation Limited
61.	West Bengal Fisheries Corporation Limited
62.	West Bengal Forest Development Corporation Limited
63.	West Bengal Tourism Development Corporation Limited
64.	Gluconate Health Limited
65.	The West Bengal Power Development Corporation Limited
66.	West Bengal Rural Energy Development Corporation Limited
67.	The West Bengal Industrial Development Corporation Limited
68.	West Bengal Film Development Corporation Limited
69.	West Bengal Wasteland Development Corporation Limited
70.	West Bengal State Warehousing Corporation
71.	West Bengal State Minor Irrigation Corporation Limited
72.	The Calcutta Tramways Company(1978) Limited
73.	West Bengal Surface Transport Corporation Limited
74.	West Bengal Transport Infrastructure Development Corporation Limited
75.	West Bengal State Electricity Board
76.	West Bengal Electricity Regulatory Commission
77.	Calcutta State Transport Corporation
78.	North Bengal State Transport Corporation
79.	South Bengal State Transport Corporation
80.	West Bengal Women Development Undertaking
81.	West Bengal Scheduled Castes & Scheduled Tribes Development & Finance Corporation
82.	West Bengal Minorities Development & Finance Corporation

Annexure 2

Questionnaire

Financial and other related Information on SLPEs

I. GENERAL INFORMATION

01a. Name of the enterprise:

____

(Please write in BLOCK LETTERS)

01b. Date of formation

____

01c. Name and Designation of the Chief Executive Officer:

____

02. Address:

____

____

Pin Code: ____________
Tel: ____________ Fax: ____________
Telex: ____________ E-mail: ____________

03. Location of Registered Office:

____

04a. Major lines of activity (put mark against the activitiy)

Manufacturing, Trading & Services, Financial, Promotional
Utility Welfare

[ ] [ ] [ ] [ ] [ ] [ ]

04b. Major reasons for establishment:

____

04c. Description of the Product

____

____

05a. Year of promotion: ____________

05b. If there was a time lag, please give reasons:

____

06. Holding company: __________
Subsidiary company: __________

07. Objectives:

08. Form of organisation (Please "tick"):

- Government company
- Public corporation
- Statutory Board
- Statutory or regulatory authority
- Departmental enterprise
- Cooperative society
- Registered society

09a. Give details of Market structure: Monopoly/Competitive

II GROWTH AND DEVELOPMENT

1. Periodisation (please describe in terms of specific landmark development)

2. Salient Features

III SOCIAL PURPOSE

1. Major line of social activities undertaken by the organisation

2. Details on outflow of funds for the social activities

S.N	*Details*	*2001-02*	*2002-03*	*2003-04*	*2004-05*	*Projected*

IV FINANCIAL INFORMATION

(Rs. in lakhs)

S.N	*Details*	*2001-02*	*2002-03*	*2003-04*	*2004-05*	*Projected*
1.	Equity					
2.	Longterm debt					
3.	Total Investment					
3.	Reserves					
4.	Surplus/losses (-)					
6	Current Assets					
7	Current liabilities					
8	Working capital					
9	Capital employed (4+8) (This may be calculated on alternate basis from the liabilities route)					
10	Net Sales / Turnover					

(Contd.)

(Contd.)

S.N	Details	2001-02	2002-03	2003-04	2004-05	Projected
11.	Accumulated Losses					
12.	Net Worth					
13.	Other income					
14.	Total income					
15.	Direct Costs					
16.	Contribution (10-15)					
17.	Gross Margin					
18.	Cost of Sales					
19.	Operating Profit					
20.	Interest					
21.	Profit Before Tax					
22.	Tax					
23.	Net Profit					
24.	Subsidies 1. Capital 2. Revenue 3. Managerial 4. Hidden 5. Total					
25.	Guarantees					
26.	Contingent Liabilities					
27.	Liabilities to be settled					
28.	Valuation of Enterprise 1. Land 2. Plant Machinery 3. Stocks 4. Patents 5. Liabilities 6. Total					
29.	Court Cases					
30.	Contribution 1. Interest 2. Dividends 3. Excise 4. Surpluses 5. Exports 6. Sales Tax 7. Depreciation 8. Write-Off					

V. PHYSICAL PERFORMANCE

1. Installed Capacity
2. Capacity Utilised
3. Manpower

    Managerial Non-Managerial Casual

4. New Products/ Services Added
5. No. of employees availing VRS
6. Costs incurred on VRS
7. Costs reimbursed on VRS

VI ORGANISATIONAL STRUCTURE

1.	Size of Board					
	(a) Government nominee(s)					
	(b) Nominee(s) of Financial Institutions					
	(c) Nominee(s) of Workers / Managers					
	(d) Nominee(s) of Foreign Collaborators					
	(e) Functional directors					
	(f) Professional part-time directors					
	(g) CMD					
	(h) Total					
	(Sanctioned strength of Directors)					

(Contd.)

(Contd.)

	(Sanctioned strength of Directors)					
	(i) Tenure of the Board of Directors					
2.	What is your Organisational Chart?					
3.	Extent of Delegation & Decentralisation					
4.	Do you practice Internal Audit					
5.	Do you have Budgeting Process					
6.	What are your Investment Policies					
7.	What Pricing methods are followed?					
8.	Do you have Man Power Planning & Performance Appraisal					
9.	Training Programmes					
10.	Status of R&D					
11.	What Performance Evaluation Methods are followed?					

VII SWOT Analysis

1. Strengths

2. Weaknesses

3. Opportunities

4. Threats

VIII RESTRUCTURING

Give details on the following aspects:

1. Product portfolio

2. Market Restructuring

3. Financial Restructuring

4. Manpower Restructuring

5. Organisational Restructuring

6. Technological Restructuring

1. What is the average tenure for the Board of Directors?

2. What is the existing Compensation Package offered to the CEO and Board of Directors ?

VI. STRATEGIC INFORMATION

1.Is your enterprise involved in:
   (i) Restructuring
   (ii) Disinvestment
   (iii) Privatisation

2. Indicate the financial costs of (including VRS, Settlement of Liabilities, rate of sale of assets, etc)
   (i) Restructuring
   (ii) Disinvestment
   (iii) Privatisation

3. Indicate the social costs of:
   (i) Restructuring
   (ii) Disinvestment
   (iii) Privatisation

4. Provide the proposed steps for:
   (i) Restructuring
   (ii) Disinvestment
   (iii) Privatisation

1. What is the market structure of the organisation?
2. Please provide the Company's Profile?
3. Give Details on Foreign Collaborations.
4. What is the present state of Technology?
5. What is the extent of spending on Advertising Expenses?
6. What is the share in Exports & Imports?
7. Please give Details on any Mergers & Acquisitions taken place?
8. What is your Corporate Vision?

Please provide exhaustive notes on:-

1. Valuation of assets.

2. Privatisation, closure and restructuring of activities, divisions, products / services, enterprise.

3. Problems faced by the enterprise.

4. How the enterprise proposes to meet the resource gap in the future due to the reduction in budgetary support by the Government.

5. Details of VRS in existence at present, and details concerning the number of employees accepting VRS, total incidence of VRS in monetary terms, and future plan of action.

Bibliography

1. A Gelb & JB Knight & RH Sabot (1991) Public Sector Employment, Rent Seeking and Economic Growth EJ Vol.101, No.408, Sept., pp.1186-1199.
2. Aaron Wildavsky (1966) The Political Economy of Efficiency: Cost-Benefit Analysis, Systems Analysis, and Program Budgeting Public Administration Review Dec., pp.292-310.
3. ABS Kilewo(1989) Management of Public Enterprises through State Holding Corporations: The Experience of The National Development Corporation of Tanzania (Paper presented in the International Workshop) mimeo April.
4. ABS Kilewo(1989) The Zimco Case Study (International Workshop on State Holdings held between 17th and 21st April at New Delhi) Deptt. of Corporate Plg., Dir. of Manpower Dev. and Corp. Plg. Zimco Ltd.
5. Ajit Singh (1972) Holding Company and the Public Sector: An Instrument of State Enterprise EPW July 22, pp.1415-1423.
6. Akilagpa Sawyerr (1977) Multinational Corporations and Development: The Case of the Rubber Industry in Ghana in Yash Ghai (Ed.) (1977).
7. Amiya Kumar Bagchi(1982). "Public Sector Industry and Quest for Self-Reliance in India", Economic and Political Weekly, IPE mimeo Annual No., Vol.XVII, Nos.14, 15 and 16, April.
8. Anand P Gupta (1982) Management of Tax Expenditures: A Study of the Indian Case mimeo Working Paper No.446.

9. Anand P Gupta(1996). "The Political Economy of Privatisation in India", mimeo Centre for Institutional Reform and the Informal Sector WP No.17.
10. Andhra Pradesh (Government) (1989) Draft White Paper on Public Enterprises mimeo.
11. Arch Vahini (1993) Sardar Sarovar Project: An Intellectual Fashion mimeo Action Research in Community Health & Development
12. Arjun Sengupta (1986) I-Public Enterprises and Planning Financial Express May 12, 13,14 & 15.
13. Ashok Rudra(1991). "Privatisation and Deregulation", Economic and Political Weekly, December 21, pp.2933-2936.
14. AV Srinivasan (1991) Evaluation of Public Enterprise and Memorandum of Understanding mimeo Administrative Staff College of India.
15. AV Srinivasan (1991) Evaluation of Public Enterprise and Memorandum of Understanding mimeo Feb.
16. Ayub M and Hegsteand.S (1985). "Public Industrial Enterprises Determinats of Performance", World Bank, Washington DC.
17. Bagaram Tulpule (1988) Industrial Relations in Public Enterprises in India: Retrospect and Prospect mimeo Centre for Studies in Public Enterprise Management, No. 3.
18. Bajaj .J.L (1994). "Divesting State Ownership : A Tale of Two Companies", Economic and Political Weekly, Vol 25, No 35, August 27, pp M120-M128.
19. Barbara Nunberg (1990) Public Sector Management Issues in Structural Adjustment Lending World Bank Discussion Paper No. 99.
20. Barberis, Nicholas, Maxim Boycko, Andrei Shleifer, and Natalia Tsukanova (1996). "How Does Privatization Work? Evidence From the Russian Shops," *Journal of Political Economy* 104, pp. 764-790.
21. Barend A de Vries (1981) Public Policy and the Private Sector (Economic Development and the Private Sector) Finance Development Sept., pp.1-5.

22. Basu,SK And Sarkar,A And Sinha, HN (1971). "Report on the Monetary and Non-Monetary Work Incentives in Public Enterprises of West Bengal", Book Exchange, Calcutta.
23. Batra, Satish K (Ed.) and JAIN,Tej K (Ed.)(1988). "State Enterprises: The Emerging Scenario", Jaipur, Printwell Publishers.
24. Ben Fine (1990) Scaling the Commanding Heights of Public Enterprise Economics CJE Vol.14, No.2, June, pp.127-142
25. Bhat K S and Nandagopal R(1991). "Role of Chairman and Managing Directors In State Level Public Enterprises: A Discussion", IPE, Hyderabad.
26. Bjorn Beckman (1977) Public Enterprise and State Capitalism Yash Ghai (Ed.) (1977).
27. Black, Bernard, Reinier Kraakman and Anna Tarassova (2000), "Russian Privatization and Corporate Governance: What Went Wrong?", Stanford Law Review.
28. Boles de Boer, D. and Evans, L. (1996). "The economic efficiency of telecommunications in a deregulated market: The case of New Zealand", The Economic Record, 72. Retrieved on September 3, 2003 from http://global.factiva.com.
29. Boubakri, N. & Cosset, J.C. (1998). "The financial and operating performance of newly privatized firms: evidence from developing countries", Retrieved June 15, 2003 from http://www.crefa.ecn.ulaval.ca/cahier/perfo-fi.pdf
30. Brendan Martin (1993) In the public interest? Privatization and Public Sector Reform NA.
31. British Industrial News (C1989) Privatisation of Public Enterprise British Industrial News pp.34-39.
32. Campbell (1977). "Workers Owners: The Monodragon Achievement", Anglo German Federation, London.
33. Catherine Eckel, Doug Eckel and Vijay Singal (1997). "Privatization and efficiency: Industry effects of the sale of British Airways", Journal of Financial Economics, Vol. 43, Issue 2, February.
34. Chauhan (1978). "Organisation and working of public enterprises in Gujarat", Vallabh Vidyanagar, Sardar Patel University, Gujarat.

35. Claessens, S., Djankov, S., and Pohl, G. (1997). "Ownership and corporate governance: Evidence from the Czech Republic", World Bank Working Papers, 1737 Retrieved on November 3, 2003 from http://econ.worldbank.org/docs/660.pdf
36. Col SP Wahi (1987) The Organizational Structure of Public Enterprise mimeo International Congress of Public Enterprises, SCOPE
37. Cook .P. and Kirkpayrick .C (1988). " Privatisaiton In Less Developed Countries", Wheat Sheaf Book, Susex, pp 3-303
38. D"Souza, J. & Megginson, W.L. (1999). "The financial and operating performance of privatized firms during the 1990s", Journal of Finance. 54, 1397-1438
39. Dihratayakinant .K.(1991). "Privatisation of Bankok Metropolitan Transit Organisation : A Case study", Geeta Gouri ed. "Privatisation of Public Enterprises : An Asia Pacific Experience", pp 467-489
40. Dina Sheikh El Din Osman (1977) Notes Towards the Study of Public Enterprise in Sudan in Yash Ghai (Ed.) (1977)
41. Djankov, Simeon (1999). "Ownership Structure and Enterprise Restructuring in Six Newly Independent States," Comparative Economic Studies 41:1, 75-95.
42. Djankov, Simeon (1999). "The Restructuring of Insider-Dominated Firms: A Comparative Analysis," Economics of Transition 7:2, pp. 467-479.
43. Douglas.R(1990). "National Policy –Makers Experience – Newzeland", Privatisation International Congress (Mimeo-IPE), Saskatoon, Canada pp 32-45
44. DR Pendse (1988) Planning for Privatisation in India - Preparatory Measures (Paper prepared for the Asian and Pacific Development Centre, Kuala Lumpur, as an Issues Paper for their project on "Privatisation of Public Enterprises".) mimeo Project Paper, Nov.
45. Du Haiyar & Zheng Hongliang(1990) Analysis of the Contract Responsibility System of State Owned Enterprises mimeo Institute of Economics, Chinese Academy of Social Sciences
46. EAC (Economic Advisory Council) (1988) White Paper on the Public Sector. Govt. of India mimeo

47. Earle, John S (1998b). "Privatization, Competition and Budget Constraints: Disciplining Enterprises in Russia," SITE working paper no. 128, Stockholm: Stockholm School of Economics.

48. Earle, John S. (1998a). "Post-Privatization Ownership Structure and Productivity in Russian Industrial Enterprises," SITE working paper, Stockholm: Stockholm School of Economics.

49. Franco A Grassini (1981) The Italian Enterprises: Political Constraints (from "StateOwned Enterprise in the Western Economics, Vermon & Yair Ahroni (Eds)) NA SOE in Western Economics.

50. Freeman.J.D.F.(1990). "The Employees Buyout of Peoples Provincial Buses: Using ESOP to Driving A Bus Company", Privatisation Internaional Congress (Mimeo –IPE), Saskatoon, Cananda.

51. Frydman, Roman, Cheryl W. Gray, Marek Hessel, and Andrzej Rapaczynski (2000). "The Limits of Discipline: Ownership and Hard Budget Constraints in the Transition Economies," C.V. Starr Center for Applied Economics working paper, New York: New York University.

52. Frydman, Roman, Marek Hessel, and Andrzej Rapaczynski (2000). "Why Ownership Matters? Entrepreneurship and the Restructuring of Enterprises in Central Europe," C.V. Starr Center for Applied Economics working paper, New York: New York University.

53. Galal, A.L.Jones, P.Tandon and Ivogelsand (1994). "Welfare Consequences of Selling Public Enterprises", Oxford University Press, New York .

54. Gareth D Myles (1989) Industry-Specific Income Taxes mimeo Economic Research Paper No.334, Dec.

55. GAVINI, Augustine L(1990). "Ancillaries of Public Enterprises in Andhra Pradesh-A Study in Structure, Growth and Performance", OU, Hyderabad.

56. Geeta Gouri (1988) Economic Liberalisation in India and Efficiency in Public Enterprises - Some Issues in TL Shankar & YV Reddy (Eds.) (1988).

57. GL Tandon (1987) Working of the Board of Directors of Public Enterprises in India mimeo International Congress of Public Enterprises, SCOPE
58. Goodman.J.(1990). "Opportunities for Privatisation in Health Care", Privatisation International Congress (Mimeo- IPE), Saskatoon, Canada pp134-141.
59. Goran Hyden (1977) The Public Enterprise in African Administrative Research in Yash Ghai (Ed.) (1977)
60. Gorwala, A D(1951). Indian Planning Commission, "Report on the Efficient Conduct of State Enterprises", New Delhi.
61. Gouri. G (1989). "Economic Liberalisation in Indian and Efficiency of Public Enterprises : Some Issues", in Sankar T.L et. al ed. "Privatisation Diversification of Ownership of Public Enterprises", pp53-70.
62. Gouri.G. (1991) ed. "Privatisation and Public Enterprises: The Asia Pacific Experience", Oxford and IBH Publishers Co. Ltd, New Delhi.
63. GR Kulkarni & C Rangarajan (1982) State Sector and the Indian Economy State Enterprise Vol.I, No.1, March
64. GR Kulkarni (1979) Management Problems in the Public Sector EPW March, RM, pp.M3-M12
65. Gyula Eorsi (1977) Two Variants of a Research Project in Yash Ghai (Ed.) (1977)
66. Harper, Joel T (2000). "The Performance of Privatized Firms in the Czech Republic," Working paper, Boca Raton: Florida Atlantic University.
67. Hassan Shabir (1987). "Public Enterprises in Economic Development", Amol Publications, New Delhi
68. HC Gandhi (1990) Management of Public Enterprises through State Holding Corporations (Paper presented by Mr HC Gandhi, Chairman-cum Managing Director, Bharat Yantra Nigam Ltd., Allahabad)
69. Hemalata Rao(1987). "Financial Performance of Public Enterprises", Printwell , Publishers, Jaipur
70. Ida R Hoos (1966) Automation, Systems Engineering, and Public Administration:Observations and Reflections on the California Experience Public Administration Review Dec., pp.311-319

71. IFC , International Finance Corporation (1995) Privatisation: Principles and Practice (Lessons of Experiene) NA International Finance Corporation
72. Ik Soo Kim & Dae Hee Song (1989) Privatisation of the Pohang Iron and Steel Company of Korea: A case study mimeo Economic Planning Board, Korea Development Institute
73. Institute Of Public Enterprise, One Week Course On State Level Public Enterprises Management For IAS Officers: June 13-18, 1988, Hyderabad, IPE, 1988.
74. Institute Of Public Enterprise, One-Week Programme On SLPEs: 24-29 October, 1988, Hyderabad, IPE, 1988.
75. Institute Of Public Enterprise, Programme On Management Of State Level Public Enterprises: 22-28 August, 1988, Hyderabad, IPE, 1988.
76. Institute Of Public Enterprise, Top Management Programme For SLPEs" In North Eastern Region: February 20-24, 1989, Hyderabad, IPE, 1989.
77. Institute Of Public Enterprise, Workshop On SLPEs: October 7, 1988. Hyderabad, IPE, 1988.
78. IPE (1989) Asian and Pacific Development Centre Project Review Meetingof Privatization of Public Enterprises: Papers presented mimeo, IPE March 28 - 30, 1989
79. J Butterworth (1987) Whither the Public Sector: The UK Scene in the 80"s mimeo
80. Jack Butterworth et. al.(1989), "Public Enterprise Management", (Course Held at Bradford& Ilkley Community College by Prof.Jack Butterworth & others), Notes, Handouts, etc. (miscellaneous)
81. James CN Paul (1977) Law, Layers, and Decision-Making in the State Enterprise in Yash Ghai (Ed.) (1977)
82. James Foreman-Peck (1989) Ownership, Competition and Productivity Growth: The Impact of Liberalisation and Privatisation Upon British Telecom mimeo Economic Research Paper No.338, July
83. James Q Wilson (1989) Bureaucracy: What Government Agencies Do and Why They Do It NA

84. Jessica, Mary V(1992). "Performance of state financial corporations: A study of APSFC and KSFC",OU, Hyderabad.
85. Joan Crokery & Roger Wettenhall (1990), "Public Enterprise Boards: A Neglected Area of Governance", mimeo December
86. John Fairbairn (1989) British Steel to be Privatised British Industrial News pp.39
87. John Heath(1989) The Role of Holding Companies in the Organization and Management of Public Entrprises: Some Comparisons (International Workshop on the Management of Public Enterprises through State Holding Corporations) mimeo Module 5, April, 20, International Workshop
88. John R Nellis (1990) Contract Plans and Public Enterprise Performance World Bank Discussion Papers The World Bank, Washington D.C.
89. Kate Jenkins & Karen Caines & Andrew Jackson (C1987) Improving Management in Government (of the UK): The Next Steps: Report to the Prime Minister Efficiency Unit HMSO
90. Kiran Kumar K(1990). "Cash Management in Selected State Level Manufacturing Public Enterprises in Andhra Pradesh", Thesis Submitted to the Osmania University for the Award of Doctor of Philosophy in Commerce , Osmania University, Hyderabad.
91. Krishnagopal Menon & Srinivasan Umapathy (1987) Control Systems for State-Owned Enterprises: A Conceptual Framework Annals of Public & Cooperative Economy Vol.58 (3), Sept., pp.287-303
92. KRS Murthy & NCB Nath (1988) Can a Holding Company be an Effective Buffer for GovernmentEnterprise Vikalpa Vol.13, No.3, July-Sept., pp.1-15
93. KRS Murthy & NCB Nath (1988) Can a Holding Company be an Effective Buffer for Government Enterprise? Vikalpa Vol.13, No.3, July-Sept., pp.3-15
94. KRS Murthy (1990) MOU: More Memorandum than Understanding EPW May 26, pp. M-59 - M-66
95. KRS Murthy (1990) MOU: More Memorandum than Understanding EPW May 26, pp.M-59 - M-66
96. KS Krishnaswamy(1980) What Ails the Public Sector Reserve Bank of India Bulletin, IPE mimeo Dec.

97. Kumah Darh (1981) India"s Tata Lands Ghana Bus DealAfrican Business Jan., p. 35.

98. La Porta, R. & Lopez- de-Silanes, F. (1999). "The benefits of privatization: evidence from Mexico", *The Quarterly Journal of Economics,* 114, 1193-1242.

99. Laurin, Claude and Yves Bozec (2000). "Privatization and Productivity Improvement: The Case of Canadian National (CN)", Working Paper, Montreal: Ecoles de HEC.

100. Laxmi Narain (1987) Public Enterprise Interface with Government and Parliament mimeo International Congress of Public Enterprises, SCOPE.

101. Leroy P Jones & Edward S Mason (1987) Role of Economic Factors in Determining the Size and Structure of the Public-Enterprise Sector in Less-Developed Countries with Mixed Economies in Leroy P Jones (Ed.), (1992).

102. Leroy P Jones (1992) Public Enterprise in Less Developed Countries NA

103. Li Dewei (1990) Reform of Public Enterprise in China mimeo

104. Lok Sabha Secretariat (1995) Action Taken by the Govt. of India on the Reccommendation contained in Third Report of the Standing Committee on Energy of the Tenth Lok Sabha (Thirteenth Report) Govt. of India Tenth Lok Sabha.

105. LP Jones & LH Wontfel (1992) Public Enterprise and Manufactured Exports in Less Developed Countries: Institutional and Market Factors Determining Comparative Advantage in LP Jones (ed) pp. 217-241.

106. Macquieira Carlos and Salvador Zurita (1996). "Privatization in Chile: Efficiency Politics, Finances", Estudios de Administration 3:2, 1-36.

107. Malcom S Adiseshiah (1989) Privatisation and State Enterprises (Centre for Studies in Public Enterprise Management) mimeo Monograph Series, No. 4.

108. Martin. S & D. Parker, (1997). "The Impact of Privatization: Ownership and Corporate Performance in the U.K", London, Routledge.

109. Maruthi Ram P(1987), "Financing of Public Enterprises - a study of the impact on cost of Funds in select Central Enterprises and Andhra Pradesh Government", Hyderabad

110. Matthew Bishop & John Kay (1988) Does Privatization Work? - Lessons from the UK NA.

111. Maxim Boycko , Andrei Shleifer & Robert W Vishney (1996). "The Theory of Privatisation" The Economic Journal Vol.106, Jan., pp. 301-319.

112. Megginson. W.L, R. Nash and Malthians Van Randenborgh (1994). "The Finaincial and Operating Performance of Newly Privatized Firms: An International Empirical Analysis", The Journal of Finance, Vol. XLIX, pp. 403-452.

113. Mike Wright & Brian Chiplin & Ken Robbie (1987) Buy-outs from State Enterprises and Elsewhere in the Public Sector

114. Mike Wright (1987) Government Divestments and the Regulation of Natural Monopolies in the UK: The Case of British Gas Energy Policy June, pp.193-216.

115. Mohapatra, S K (1996). "Public Sector Restructuring: The Case of GSTC (Gujarat State Textile Corporation)", mimeo

116. Moosa Raza (1987) Working of Board of Directors mimeo International Congress of Public Enterprises, SCOPE.

117. Murthy, K S N(1985). "Industrial Relations in Andhra Pradesh State Electricity Board", IPE Hyderabad.

118. N Krishnaji (1989) Measuring Tax Potential: A Note on the Finance Commission"s Approach EPW Feb.4, pp. 265-267.

119. Nagraj.R(1991). "Public Sector and Public Interest : Some Tentative Findings", The Economic and Political Weekly, December 14, Vol. 25, No. 44, Bombay.

120. Narayana Murthy A S Y(1984). "Project Report on Industrial Sickness-causes and cures (a study in APSFC's experience)", IPE, Hyderabad.

121. Newberry, D.M. & Pollitt, M.G. (1997). "The restructuring and privatization of Britain's CEGB – Was it worth it?", The Journal of Industrial Economics, 45, 269-303. Retrieved November 3, 2003 from www.jstor.org.

122. Nitish De (1988) Open System Logic for Public Enterprises NA Monograph Series : 2

123. NK Singh (1987) Organizational Structure of Public Enterprises: Some Basic Issues mimeo International Congress of Public Enterprises, SCOPE

124. Oliver Leftwin (1983) Privatising the World: A Study of International Privatisation in theory and practice NA.

125. Olu Fadahunsi (1989) State Holding Corporation in Nigeria: The Evolution of New Nigeria Development Company Ltd and ODU"A Investment Ltd.

126. PC Luthar (1987) Interface Relationship of Public Enterprise with Government mimeo International Congress of Public Enterprises, SCOPE.

127. Peter Bauer (1989) Marketing Boards in The New Palgrave Economic Development,1989.

128. Petrazzini, Ben and Theodore.Clark (1996). "Costs and Benefits of Telecom"s Liberalization in Developing Countries", Mimeo.

129. Pheroze Nowrojee (1977) Public Enterprise in Kenya in Yash Ghai (Ed.) (1977).

130. Philip Marsh & Vladimir Kreacic (1986) Towards Excellence in Public Enterprises in Developing Countries mimeo Discussion Paper No.1.

131. Philip Thomas (1972) Holding Companies for Government Enterprises: The Italian Experience EPW June 10, pp.1156-1158.

132. Philippe Lasserre (1988) Sanofi-Lifeguard (A) INSEAD mimeo INSEAD - Euro-Asia Centre.

133. Pohl, Gerhard, Robert E. Anderson, Stijn Claessens, and Simeon Djankov (1997). "Privatization and Restructuring in Central and Eastern Europe: Evidence and Policy Options, (Working Paper: World Bank Technical Paper No.368, Washington D.C.).

134. Prajapati Trivedi (1989) Public Enterprise Performance Improvement and Holding Companies: (A Case Study of Bharat Bhari Udyog Nigam, Limited) IJPE Dec., pp. 29-43.

135. Prajapati Trivedi (1990) Lack of Understanding on Memorandum of Understanding EPW Nov.24, pp. M-175 - 182.

136. R G Nambiar (c1995) A New Vision of Federalism for Improving Health of the Indian Economy mimeo Sardar Patel Institute of Economic & Social Research.

137. R Hema (C1991) Regulation of Electricity in India: Features and Implications mimeo Paper submitted to the Ford Foundation.
138. R K Mishra & Ravishankar (1987) Capacity Utilisation in State Level Public Enterprises in Andhra Pradesh Udyog Pragati July-Sept., pp. 24-40.
139. Ramamurti, R (1996). "Privatizing Monopolies: Lessons from the Telecommunications and Transport Sectors in Latin America. Baltimore: The Johns Hopkins University Press.
140. Ramaswamy R Iyer (1989) Public Sector Holding Companies: Relationship with the Government and Allied Issues ICPE/BPE/COMSEC International Workshop on Holding Companies April 17-21.
141. Ramaswamy R Iyer (1989) Red Herring of Privatisation (Book Review: TL Sankar, YV Reddy, "Diversification of Ownership of Public Enterprise", IPE and Booklinks) EPW Oct.7, pp.2244-45.
142. Ramaswamy R Iyer (1989) The Profitability of Public Enterprises Economic Times Jan. 25, pp.1-2.
143. Ramaswamy R Iyer (1990) Public Enterprises: The Holding Company Idea (Theme Paper Presented at the Seminar on "Holding Companies - A Retrospection") Nov. 28.
144. Ramprasad Sengupta (1984). "Technical Change in the Public Sector Steel Industry", Economic and Political Weekly, Feb.4, pp.206-215.
145. Ratnam.C.S.V (1993). "Adjustment Through Privatisaiton : The Indian Agenda", ASCI Journal of Management, Vol. 22 No 4 March, Hyderabad.
146. Reddy.Y.V (1990). "Public Enterprises – Towards A White Paper", Booklinks Publication House, Hyderabad. p. 3-307
147. Reddy.Y.V(1991). "Privatisaiton Approaches, Process and Issues", Galgotia Publications, New Delhi.
148. Reginald Herbold Green (1977) Historical Decision Taking, Firm and Sectoral Dimensions of Public Sector Enterprise. Some Aspects of and Angles of Attack for Research in Yash Ghai (Ed.) (1977).
149. Reginald Herbold Green (1977) Law, Laws and Public Enterprise Planning in Africa. Preliminary Analytical Notes

towards More Productive Interaction in Yash Ghai (Ed.) (1977).

150. Reginald Herbold Green(1977) Public Directly Productive Units/Sectors in Africa and Political Economy. Some Notes on Methodological Pitfalls in Yash Ghai (Ed.) (1977).

151. Rehman Sobhan (1982) Public Enterprise and the Nature of the State State Enterprise Vol.XI, No.2, April-June.

152. Rehman Sobhan The Nature of the State and its Implications for the Development of Public Enterprises in Asia Journal of Contemporary Asia, pp. 410-433.

153. RK Mishra & R Nandagopal (1988) Capital Market and Privatisation of Public Enterprises: A Case of India in TL Sankar & YV Reddy (Eds.) (1988).

154. RK Mishra & R Nandagopal (1990) Do State Level Public Enterprises Need Memorandum of Understanding mimeo.

155. RN Tata & AK Khosla & SP Acharya & P Singh & DM Shawhney & MB Athreya (1987) Report of the Advisory Council on Project Implementation: Submitted to the Ministry of Programme Implementation Government of India Oct.

156. Robert J Barro (1980) The Ricardian Approach to Budget Deficits JEP Vol.3, No.2, Spring, pp. 37-54.

157. Robert Oakeshott (1985) The Beginnings of an Employee-Owned Sector Lloyds Bank Review Jan., pp.174-186.

158. Roman Frydman, Cheryl Gray, Marek Hessel and Andrzej Rapaczynski (1999). "When Does Privatization Work? The Impact of Private Ownership on Corporate Performance in the Transition Economies", The Quarterly Journal of Economics, vol. 114, issue 4, pp. 1153-1191.

159. Ros, A.J. (1999). "Does ownership or competition matter? The effects of telecommunications reform on network expansion and efficiency", Journal of Regulatory Economics, 49, 1-20.

160. Roy, R C(1985). "State Public Enterprise in India", Uppal Publishing House, New Delhi.

161. RS Ganapathy (etal) (1985) Public Policy and Policy Analysis in India NA.

162. RS Ganapathy (etal) (Eds.) (1985) On Methodologies and Policy Analysis in Public Policy and Policy Analysis in India.

163. S Guhan (1985) Towards a Policy Analysis in R.S. Ganapathy, et al (eds.).

164. Sankar, T L and Mishra, R K and Nanada Gopal, R, (1990). "State Level Public Enterprises in India: An Overview", Bombay .

165. Sankar, T L and Mishra, R K and Nanada Gopal, R, (1991). "Working of State-Level Manufacturing Public Enterprises: Promise and Performance", IPE, Hyderabad.

166. Saraswathy Rao, Y(1986). "Public Enterprises: A State Level Perspective", B.R.Publishing Company, New Delhi.

167. Sarma R P(1987). "Investment Pattern of Public Undertakings in India: A Study of Orissa Enterprises", Mittal Publications, New Delhi.

168. Sarma S D(1985). "Study of Project Appraisal Systems in Financial Institutions with special reference to APSFC", IPE, Hyderabad.

169. Savas.E.S(1982). "Privatisation The Key To Better Government", Tata Macgraw-Hill Publication Co. Ltd, New Delhi.

170. Sebastian Morris (1991) Holding Companies, Performance Contracts and Task Orientation in Public Sector Economic and Political Weekly, vol xxvi, no. 48, Nov. 30.

171. Sebastian Morris (1992) Export of Technology from the Public Sector: 1968-88 Sponsored by the DSIR, 18-2-1992.

172. Sebastian Morris (1996). "Technology Export from the Indian Public Sector: Case Study of BHEL", The Journal of Entrepreneurship Vol.5, No. 2, July-Dec., pp.223-251.

173. Selvarani,S(1993). "Employees Welfare Measures In Select Public Enterprises in Andhra Pradesh", Osmania University, Hyderabad.

174. Shikha Jha (1992) Consumer Subsidies in India: Is Targeting Effective? Development and Change Vol.23, No.4, pp.101-128.

175. Shirley, Mary M,(1983). "Managing State-owned Enterprises", World Bank, Washington.

176. SM Patil (1987) A Challenge for Professional Managers of Public Enterprises in India mimeo International Congress of Public Enterprises, SCOPE.

177. Smith, Stephen C., Beon-Cheol Cin, and Milan Vodopivec(1997). "Privatization Incidence, Ownership Forms, and Firm performance: Evidence From Slovenia," Journal of Comparative Economics 25, pp. 158-179.

178. Sudip Chaudhuri (1993) Public Enterprises and Private Purposes Working Paper, IIMC June, 1993, WPS-204(93).

179. Sukhamoy Chakrabarty (1987) Report of the Economic Advisory Council to the Prime MInister: Public Enterprise in India - Some Current Issues mimeo, Economic Advisory Council, Planning Commission Government of India, New Delhi.

180. Sunil Mani (1997) Divestment in Public Sector Enterprise Reforms: Indian Experience since 1991 memio Working Paper No.272, Feb., Centre for Development Studies, Triva.

181. Sunil Mani (1997). "Divestment and Public Sector Enterprise Reforms: Indian experience since 1991", mimeo CDS.

182. Suryanarayana. M(1986). "Monograph on Andhra Pradesh State Financial Corporation a catalyst of Industrial Development in Andhra Pradesh", IPE, Hyderabad.

183. Swamy,K,(1992). "Financial performance of manufacturing state level public enterprises in Andhra Pradesh", JNTU, Hyderabad.

184. Tamas Sarkozy (1977) The Legal Status of State Enterprises in Socialist Countries, with Special Reference to Hungary in Yash Ghai (Ed.) (1977).

185. Tandon, B C.(1987). "Public Enterprises In India", Chaitanya Publishing House, Allahabad.

186. Taxman (1991) Taxmann"s New Industrial Policy 1991 (Free with Tamann"s Budget 1991-92) Taxmann (1991).

187. Tenth Lok Sabha & Planning Commission (c1996) Energy for 90"s and Beyond: (Standing Committee on Energy 1995-96), Prospects, Reality and Challenges Govt. of India Ministry of Power, Coal, Petroleum, Natural Gas, Non-Convetional.

188. The British Council (1984) Annotated Bibliography on Public Administration mimeo Central Information Service No.3.

189. The Efficiency Unit(1985) An Introduction to the Efficiency Unit (of the Prime Minister (UK"s) office) The Efficiency Unit Oct.

190. The World Bank, Industry and Finance Division, Asia Country Department IV (1988) India Review of Public enterprises Propositions for Greater Efficiency in the Central government Public enterprises Sector Report, Vol. III - Appendices and Annexes NA.

191. TL Sankar & RK Mishra (1990) Review of Research on Governance of Public Sector in India mimeo Working Paper No.5/90.

192. TL Sankar & YV Reddy (1988) Privatisation: Diversification of Ownership of Public Enterprises NA.

193. TL Sankar (1990) Privatisation of Public Enterprises - The Experience of India (Paper presented at the conference: "Making Public Sector Engerprises Viable; Is Privatisation the Answer", 20-21 December, New Delhi) mimeo Proceedings of a Conference.

194. Trivedi.P (1993). "What is India's Privatisation Policy", The Economic and Political Weekly", May 29, Vol. 28 No. 22.

195. US Aswathi (1987) Interface Relationship of Public Enterprises with the Government mimeo International Congress of Public Enterprises, SCOPE.

196. Venkataramana.C.S (1993). "Adjustment Through Privatisaiton : The Indian Agenda", ASCI Journal of Management, Vol 22, No. 4, March pp. 173.

197. Venkatswamy, G.(1987). "Management Of State Government Enterprises", Archives Publishers, New Delhi.

198. Vidar Christiansen (1990) Subsidization of Risky Investment Under Income Taxation andMoral Hazard mimeo Economic Research Paper No.357, June.

199. Vidar Christiansen (1990) A Normative Analysis of Capital Income Taxes in the Presence of Aggregate Risk mimeo Economic Research Paper No. 343, April.

200. Vidar Christiansen(1990) Normative Aspects of State-Contingent Capital Income Taxation mimeo Economic Research Paper No. 3 44.

201. Vinod Vyasulu (1993) Public Enterprise in a Restructuring Economy: An inagural Lecture NA IPE, Hyderabad.

202. Voravidh Charoenloet (1989)The Crisis of State Enterprises in Thailand JCA Vol.19, No.2, pp. 206-217.

203. Voravidh Charoenloet (1989) The Crisis of Asian State Enterprises in Thailand JCA Vol.19, No.2, pp.206-217.

204. Vyasulu.V. (1993). "Public Enterprises in Restructuring Economy (Lecture)", IPE, Hyderabad.

205. Wallsten, Scott J. (2000). An Econometric Analysis of Telecom Competition, Privatization, and Regulation in Africa and Latin America. Journal of Industrial Economics, 44(1), 1-19.

206. Waris R Kidwai (1987) The Threatening Storm over the Public Sector in Indiamimeo International Congress of Public Enterprises, SCOPE.

207. Weiss, Andrew and Georgiy Nikitin. (1998). "Effects of Ownership by Investment Funds on the Performance of Czech Firms," Working paper, Boston University, Boston.

208. World Bank (1988) India Review of Public Enterprises Propositions for GreaterEfficiency in the Central Government Public Enterprises Sector Report, Vol.II - Main Text World Bank, Industry and Finance Division, Asia Country Dept.IV.

209. Yash Ghai & Susanne Linderos (1977) Selective Bibliography in Yash Ghai (Ed.) (1977).

210. Yash Ghai & TC Choong (1988) Management Contracts and Public Enterprises in Developing Countries NA ICPE Monograph Series No.20, May.

211. Yash Ghai (1977) Control and Management of the Economy: Research Perspectives on Public Enterprise in Yash Ghai (Ed.) (1977).

212. Yash Ghai (1977) Introduction in Yash Ghai (ed.) (1977), pp. 9-12.

213. Yash Ghai (1977) Law and Public Enterprise in Tanzania in Yash Ghai (Ed.) (1977).

214. Yash Ghai (1977) Law and Public Enterprise in Tanzania in Yash Ghai (ed) (1977) pp.206-266.

215. Yash Ghai (1977) Law in the Political Economy of Public Enterprise, African Perspectives NA ed.

216. Yash Ghai (1990) Entrepreneurship and Public Enterprise Legislation mimeo

217. ZahurAhmad Khan(1989) Financing of the National Fertilizer Corporation of Pakistan (Pvt.) Ltd. (International Workshop

on Management of Public Enterprises through State Holding Corporations by ICPE, Commonwealth Secretariat and BPE) mimeo April 17-21.